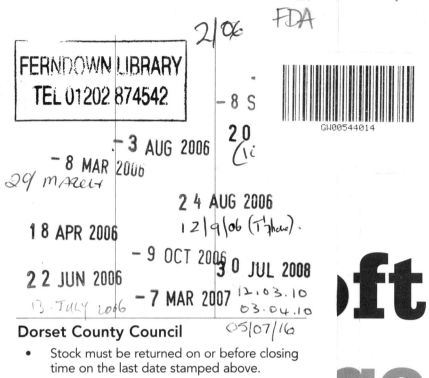

...oft
...ce
...llection

by Maria Langer and Tom Negrino

Peachpit Press

Microsoft Office Visual QuickProject Guide Collection

Maria Langer and Tom Negrino

Peachpit Press

1249 Eighth Street
Berkeley, CA 94710
510/524-2178
800/283-9444
510/524-2221 (fax)

Find us on the Web at: www.peachpit.com
To report errors, please send a note to errata@peachpit.com

Peachpit Press is a division of Pearson Education

A Note About This Collection

Thank you for purchasing the Microsoft Office Visual QuickProject Guide Collection. By combining three books into one, you save money and learn just what you need to get the job done.

Creating Résumés, Letters, Business Cards, and Flyers in Word: Visual Quick-Project Guide is the first book in this combined volume, with the index for the book following immediately after the text. This is followed by Creating Spreadsheets and Charts in Excel: Visual QuickProject Guide and Creating a Presentation in PowerPoint: Visual QuickProject Guide, with their respective indexes following immediately after each book, as well.

Two of these titles have companion Web sites where you can find project files and updates.

Creating Résumés, Letters, Business Cards, and Flyers in Word: Visual QuickProject Guide
Companion Web site at http://www.langerbooks.com/wordquickproject/ gives you sample files to download, links to related information, and more.

Creating Spreadsheets and Charts in Excel: Visual QuickProject Guide
Companion Web site at http://www.langerbooks.com/excelquickproject/ gives you sample files to download, links to related information, and more.

Full-color projects
from the folks
who bring you
Visual QuickStart
Guides…

Visual QuickProject

Creating Résumés, Letters, Business Cards, and Flyers in Word

MARIA LANGER

creating résumés, letters, business cards, and flyers in Word

Visual QuickProject Guide

by Maria Langer

Peachpit
Press

Visual QuickProject Guide
Creating Résumés, Letters,
Business Cards, and Flyers in Word
Maria Langer

Peachpit Press

1249 Eighth Street
Berkeley, CA 94710
510/524-2178
800/283-9444
510/524-2221 (fax)

Find us on the World Wide Web at: www.peachpit.com
To report errors, please send a note to errata@peachpit.com
Peachpit Press is a division of Pearson Education

Editor: Nancy Davis
Production Editor: Lisa Brazieal
Compositor: Maria Langer
Indexer: Julie Bess
Cover design: The Visual Group with Aren Howell
Interior design: Elizabeth Castro
Cover photo credit: Photodisc

ISBN 0-321-24751-5

Printed and bound in the United States of America

 To Mike,
on the 20th anniversary
of our engagement.

I still love you.

Special Thanks to...

Nancy Davis, for thinking of me for this great project—my first color book! And for helping me keep on track throughout the writing and production process.

Lisa Brazieal, for helping me fine-tune the book's layout and appearance.

Julie Bess, for coming to my rescue when I needed an index on short notice (again).

Microsoft Corporation, for continuing to improve the world's best word processing program for Windows and Macintosh users.

To Mike, for the usual things.

contents

contents

contents

introduction

This Visual QuickProject Guide offers a unique way to learn about new technologies. Instead of drowning you in theoretical possibilities and lengthy explanations, this Visual QuickProject Guide uses big, color illustrations coupled with clear, concise step-by-step instructions to show you how to complete a few specific projects in a matter of hours.

Our projects in this book are to create Word documents that you can use to simplify and improve your working life. Why go to a print shop to create letterhead and business cards? Or a graphic designer to create flyers? Why address envelopes by hand? If you have Microsoft Word, you can do it all yourself and make it look great. After all, Word is more than just a glorified typewriter. It has all the tools you need to create useful, professional-looking documents that bring out the best of you and your business.

Word may be the most useful program you have in your computer. It empowers you to tap into your own creativity. In doing so, not only will you save money, but you'll retain complete control over the documents you create. For example, suppose you follow the instructions in Chapter 3 to create a personal or business letterhead template. Three months later, the phone company changes your area code. Or your ISP goes out of business and you get a new e-mail address. Making changes to your letterhead template is as simple as editing a Word file. There's no need to pay a print shop to correct and reprint hundreds of sheets of letterhead paper that you'll have to throw away. And no need to compromise your professionalism by making handwritten corrections to your letterhead while waiting for new letterhead to arrive.

That's one example of how using Word to create these documents can help you. As you work through the projects in this book, you'll learn even more.

what you'll create

Create a custom letterhead template with formatted text.

Import and resize an image or logo to reinforce your company identity.

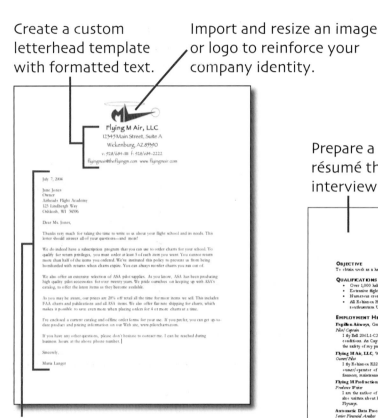

Use your custom letterhead to write professional-looking letters that get results.

Prepare a professionally formatted résumé that'll help you get an interview for your next job.

Mail your correspondence in perfectly printed envelopes.

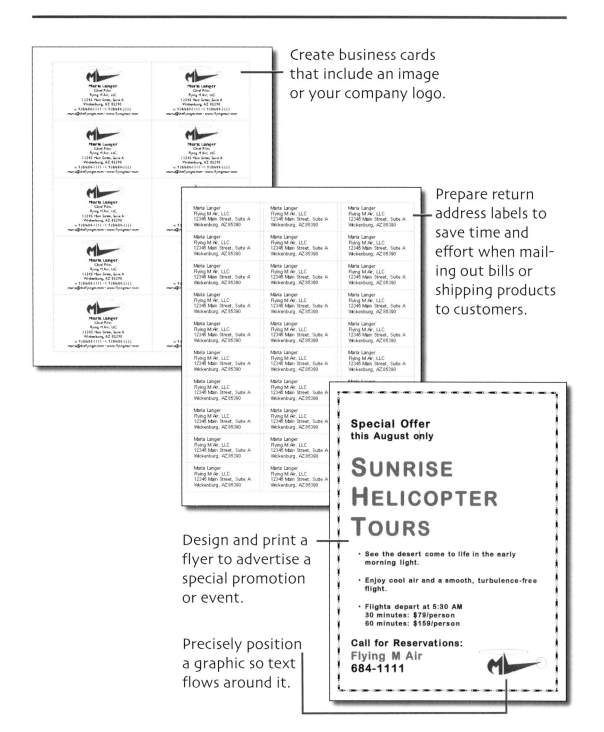

Create business cards that include an image or your company logo.

Prepare return address labels to save time and effort when mailing out bills or shipping products to customers.

Design and print a flyer to advertise a special promotion or event.

Precisely position a graphic so text flows around it.

Special Offer
this August only

SUNRISE
HELICOPTER
TOURS

- See the desert come to life in the early morning light.

- Enjoy cool air and a smooth, turbulence-free flight.

- Flights depart at 5:30 AM
  30 minutes: $79/person
  60 minutes: $159/person

Call for Reservations:
Flying M Air
684-1111

how this book works

The title of each section explains what is covered on that page.

An introductory sentence or paragraph summarizes what you'll do.

Numbered steps explain actions to perform in a specific order.

Important terms, names of interface elements, and text you should type exactly as shown appear in orange.

Captions explain what you're seeing and why. They also point to relevant parts of Word's interface.

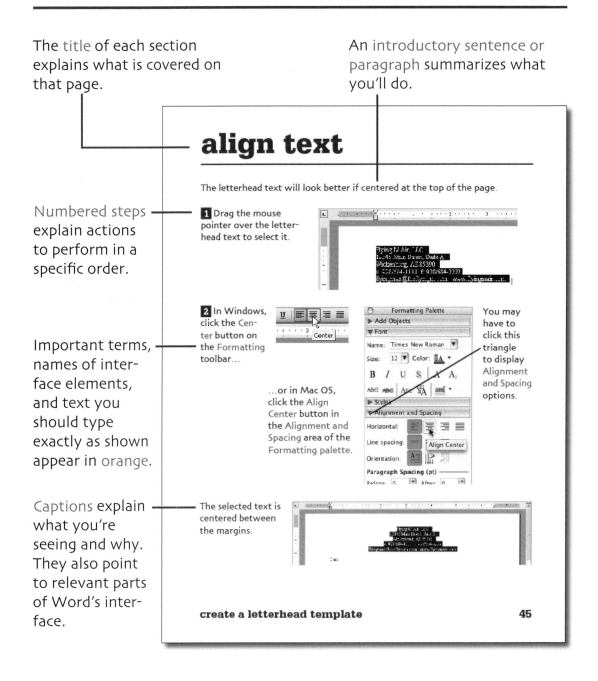

align text

The letterhead text will look better if centered at the top of the page.

1 Drag the mouse pointer over the letterhead text to select it.

2 In Windows, click the Center button on the Formatting toolbar...

...or in Mac OS, click the Align Center button in the Alignment and Spacing area of the Formatting palette.

You may have to click this triangle to display Alignment and Spacing options.

The selected text is centered between the margins.

create a letterhead template   45

The extra bits section at the end of each chapter contains additional tips and tricks that you might like to know—but that aren't absolutely necessary.

prepare a document

The heading for each group of tips matches the section title.

extra bits

prepare a document p. 40
- Print Layout View and Page Layout View are the same. For some reason, Microsoft gave this view different names for Windows and Mac OS.
- You can create a letterhead in any document view. Print Layout View (Windows) or Page Layout View (Mac OS) is best when working with headers and footers or positioning graphics.

set margins p. 41-42
- If you're creating a template for use with preprinted letterhead, measure the distance from the top of the letterhead paper to the bottom of any text or graphics printed there. Then add a tiny bit—perhaps 0.1 or 0.2 inches—and use that as your top margin measurement. If there's printing on the bottom of the page, measure from the bottom of the paper to the top of the text or graphics there, add a tiny bit, and use that as your bottom margin measurement. This ensures that any letter you write with your letterhead template will not overprint preprinted text or graphics.

- The Gutter box in Margins options is for spacing on bound documents. Keep it set to 0 for single-page documents like a letterhead template.
- Clicking the Default button in the Page Setup (Windows) or Document (Mac OS) dialog, enables you to establish the current settings as the default settings for all new blank documents.

enter letterhead text p. 43
- If Smart Tag underlines bother you—they drive me nuts!— point to the underlined text, click on the Smart Tag menu icon that appears, and choose Remove this Smart Tag from the menu.

- What you include in your letterhead is entirely up to you. I like to include the same information that can be found on my business card.

The page number next to the heading makes it easy to refer back to the main content.

create a letterhead template 51

the web site

Find this book's companion Web site at:
http://www.langerbooks.com/wordquickproject/.

Content is up-
dated regularly
with news, tips,
and more.

Read timely
articles about
getting the most
out of Word.

Download
sample files
used in the
book.

Access other
valuable online
resources.

Share your com-
ments and tips
with other site
visitors.

the next step

While this Visual QuickProject Guide will walk you through all of the steps required to create letterhead, letters, business cards, résumés, flyers, envelopes, and labels, there's more to learn about Word. After you complete your documents, consider picking up one of my books about Word—Microsoft Office Word 2003 for Windows: Visual QuickStart Guide or Microsoft Word 2004 for Macintosh: Visual QuickStart Guide—as a handy, in-depth reference.

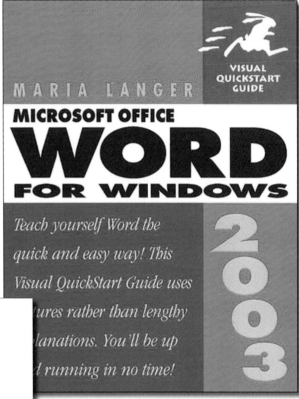

Both books include more advanced information about using Word to create documents. They tell you about all the options you see in Word dialogs, explain how to customize Word so it works the way you need it to, and provide detailed, step-by-step instructions for using basic, intermediate, and advanced Word features.

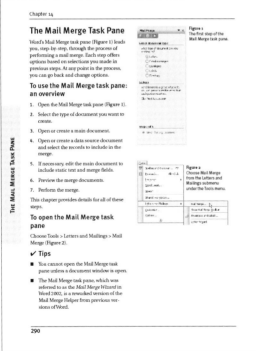

1. meet microsoft word

Microsoft Word is a full-featured word processing program that you can use to create all kinds of text-based documents, including the letters, résumés, business cards, flyers, and labels you'll create with this book.

As you work with Word, you'll see that it has a lot of the same interface elements you're familiar with from using your other Windows or Mac OS programs: windows, menus, dialogs, and buttons. And, as you work your way through this book you'll see that the Windows and Mac OS versions of Word are remarkably similar—so similar that instructions for one version of the program usually work for the other.

In this chapter, I introduce you to Word's interface elements and tell you about the techniques you'll need to know to use Word. If this project is your first hands-on experience with Word or your computer, be sure to read through this chapter!

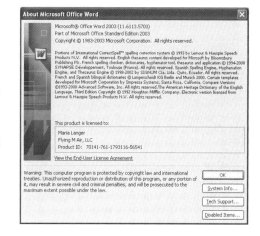

This book covers Word 2003 for Windows...

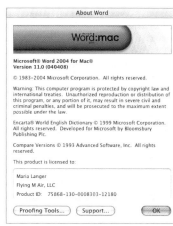

...and Word 2004 for Macintosh.

But if you have an earlier version of Word, you should still be able to follow most of the instructions in this book.

learn the lingo

Before you start working with Word, let me review a few of the terms I'll use throughout this book. If you've been working with your computer for a while, this may seem a bit basic, but I do want to make sure we're on the same page (so to speak) as we work through this project.

An icon is a graphical representation of a file.

WINWORD   Microsoft Word

Here's what the Word program icons look like in Windows (left) and Mac OS X (right).

Letter   Letter

And here's what a Word document icon looks like in Windows (left) and Mac OS X (right).

Windows Explorer is the Windows program that you use to work with files.

If you need to learn more about using Windows, be sure to check out Windows XP: Visual QuickStart Guide by Chris Fehily.

Finder is the Mac OS program that you use to work with files.

If you need to learn how to use Mac OS X, check out Mac OS X Panther: Visual Quick-Start Guide by Maria Langer. (Yes, that's me.)

mouse around

The white (Windows) or black (Mac OS) arrow that appears on your screen is the mouse pointer. Move your mouse and the mouse pointer moves.

Point means to position the tip of the mouse pointer on something. For example, you can point to a menu,...

...point to a button,...

...or point to some selected text.

The mouse pointer can also change its appearance when you point to other things. For example, if you point to text or a text area of a Word document window, it changes into an I-beam pointer. —————————]Fourscore and seven years

You use the button(s) on your computer's mouse to click, double-click, and drag.

Click means to press and release the left mouse button on a Windows computer or the only mouse button on a Mac OS computer.

Right-click means to press and release the right mouse button on a Windows computer. (You can't right-click on a Mac unless your Mac has a two-button mouse.)

Double-click means to click twice fast— without moving the mouse between clicks.

Drag means to point to something, hold the mouse button down, and move the mouse. You use this technique to move icons, select text, and perform other tasks.

A typical Windows mouse has two buttons.

A standard Mac OS mouse has only one button. On the Apple Pro Mouse shown here, the whole top of the mouse is a button.

start or open word

In Windows, you start a program. In Mac OS, you open a program. To keep things simple, I'll use the word start for both platforms.

In Windows:

1 Click Start to display the Start menu.

2 Click All Programs.

3 Click Microsoft Office.

4 Click Microsoft Office Word 2003.

In Mac OS:

1 Double-click your hard disk icon to open its window.

2 Double-click Applications.

3 Double-click Microsoft Office 2004.

4 Double-click Microsoft Word.

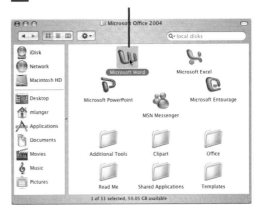

Word starts. If a Project Gallery window appears, click Cancel to dismiss it. An untitled document window appears, as shown on page 6.

Word starts and an untitled document window appears, as shown on page 5.

meet microsoft word

look at word (Windows)

Here are some of the important interface elements in Word for Windows.

title bar   menu bar   Standard toolbar   Formatting toolbar

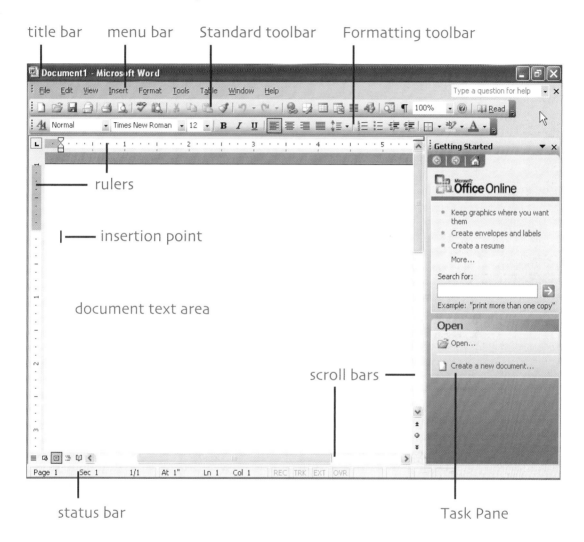

rulers

insertion point

document text area

scroll bars

status bar   Task Pane

look at word (Mac OS)

Here are some of the important interface elements in Word for Mac OS X.

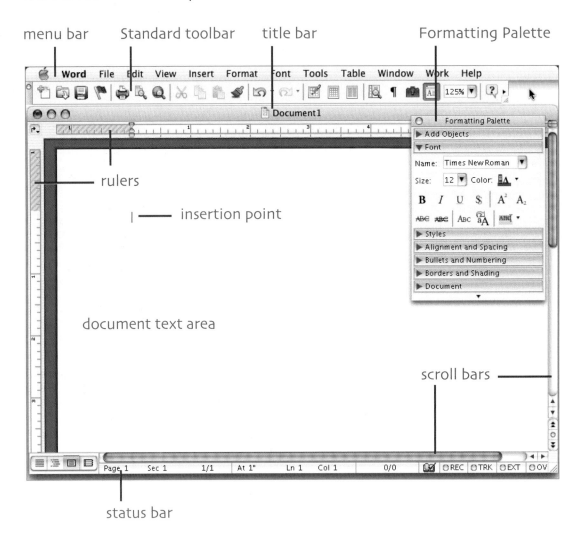

menu bar   Standard toolbar   title bar   Formatting Palette

rulers

insertion point

document text area

scroll bars

status bar

meet microsoft word

change the view

Word for Windows has five views: Normal, Web Layout, Print Layout, Reading Layout, and Outline.

Word for Mac OS has five views: Normal, Online Layout, Page Layout, Outline, and Notebook Layout.

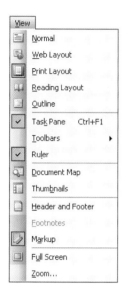

You can change a window's view by choosing the name of the view you want from the View menu...

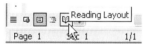

...or by clicking one of the View buttons at the bottom of the window. As shown here, you can point to a button to determine which view it's for.

Throughout this book, we'll stick to two views: Normal, and Print Layout (Windows) or Page Layout (Mac OS).

scroll a window

Scroll bars on a window make it possible to shift window contents up or down (or sideways) to see hidden contents.

A Windows
scroll bar.

A Mac OS
scroll bar.

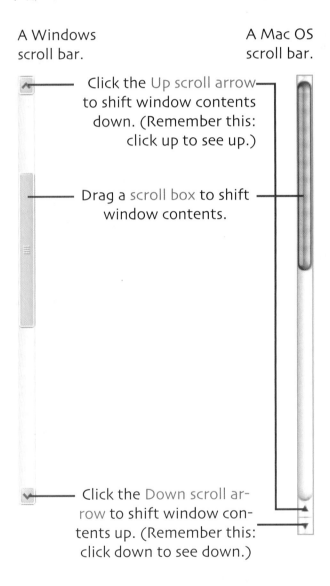

Click the Up scroll arrow
to shift window contents
down. (Remember this:
click up to see up.)

Drag a scroll box to shift
window contents.

Click the Down scroll ar-
row to shift window con-
tents up. (Remember this:
click down to see down.)

meet microsoft word

choose from a menu

A menu is a list of commands that can be accessed from the menu bar at the top of the program window (Windows) or screen (Mac OS).

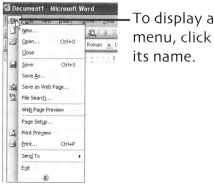 To display a menu, click its name.

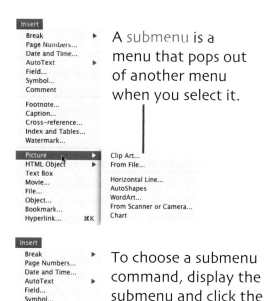 A submenu is a menu that pops out of another menu when you select it.

 To choose a menu command, click it.

To choose a submenu command, display the submenu and click the command.

 A contextual menu appears when you right-click something (Windows) or hold down the Control key while clicking something (Mac OS).

 To choose a contextual menu command, display the menu and click the command.

meet microsoft word

use a toolbar

Word has a number of toolbars with buttons you can click to access commands quickly.

In Word for Windows, two toolbars appear automatically: the Standard toolbar and the Formatting toolbar.

In Word for Mac OS, one toolbar and a palette appear automatically: the Standard toolbar and the Formatting palette.

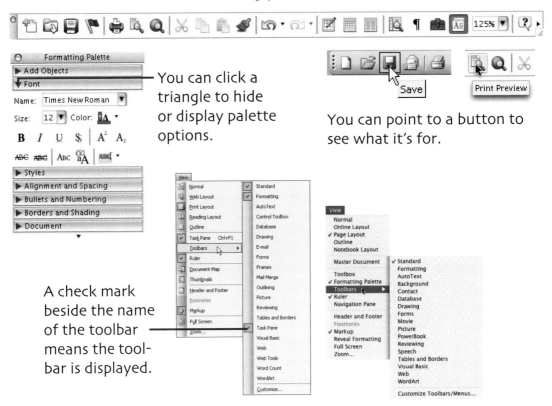

You can click a triangle to hide or display palette options.

You can point to a button to see what it's for.

A check mark beside the name of the toolbar means the toolbar is displayed.

To display a toolbar, choose its name from the Toolbars submenu under the View menu.

meet microsoft word

have a dialog

A dialog (or dialog box) is a window that appears onscreen when your computer needs to communicate with you.

When a dialog offers options for you to complete a task, it can display the options in a number of ways:

Tabs or buttons let you switch from one group of settings to another.

Scrolling lists offer multiple options in a list.

Check boxes are toggles for turning an option on or off. Click a check box to toggle its setting.

Text boxes are fields you can fill in by typing.

Drop-down lists (Windows) and pop-up menus (Mac OS) are menus within a dialog.

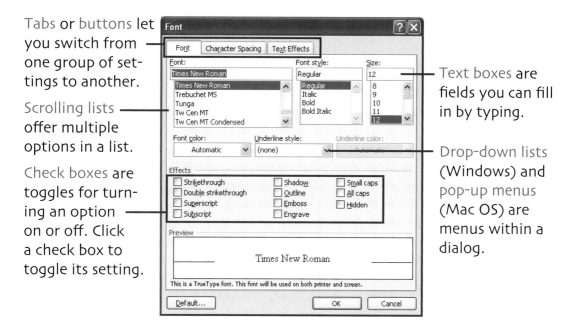

Option buttons (Windows) or radio buttons (Mac OS) let you select one option in a group.

Push buttons enable you to cancel or accept the choices in the dialog. Sometimes, push buttons can display other dialogs with other options.

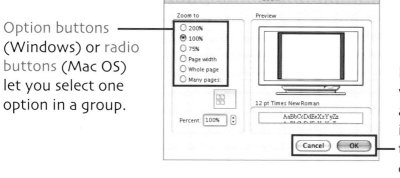

exit or quit word

When you're finished using Word, you should exit or quit it.

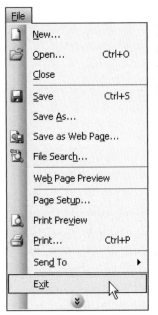

In Windows: choose Exit from the File menu.

In Mac OS: choose Quit Word from the Word menu.

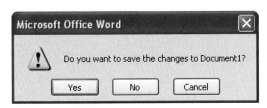

If a document with unsaved changes is open, Word displays a dialog that tells you and gives you a chance to save the document. (I tell you how to save documents in Chapter 2.)

extra bits

mouse around p. 3

- It is possible to get a multiple-button mouse for your Macintosh. But this book assumes you have a standard mouse with only one button.

- It's also possible to get a three-button mouse for your Windows PC. Frankly, I think two buttons are confusing enough, so I'll assume that's all your mouse has.

- You can also get a mouse with a roller—for Windows or Mac OS. (It's pretty common on Windows mice.) You can use the roller to scroll an active window. Since this feature doesn't work consistently, I don't bother talking about it in this book.

start or open word p. 4

- These instructions assume you have installed the entire Microsoft Office suite of products, including Word, Excel, PowerPoint, and Outlook (or Entourage). If you have installed just Word on your computer, consult the manual that came with it for instructions on how to start it.

- If you have a version of Word other than Word 2003 for Windows or Word 2004 for Mac OS, you might have to follow a different procedure for starting Word. Check the documentation that came with your version of Word to learn how to start it.

- Chances are, your Start menu won't look exactly like mine. But if you follow the instructions, you should be able to find and start Word using your Start menu.

- There are lots of ways to start Word in Windows and Mac OS. If you have a method you prefer, go for it!

extra bits

scroll a window p. 8

- It's possible to customize Mac OS X so the scroll arrows are at either end of the scroll bars. You do this with System Preferences. Choose System Preferences from the Apple menu and click the Appearance tab to get started. (As a long-time Mac user, I prefer them on either end; you may also.)

choose from a menu p. 9

- Contextual menus are sometimes known as shortcut menus.

- If a menu command has a shortcut key, it appears on the menu beside the command. For example, the Save command has a shortcut key of Ctrl-S (in Windows) or Command-S (in Mac OS). Pressing that key combination invokes the Save command without displaying the File menu.

use a toolbar p. 10

- In Windows, the Standard and Formatting toolbars sometimes appear on the same line. If so, not all buttons may appear. You can display the toolbars on separate lines by dragging the move handle of either toolbar down until it appears on its own line.

have a dialog p. 11

- You can select any number of check boxes in a group, but you can select only one option or radio button in a group.

2. work with a word document

As you build the documents in this project, you'll use a number of basic techniques for creating, opening, editing, formatting, and saving Word documents. Think of these techniques as a toolbox of skills that you'll use every time you work with Word.

Rather than present these skills over and over in every chapter in which they're used—which would probably waste a lot of pages and make me sound like a broken record—I've presented them just once: here, in this chapter.

If you're new to Word, please go through the practice exercises in this chapter. They explain how to work with a Word document. Throughout this book, I'll be referring to this chapter's tasks, so you can avoid a lot of page flipping if you understand its contents now, before you start building project documents.

If you've been using Word for a while, you may want to skip this chapter. Go ahead. But I recommend that you at least browse through it. You might be surprised by the tips you pick up in its pages.

create a document

Word offers a number of ways to create a new blank document. Here are a few of them.

Click the New Blank Document button on the Standard toolbar. Here's what it looks like in Windows (top) and Mac OS (bottom).

New Blank Document

New Blank Document

As you'll see through-out this book, this is the technique I personally recommend. It's quick and easy!

In Windows, choose New from the File menu...

...and then click Blank document in the New Document task pane that appears.

In Mac OS, choose New Blank Document from the File menu.

Use shortcut keys:

• In Windows, press Control-N.

• In Mac OS, press Command-N.

open a document (Windows)

You can open a saved document to work with it. From within Word, you do this with the Open dialog.

1 If the document is on a diskette, CD, or other removable media, insert it into your computer.

2 Choose Open from the File menu.

The Open dialog appears. You use this dialog to find the file you want to open.

3 Choose All Word Documents from the Files of type drop-down list.

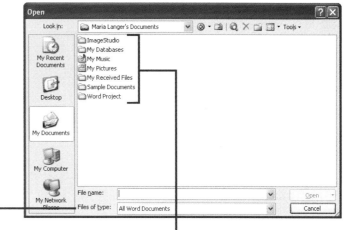

4 To look in a different disk or folder, choose the disk or folder from the Look in drop-down list.

5 To open a folder that appears in the list, double-click it. Repeat this step until you see the file you want to open.

6 Double-click the name of the file.

open a document (Mac OS)

You can open a saved document to work with it. From within Word, you do this with the Open dialog.

1 If the document is on a CD disc or other removable media, insert it into your computer.

2 Choose Open from the File menu.

The Open dialog appears. You use this dialog to find the file you want to open.

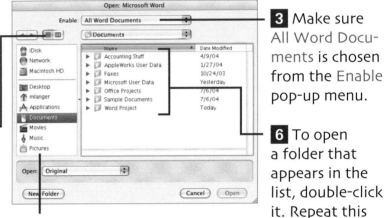

Click this button to display files in a list as shown here.

3 Make sure All Word Documents is chosen from the Enable pop-up menu.

6 To open a folder that appears in the list, double-click it. Repeat this step until you see the file you want to open.

4 To look in a different disk or folder, click the disk or folder in the Sidebar.

5 To backtrack through the file hierarchy or open a recently accessed folder, choose a location from the second pop-up menu.

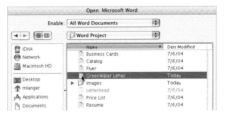

7 Double-click the name of the file.

work with a word document

enter and edit text

You enter text by typing. Text appears at the blinking insertion point cursor. Create a new document and give it a try.

Here's some sample text to type. As you can see in this example, when you type too much text to fit on a line, the text automatically wraps to the next line. This is called word wrap and it's why we all threw away our typewriters.|

Text automatically wraps to the next line when you've typed too much to fit on a line.

Here's some sample text to type. As you can see in this example, when you type too much text to fit on a line, the text automatically wraps to the next line. This is called word wrap and it's why we all threw away our typewriters.
I just pressed Enter (this is a Windows PC) to start a new paragraph.|

Press Enter (Windows) or Return (Mac OS) at the end of a paragraph or when you want to start a new line.

If I make a misteak| If you make a mistake while typing…

If I make a mist| …you can press the Backspace key (Windows) or Delete key (Mac OS) to delete the last character(s) you typed…

If I make a mistake| …and then type the correct characters.

enter and edit text (cont'd)

Here's some sample text to type. As you can see in this example, when you type too much text to fit on a line, the text automatically wraps to the next line. This is called word wrap and it's why we all threw away our typewriters. I can also insert text anywhere in my document.
I just pressed Enter (this is a Windows PC) to start a new paragraph.
If I make a mistake, I can delete the bad characters and type in good ones.

Inserted text.

Use the arrow keys to move the blinking insertion point. This makes it easy to insert text. Just position the insertion point where you want to insert text and type.

paragraph.[
pe in good ones.|

You can also move the blinking insertion point by clicking where you want the insertion point to be. Just point…

paragraph.[[
pe in good ones.

…and click. The blinking insertion point moves. But only if you click!

work with a word document

select text

Selecting text is the first step to changing it. For example, you select text before you format it, copy it, or cut it. Word offers lots of ways to select text. Here are the ones I use most.

To select a single word (and any space immediately after it), double-click the word.

> Here's some sample text to type.
> much text to fit on a line, the text
> wrap and it's why we all threw av

To select any amount of text, drag over the text.

> As you can see in this example, v
> t automatically wraps to the next l
> way our typewriters. I can also in:

To select any amount of text without dragging, position the insertion point at the beginning of the text…

> Here's some sample text to type.
> much text to fit on a line, the text
> wrap and it's why we all threw av

…and then hold down the Shift key and click at the end of the text. (This technique is known as Shift-click.)

> Here's some sample text to type.
> much text to fit on a line, the text
> wrap and it's why we all threw av

> Here's some sample text to type. As you can see in this example, when you type too
> much text to fit on a line, the text automatically wraps to the next line. This is called word
> wrap and it's why we all threw away our typewriters. I can also insert text anywhere in

To select an entire line of text, position the mouse pointer in the left margin so it turns into an arrow pointing to the upper-right. Then click.

> Here's some sample text to type. As you can see in this example, when you type too
> much text to fit on a line, the text automatically wraps to the next line. This is called word
> wrap and it's why we all threw away our typewriters. I can also insert text anywhere in
> my document.

To select an entire paragraph of text, triple-click it.

copy and paste text

When you copy text, you place a copy of it in Word's clipboard so you can paste it elsewhere—in the same document or a different document. The original text remains in the document, right where it was when you copied it.

It's easy to repeat yourself with Word.

1 Select the text you want to copy.

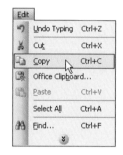

2 Choose Copy from the Edit menu.

It's easy to repeat yourself with Word.

3 Position the insertion point where you want the text to appear.

4 Choose Paste from the Edit menu.

It's easy to repeat yourself with Word.
It's easy to repeat yourself with Word.

A copy of the text appears at the insertion point.

This is a Paste Options button. See extra bits.

work with a word document

cut and paste text

When you cut text, you remove it from the document and place it in Word's clipboard so you can paste it elsewhere—in the same document or a different document.

1 Select the text you want to cut.

Try this: It's easy to move text with Word. Just use Cut and Paste.

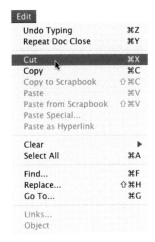

2 Choose Cut from the Edit menu.

Try this: |
Just use Cut and Paste.

The text disappears.

Try this:
Just use Cut and Paste.
|

3 Position the insertion point where you want the text to appear.

4 Choose Paste from the Edit menu.

This is a Paste Options button. See extra bits.

Try this:
Just use Cut and Paste.
It's easy to move text with Word.|

The text you cut appears at the insertion point.

drag and drop

Another way to move or copy text is to drag it to a new location.

To move text:

1 Select the text you want to move.

2 Position the mouse pointer on the text. It should look like an arrow.

3 Drag the text into a new position.

> You can move text from one place to another by just dragging it. Drag and drop is a little quicker than cut and paste, but it requires a steady hand.

As you drag, an insertion point appears to indicate where the text will be moved.

4 Release the mouse button. The

> Drag and drop is a little quicker than cut and paste, but it requires a steady hand. You can move text from one place to another by just dragging it.

text appears in the new location.

To copy text:

1 Select the text you want to copy.

2 Position the mouse pointer on the text. It should look like an arrow.

3 Hold down the Control key (Windows) or

> You can also copy text by dragging it. Remember to hold down the Control (Windows) or Option (Mac OS) key while dragging it.

Option key (Mac OS) and drag the text into a new position. A plus sign icon appears to indicate that the text will be copied. As you drag, an insertion point also appears to indicate where the text will be copied.

4 Release the mouse button. The text is copied to the location.

> You can also copy text by dragging it. Remember to hold down the Control (Windows) or Option (Mac OS) key while dragging. You can also copy text by dragging it.

work with a word document

undo actions

Ever do something on your computer and immediately say "Oops"? (Or something a little less polite?) If so, you should know about the Undo command. Available under the Edit menu of most programs—including Word—Undo can reverse the last thing you did.

Suppose you used drag and drop to move some text and your finger slipped off the mouse button before you had the text right where you wanted it. Oops! Choose Undo from the Edit menu to put it back where it was so you can start all over again.

Word supports multiple levels of undo. That means if you made a string of mistakes, you can undo all of them. Just keep choosing that Undo command until the document is restored to the way you want it.

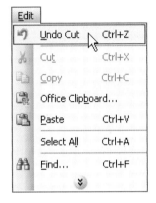

As shown in these two screen-shots, the exact wording of the Undo command varies depending on your last action.

format characters

Word has extensive formatting capabilities. The most basic formatting is font formatting, which enables you to change the appearance of text characters by applying different fonts (or typefaces), font sizes, font styles, and other effects.

One way to format text characters is with the Formatting toolbar (Windows)…

…or Formatting Palette (Mac OS).

As you can see, when you type too much text to fit on a line, the text automatically wraps to the next line. This is called word wrap and it's why we all threw away our typewriters.

1 Select the text you want to format.

2 Click a button…

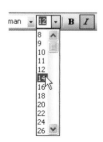

…or choose a menu option to apply formatting.

As you can see, when you type too much text to fit on a line, the text automatically wraps to the next line. This is called word wrap and it's why we all threw away our typewriters.

Formatting is applied immediately.

work with a word document

format characters (cont'd)

Another way to format text characters is with the Font dialog.

1 Select the text you want to format.

2 Choose Font from the Format menu.

3 If necessary, click the Font tab (Windows) or Font button (Mac OS) in the Font dialog that appears.

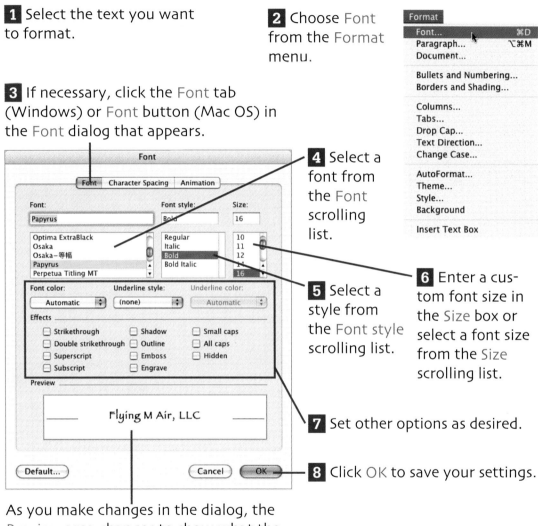

4 Select a font from the Font scrolling list.

5 Select a style from the Font style scrolling list.

6 Enter a custom font size in the Size box or select a font size from the Size scrolling list.

7 Set other options as desired.

8 Click OK to save your settings.

As you make changes in the dialog, the Preview area changes to show what the text will look like.

format paragraphs

Word's paragraph formatting features affect the appearance of an entire paragraph of text. Paragraph formatting includes alignment, line spacing, and indentation.

One way to format a paragraph is with the Formatting toolbar (Windows)...

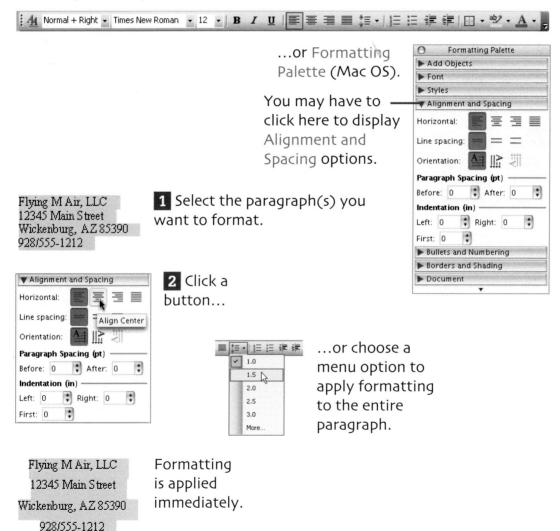

...or Formatting Palette (Mac OS).

You may have to click here to display Alignment and Spacing options.

1 Select the paragraph(s) you want to format.

2 Click a button...

...or choose a menu option to apply formatting to the entire paragraph.

Formatting is applied immediately.

work with a word document

format paragraphs (cont'd)

Another way to format paragraphs is with the Paragraph dialog.

1 Select the paragraph(s) you want to format.

2 Choose Paragraph from the Format menu.

3 In the Paragraph dialog, click the Indents and Spacing tab (Windows) or Indents and Spacing button (Mac OS).

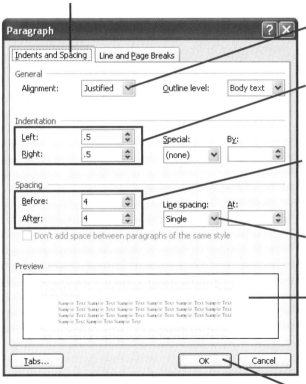

4 Choose an Alignment option.

5 Enter Indentation measurements in the Left and Right boxes.

6 Enter paragraph spacing options in the Before and After boxes.

7 Choose a Line spacing option.

As you make changes in the dialog, the Preview area changes to show what the paragraph will look like.

8 Click OK to save your settings.

print a document (Windows)

When you're finished creating a document, you can print it.

1 With the document you want to print displayed, choose Print from the File menu to display the Print dialog.

2 Choose the name of the printer you want to print to from the Name drop-down list.

4 To print only some of the pages, select the Pages option and enter the appropriate page range in the box beside it.

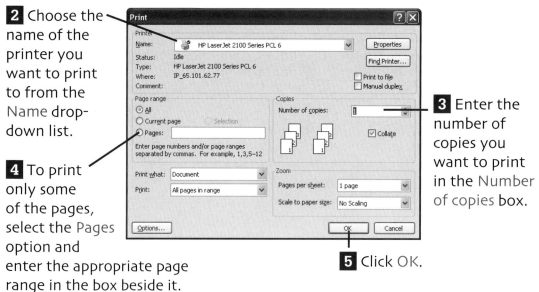

3 Enter the number of copies you want to print in the Number of copies box.

5 Click OK.

print a document (Mac OS)

When you're finished creating a document, you can print it.

1 With the document you want to print displayed, choose Print from the File menu to display the Print dialog.

2 Choose the name of the printer you want to print to from the Printer pop-up menu.

3 Enter the number of copies you want to print in the Copies box.

4 To print only some of the pages, select the Page range option and enter the appropriate page range in the box beneath it.

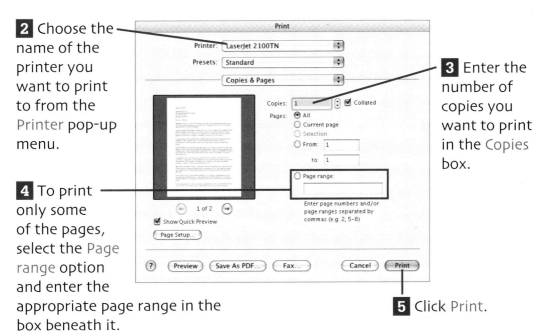

5 Click Print.

save a document (Windows)

You can save a document to keep a record of it on disk or so you can open and work with it at a later date.

1 With the document you want to save displayed, choose Save from the File menu.

The Save As dialog appears. You use this dialog to navigate to the location where you want to save the file.

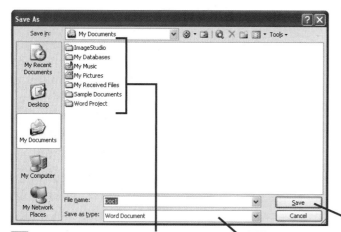

2 To open a different disk or folder, choose the disk or folder from the Save in drop-down list.

3 To open a folder that appears in the list, double-click it. Repeat this step until you open the folder in which you want to save the file.

5 Choose Word Document from the Save as type drop-down list.

6 Click Save.

4 Enter a name for the file in the File name box.

GreenWater Letter - Microsoft Word

The document is saved in the location you specified. Its name appears in the title bar.

work with a word document

save a document (Mac OS)

You can save a document to keep a record of it on disk or so you can open and work with it at a later date.

1 With the document you want to save displayed, choose Save from the File menu.

The Save As dialog appears. You use this dialog to navigate to the location where you want to save the file.

Click this button to display files in a list as shown here.

Click this button to expand the dialog and show the file list.

3 To backtrack through the file hierarchy or open a recently accessed folder, choose a location from the pop-up menu.

2 To open a different disk or folder, click the disk or folder in the Sidebar.

4 To open a folder that appears in the list, double-click it. Repeat this step until you open the folder in which you want to save the file.

6 Choose Word Document from the Format pop-up menu.

7 Click Save.

5 Enter a name for the file in the Save As box.

The document is saved in the location you specified. Its name appears in the title bar.

close a document

There are two ways to close a document.

Click the window's Close button.

Here's what it looks like in Windows...

...and here's what it looks like in Mac OS X.

Choose Close from the File menu.

If you close a document that contains unsaved changes, a dialog like this appears in Windows (top) or Mac OS (bottom). Click a button:

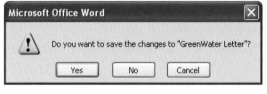

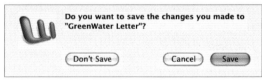

• Yes (Windows) or Save (Mac OS) saves the document. If the document has never been saved, the Save As dialog—see pages 32 and 33—appears. Follow the instructions on those pages to save the document.

• No (Windows) or Don't Save (Mac OS) closes the document without saving it. Any changes you made since it was last saved will be lost.

• Cancel tells Word not to close the document.

extra bits

open a document (Windows) p. 17

- You can also open a Word document from within Windows Explorer. Locate the icon for the document you want to open and double-click it.

open a document (Mac OS) p. 18

- The Sidebar appears in the Open dialog in Mac OS X 10.3 (Panther) and later only.

- You can also open a Word document from within the Finder. Locate the icon for the document you want to open and double-click it.

enter and edit text pp. 19-20

- You can delete the character immediately to the right of the insertion point by pressing the Delete key (Windows) or Del key (Mac OS).

- Pressing the Backspace key (Windows) or Delete key (Mac OS) while text is selected deletes the selected text.

- If you see black (Windows) or gray (Mac OS) dots between words and a ¶ symbol at the end of paragraphs, don't panic. This is the formatting marks (Windows) or non-printing characters (Mac OS) feature in action. The characters don't print. But if seeing them bugs you, click the Show/Hide ¶ button on the Standard toolbar and they'll go away.

Dear·Sir·or·Madam ¶
¶
Flying·M·Air·has·been·conducting·helicopter·rides·and·tours·in·the·Wickenburg,·
AZ·area·since·2001.·This·winter/spring·season,·we're·interested·in·expanding·our·
business·to·offer·helicopter·rides·and·tours·in·a·resort·environment ¶

- As you type, you may see red or green squiggly underlines beneath certain text. Red underlines indicate potential spelling errors and green underlines indicate potential grammar errors. I explain how to resolve spelling and grammar errors in Chapter 4.

I recently visited the GreenWater and liked what I saw. I am very
interested in bringing our 2004 Robinson R44 Raven helicopter to your
resort to conduct rides and tours either on a regular basis (for example,
every weekend or every Saturday) or in conjunction with other activities
planned at your resort (for example, on weekends of boat races or ATV
events).

work with a word document

extra bits

select text p. 21

- Word may automatically select entire words whenever you select more than just one word. If you find this feature as annoying as I do, you can turn it off. In Windows, choose Options from the Tools menu to display the Options dialog. In Mac OS, choose Preferences from the Word menu to display the Preferences dialog. Click the Edit tab (Windows) or the Edit list item (Mac OS). Then turn off the check box marked When selecting, automatically select entire word. Click OK.

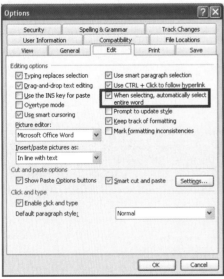

copy and paste text p. 22
cut and paste text p. 23

- You can also use shortcut keys for the Copy, Cut, and Paste commands. In Windows, they are Control-C, Control-X, and Control V. In Mac OS, they are Command-C, Command-X, and Command-V.

- Word's smart cut-and-paste feature automatically adds or removes space characters when you paste text.

- The Paste Options button appears when you use the Paste command. Click this button to display a menu of options for the text you pasted.

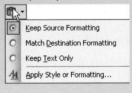

- If you don't want to see the Paste Options button every time you use the Paste command, you can turn off this feature. In Windows, choose Options from the Tools menu to display the Options dialog. In Mac OS, choose Preferences from the Word menu to display the Preferences dialog. Click the Edit tab (Windows) or the Edit list item (Mac OS). Then turn off the check box marked Show Paste Options buttons. Click OK to save this change.

undo actions p. 25

- You can also use a shortcut key for the Undo command: Control-Z in Windows and Command-Z in Mac OS.

- The Undo button on the Standard toolbar is really a menu. Use it to choose multiple actions to undo at once.

- If you say "Oops!" right after using the Undo command, you probably need to undo the Undo. Choose Redo from the Edit menu. If it's available, it will appear right beneath the Undo command.

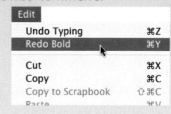

work with a word document 37

extra bits

print a document pp. 30-31

- You can also use a shortcut key for the Print command: Control-P in Windows and Command-P in Mac OS.

- The instructions in this book assume you have already set up at least one printer for use with your computer. If you have not, you can learn how by checking the documentation that came with your computer or with your printer.

save a document pp. 32-33

- You can also use a shortcut key for the Save command: Control-S in Windows and Command-S in Mac OS.

- Once a document has been saved, using the Save command automatically saves it with the same name in the same location on disk as the last time you saved it. It does not display the Save As dialog again.

- If you want to save a document with a different name or in a different location on disk, use the Save As command. This command always displays the Save As dialog, so you can give the document a name and choose a save location.

close a document p. 34

- All open documents automatically close when you use the Exit (Windows) or Quit (Mac OS) command. I tell you more about exiting or quitting Word in Chapter 1.

work with a word document

3. create a
letterhead template

Letterhead. It sounds so formal, like something a big business would use to send letters to stockholders.

But whether you're building a business from the ground up or are just using Word to handle personal writing tasks, letterhead should be one of your writing tools. At the very minimum, it provides contact information for you or your business. It can also help reinforce your company identity by displaying your logo or other brand information where it will be seen by everyone you write to.

Microsoft Word's template feature enables you to create two kinds of preformatted letterhead documents:

One kind is designed to be printed on blank paper. It includes all the text and graphics on every letter you write. Then, when you write and print the letter, the letterhead is printed as part of the letter. Here's an example.

The other kind is designed to be printed on preprinted letterhead. It just includes formatting settings. Then, when you write and print the letter, the body of your letter is formatted properly.

This chapter explains how to create the first kind of template.

prepare a document

1 Click the New Blank Document button on the Standard toolbar.

Here's what it looks like in Windows...	...and here's what it looks like in Mac OS X.

 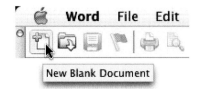

A blank document window appears.

2 Click the Print Layout View button (Windows)...   ...or Page Layout View button (Mac OS) at the bottom of the window.

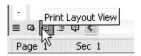 

This switches you to a layout view where you can see exactly how each page of your document will look as you work with it.

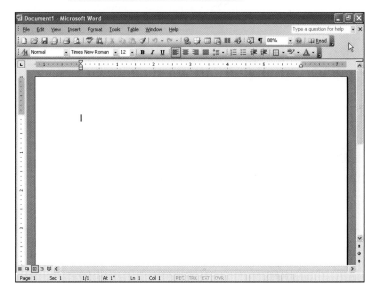

40   **create a letterhead template**

set margins

In Windows:

1 Choose Page Setup from the File menu.

In Mac OS:

1 Choose Document from the Format menu.

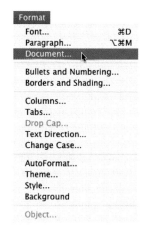

2 If necessary, click the Margins tab in the Page Setup dialog that appears.

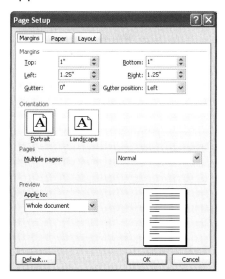

2 If necessary, click the Margins button in the Document dialog that appears.

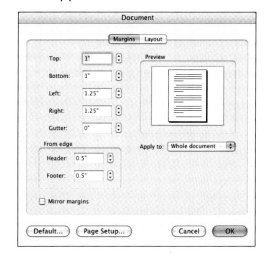

set margins (cont'd)

3 Enter margin measurements in the Top, Bottom, Left, and Right boxes.

You don't have to enter the inches character; Word knows the measurement will be in inches.

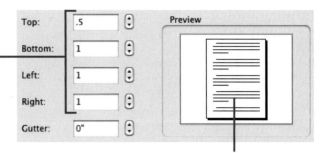

As you make changes in the measurement boxes, the Preview area changes to give you an idea of what the document will look like.

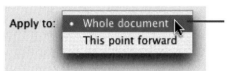

4 Make sure Whole document is selected from the Apply to menu.

5 Click OK to save your settings.

create a letterhead template

enter letterhead text

Letterhead text is the formatted text that appears at the top of every letter. You'll enter it in this step and format it in a later step.

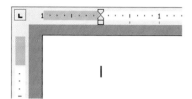 With the blinking insertion point at the top-left corner of the page…

…type in the text that you want to appear at the top of every page. Press Enter (Windows) or Return (Mac OS) after each line. For my letterhead, I want to display my company name, address, phone numbers, e-mail address, and Web site, as shown below.

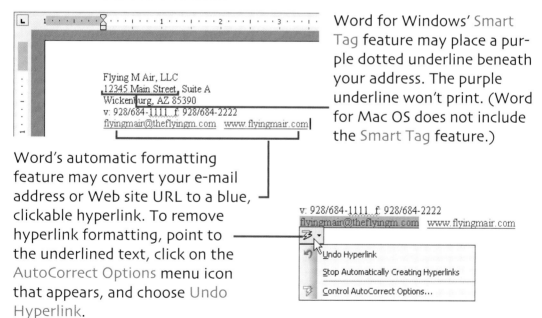

Flying M Air, LLC
12345 Main Street, Suite A
Wickenburg, AZ 85390
v: 928/684-1111   f: 928/684-2222
flyingmair@theflyingm.com   www.flyingmair.com

Word for Windows' Smart Tag feature may place a purple dotted underline beneath your address. The purple underline won't print. (Word for Mac OS does not include the Smart Tag feature.)

Word's automatic formatting feature may convert your e-mail address or Web site URL to a blue, clickable hyperlink. To remove hyperlink formatting, point to the underlined text, click on the AutoCorrect Options menu icon that appears, and choose Undo Hyperlink.

create placeholders

Text placeholders will help guide you when it comes time to write the letter. They also make it easy to apply consistent formatting to the body of the letter before the letter is written.

1 Make sure the blinking insertion point is at the end of the letterhead text. Then press Enter (Windows) or Return (Mac OS) twice to move it down two lines. —————

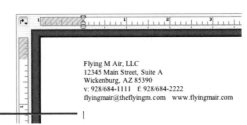

Flying M Air, LLC
12345 Main Street, Suite A
Wickenburg, AZ 85390
v: 928/684-1111   f: 928/684-2222
flyingmair@theflyingm.com   www.flyingmair.com

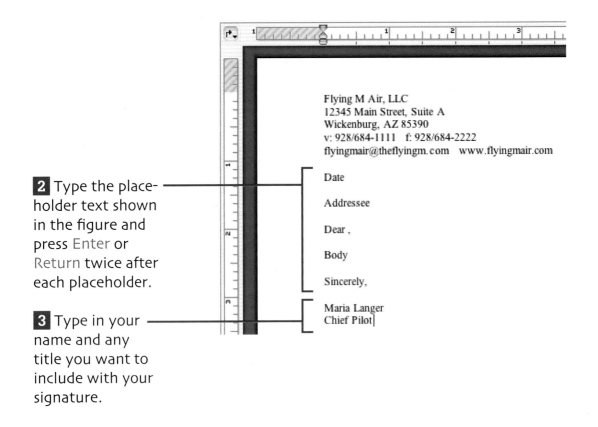

Flying M Air, LLC
12345 Main Street, Suite A
Wickenburg, AZ 85390
v: 928/684-1111   f: 928/684-2222
flyingmair@theflyingm.com   www.flyingmair.com

Date

2 Type the placeholder text shown in the figure and press Enter or Return twice after each placeholder.

Addressee

Dear ,

Body

Sincerely,

Maria Langer
Chief Pilot

3 Type in your name and any title you want to include with your signature.

create a letterhead template

align text

The letterhead text will look better if centered at the top of the page.

1 Drag the mouse pointer over the letterhead text to select it.

2 In Windows, click the Center button on the Formatting toolbar...

...or in Mac OS, click the Align Center button in the Alignment and Spacing area of the Formatting Palette.

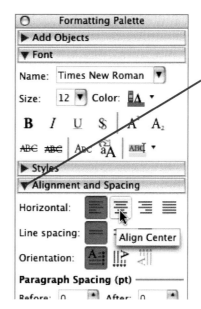

You may have to click this triangle to display Alignment and Spacing options.

The selected text is centered between the margins.

apply font formatting

You can format the letterhead text so it stands out by applying font formatting. You should also format the placeholder text with a typeface that's easy to read.

1 Drag the mouse pointer over the text you want to format to select it.

2 Choose Font from the Format menu.

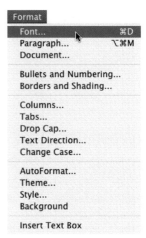

3 Set options in the Font screen of the Font dialog. I tell you more about using this dialog in Chapter 2.

4 Click OK.

5 Repeat this process for any letterhead or placeholder text in the document.

Here's what my letterhead looks like with various sizes and styles of Papyrus font applied to letterhead text and Garamond font applied to placeholder text.

create a letterhead template

insert an image

Since my company uses an image as its logo, I want to place it on the letter-head, right at the top.

1 Click to the left of the first character in the letterhead text to position the blinking insertion point there.

2 Press Enter (Windows) or Return (Mac OS) to shift the text down one line, then press the Up Arrow key once to move the insertion point up to the blank line.

3 Choose From File from the Picture submenu under the Insert menu.

The Insert Picture (Windows) or Choose a Picture (Mac OS) dialog appears, as shown on the next page.

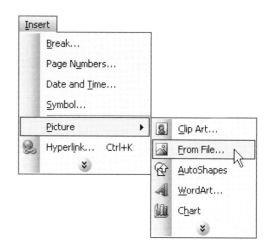

insert an image (cont'd)

4 Use tools within the dialog to navigate to and open the folder in which the image file resides. (I explain how to use a dialog like this in Chapter 2.)

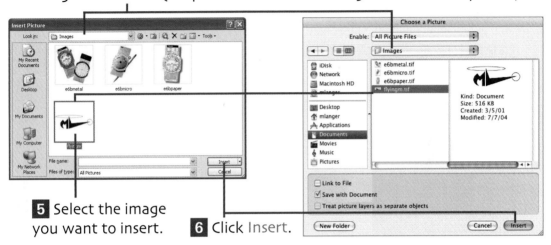

5 Select the image you want to insert.

6 Click Insert.

The image appears in the document.

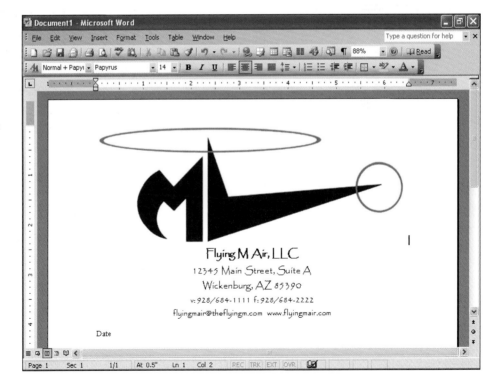

create a letterhead template

resize an image

Although I love the image that artist Gary-Paul Prince created for my company logo, I really don't want it to take up so much space on my letterhead. So I'll resize it.

1 Click the logo to select it. A box with resizing handles appears around the image.

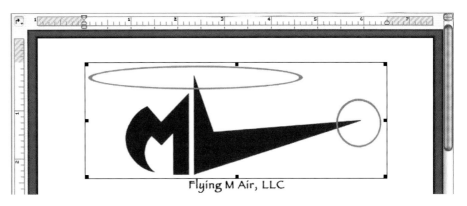

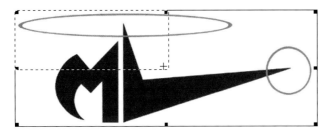

2 Position the mouse pointer on a corner resizing handle, press the mouse button down, and drag toward the middle of the image. A dotted-line box indicates the size the image will be when you release the mouse button.

3 When the image box is the size you want, release the mouse button. The image resizes.

Flying M Air, LLC
12345 Main Street, Suite A
Wickenburg, AZ 85390
v: 928/684-1111 f: 928/684-2222
flyingmair@theflyingm.com www.flyingmair.com

create a letterhead template

save as a template

When the letterhead document is just the way you want it, you can save it as a template. A template is a special type of Word document that you can use as a starting point for creating other documents.

1 Choose Save As from the File menu to display the Save As dialog.

When you save a document as a template, Word automatically displays the contents of the Templates (Windows) or My Templates (Mac OS) folder.

3 Enter Letterhead in the File name (Windows) or Save As (Mac OS) box.

2 Choose Document Template from the Save as type drop-down list (Windows) or Format pop-up menu (Mac OS).

In Mac OS, you may have to click here to see the file list area of the dialog.

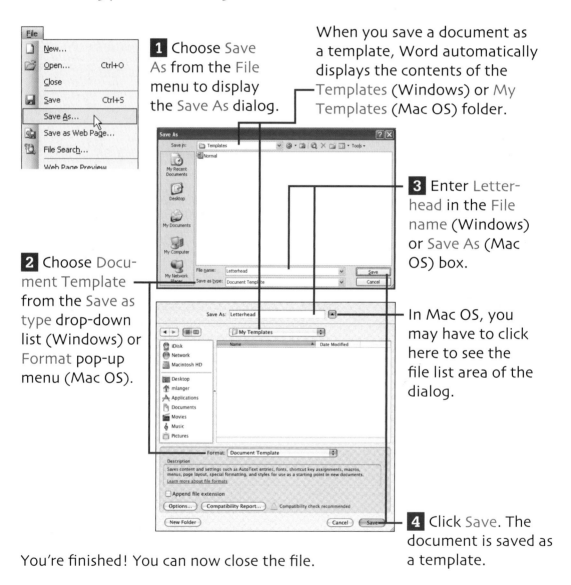

4 Click Save. The document is saved as a template.

You're finished! You can now close the file.

extra bits

prepare a document p. 40

- Print Layout View and Page Layout View are the same. For some reason, Microsoft gave this view different names for Windows and Mac OS.

- You can create a letterhead in any document view. Print Layout View (Windows) or Page Layout View (Mac OS) is best when working with headers and footers or positioning graphics.

set margins pp. 41-42

- If you're creating a template for use with preprinted letterhead, measure the distance from the top of the letterhead paper to the bottom of any text or graphics printed there. Then add a tiny bit—perhaps 0.1 or 0.2 inches—and use that as your top margin measurement. If there's printing on the bottom of the page, measure from the bottom of the paper to the top of the text or graphics there, add a tiny bit, and use that as your bottom margin measurement. This ensures that any letter you write with your letterhead template will not overprint preprinted text or graphics.

- The Gutter box in Margins options is for spacing on bound documents. Keep it set to 0 for single-page documents like a letterhead template.

- Clicking the Default button in the Page Setup (Windows) or Document (Mac OS) dialog enables you to establish the current settings as the default settings for all new blank documents.

enter letterhead text p. 43

- If Smart Tag underlines bother you—they drive me nuts!— point to the underlined text, click on the Smart Tag menu icon that appears, and choose Remove this Smart Tag from the menu.

- What you include in your letterhead is entirely up to you. I like to include the same information that can be found on my business card.

extra bits

create placeholders p. 44

- You don't have to create place-holder text if you don't want to.
- The main benefit of using place-holder text is that it enables you to set formatting for the text that will make up your letter.

apply font formatting p. 46

- Although applying colors to text makes it look great on screen, you'll need a color printer for the colors to appear when the letterhead is printed.
- Don't get carried away with font formatting! Although it's a lot of fun to play with fonts, sizes, and styles, too much for-matting can make a document look trashy. Limit yourself to no more than three fonts in your document. (I used only two.)
- When applying font formatting to placeholder text, be sure to choose a font that is legible. What good is a letter if the re-cipient can't read it?
- You don't have to change the formatting of placeholder text. The default Word font—New Times Roman for Windows and Times for Mac OS— is fine.

insert an image pp. 47-48

- The exact appearance of the Insert Picture (Windows) or Choose a Picture (Mac OS) dia-log varies depending on settings within the dialog. Don't panic if your dialog doesn't look exactly like the ones shown here.

resize an image p. 49

- You can also resize an image by double-clicking it and using the Size options of the Format Picture dialog that appears.

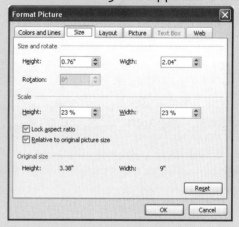

save as a template p. 50

- In Mac OS, turn on the Append file extension check box if you plan to share the template with a Word for Windows user.

create a letterhead template

4. write a letter

Once you've created a letterhead template, you can use that template to create professional-looking letters on your very own letterhead.

Here's how it works. Think of your letterhead template as a box of letterhead paper that never runs out. When you're ready to write a letter, you create a new document based on the template. (That's like pulling a sheet of letterhead paper out of the box.) You replace placeholder text with the text of your letter. (That's like typing the letter on the letterhead paper.) You take care of potential spelling and grammar errors. (That's like proofreading, but Word does a lot of the work.) Then you save, print, and close the document. (That's like making a copy of the letter and filing it where you can find it later on.)

If you've been using Word for a while, you may already create new documents based on existing ones that are similar. But using a template is much better. Why? Because it's virtually impossible to accidentally overwrite the original document with the new one.

In this chapter, you'll create a new document based on a template, replace placeholder text with your letter's text, use Word's proofing tools to fix potential errors, and finish up the document by formatting, saving, printing, and closing it.

Important Note: This chapter assumes that you have already created and saved a letterhead template as instructed in Chapter 3. If you haven't, go back to that chapter and work through the exercise there before continuing here.

create a letter (Windows)

When you create a letter from a template, you are creating a brand new Word document based on an existing template file.

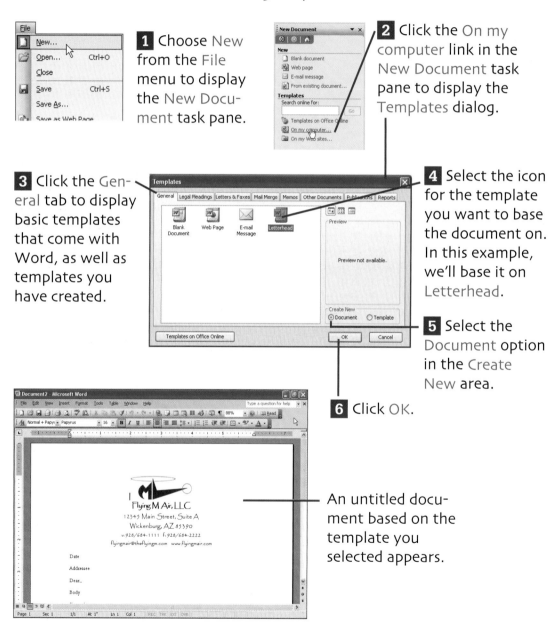

1 Choose New from the File menu to display the New Document task pane.

2 Click the On my computer link in the New Document task pane to display the Templates dialog.

3 Click the General tab to display basic templates that come with Word, as well as templates you have created.

4 Select the icon for the template you want to base the document on. In this example, we'll base it on Letterhead.

5 Select the Document option in the Create New area.

6 Click OK.

An untitled document based on the template you selected appears.

write a letter

create a letter (Mac OS)

When you create a letter from a template, you are creating a brand new Word document based on an existing template file.

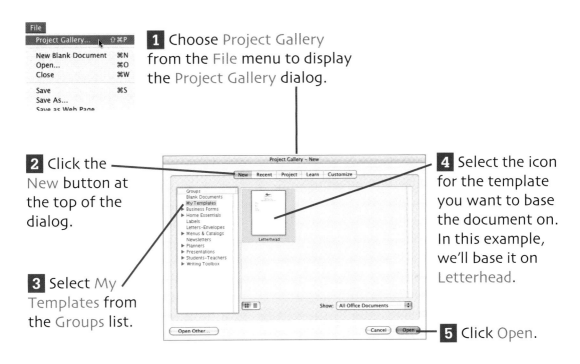

1 Choose Project Gallery from the File menu to display the Project Gallery dialog.

2 Click the New button at the top of the dialog.

3 Select My Templates from the Groups list.

4 Select the icon for the template you want to base the document on. In this example, we'll base it on Letterhead.

5 Click Open.

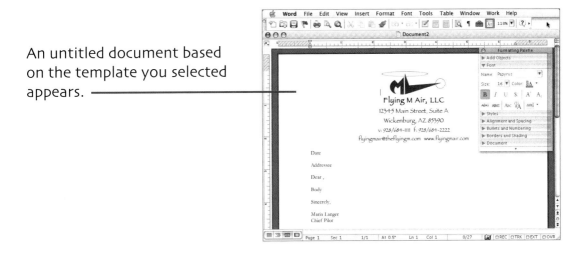

An untitled document based on the template you selected appears.

turn on proofing (Windows)

Word can check your spelling and grammar as you type. Although these proofing tools should be on by default, they may have been disabled. Before you start typing, you may want to confirm that they are on and ready to work.

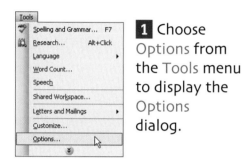

1 Choose Options from the Tools menu to display the Options dialog.

2 Click the Spelling & Grammar tab.

3 Turn on the check boxes marked Check spelling as you type and Check grammar as you type.

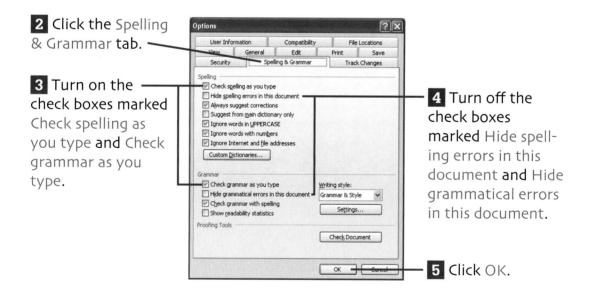

4 Turn off the check boxes marked Hide spelling errors in this document and Hide grammatical errors in this document.

5 Click OK.

write a letter

turn on proofing (Mac OS)

Word can check your spelling and grammar as you type. Although these proofing tools should be on by default, they may have been disabled. Before you start typing, you may want to confirm that they are on and ready to work.

1 Choose Preferences from the Word menu to display the Preferences dialog.

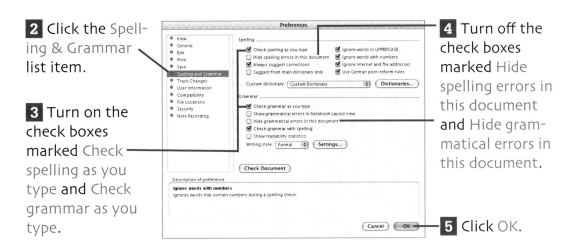

2 Click the Spelling & Grammar list item.

3 Turn on the check boxes marked Check spelling as you type and Check grammar as you type.

4 Turn off the check boxes marked Hide spelling errors in this document and Hide grammatical errors in this document.

5 Click OK.

enter text

Your next task is to replace placeholder text with the text of your letter.

Date

1 Double-click the word Date to select it.

October 21, 2004|

2 Type in today's date the way you want it to appear.

Addressee

3 Double-click the word Addressee to select it.

John Smith
Amenities Director
The GreenWater Resort and Casino
12345 Resort Drive
Quartzsite, AZ 85344|

4 Type in the name, title, company, and address of the recipient. Be sure to press Enter (Windows) or Return (Mac OS) after each line. When you're finished, the single word should be replaced with multiple lines of text.

Dear|

5 Position the blinking insertion point immediately in front of the comma after Dear.

Dear Mr. Smith|

6 Type in the name of the person you are writing to.

Body **7** Double-click the word Body to select it.

My ground crew and I will be in the Quartzsite area next Tuesday, October 26, with our new 2004 Robinson R44 Raven II helicopter and I'd like the opportunity to show you this ship and take you and one or two members of your staff for a ride and I think you'll agree that our rides would make a great activity for resort guests.

I'll be in touch later this week to confirm a time for our visit. At that time, I'll also make arrangments with you for a landing zone on the outer edges of your parking area.

I look forward to seeing you next week|

Remember, green and red squiggles under text indicate potential grammar and spelling problems. I explain how to resolve these on the next page.

8 Type in the body of your letter. Be sure to press Enter (Windows) or Return (Mac OS) at the end of each paragraph—not at the end of each line! If you need help, refer to Chapter 2.

resolve spelling errors

If Word's proofing tools are enabled, Word may indicate potential errors as you type. Red squiggly lines under text indicate possible spelling errors or repeated words. You can use a contextual menu to resolve these errors.

1 Right-click (Windows) or hold down the Control key and click (Mac OS) on a possible spelling error to display a menu of options.

2 Choose an appropriate option from the menu.

Add to Dictionary (Windows) or Add (Mac OS) tells Word to add the word to your dictionary so it knows it for the future. The red squiggles disappear and Word will never mark the word as a possible error again.

Here's an example of a contextual menu full of options for a possible spelling error in Windows.

to confirm a time for our visit. At that
nding 2days c   p:
next week!

| confirm |
| confirms |
| conform |
| Ignore All |
| Add to Dictionary |
| AutoCorrect ▶ |
| Language ▶ |
| Spelling... |
| Look Up... |
| Cut |
| Copy |
| Paste |

Possible corrections are listed at the top of the menu. Choose a correction to replace the marked word.

Ignore All tells Word to ignore all occurrences of the word in this document. The red squiggles disappear.

resolve grammar errors

Green squiggly lines under text indicate possible grammar or style errors. You can also use a contextual menu to learn more about and resolve these errors.

1 Right-click (Windows) or hold down the Control key and click (Mac OS) on a possible grammar error to display a menu of options.

2 Choose an appropriate option from the menu.

Ignore Once (Windows) or Ignore (Mac OS) tells Word to ignore this potential problem. This removes the green squiggles.

Here's what the letter's text might look like once the errors have been resolved. I manually rewrote the first paragraph to break it into three separate sentences.

Here are two examples of contextual menus full of options for possible grammar errors in Mac OS.

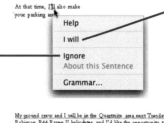

Possible replacement text appears near the top of the menu. Choose a correction to replace the marked word or phrase.

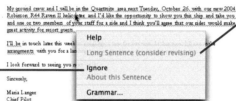

A brief description of the problem with advice on how to fix it may appear in gray. You cannot choose this item. Instead, use it as guidance for fixing the problem.

October 21, 2004

John Smith
Amenities Director
The GreenWater Resort & Casino
12345 Resort Drive
Quartzite, AZ 85344

Dear Mr. Smith,

My ground crew and I will be in the Quartzite area next Tuesday, October 26, with our new 2004 Robinson R44 Raven II helicopter. I'd like the opportunity to show you this ship and take you and one or two members of your staff for a ride. I think you'll agree that our rides would make a great activity for resort guests.

I'll be in touch later this week to confirm a time for our visit. At that time, I'll also make arrangements with you for a landing zone on the outer edges of your parking area.

I look forward to seeing you next week!

Sincerely,

Maria Langer
Chief Pilot

write a letter

finish up

Once you're satisfied with the content of your letter, it's time to finish up. For more information, consult Chapter 2.

1 Apply formatting. There shouldn't be much

My ground crew and I will be in the Quartzsite area next Tuesday, October 26, with our **new 2004 Robinson R44 Raven II helicopter**. I'd like the opportunity to show you this ship and take you and one or two members of your staff for a ride. I think you'll agree that our rides would make a *great* activity for resort guests.

need for this, since you've already formatted both the letterhead text and the placeholder text. But there may be some words or phrases that you want to underline, boldface, or italicize for emphasis.

2 Save the letter. When you use the Save command, Word displays the Save As dialog, just as if you'd started with a blank new document. This makes it virtually impossible to accidentally over-write the existing template file. Be sure to save the document in your My Documents (Windows) or Documents (Mac OS) folder or some other location where you can easily find it.

3 Print the letter. If you're ready to send the letter, print out a copy to send. Don't forget to sign it before you send it out!

4 Close the document. If you're done working with the letter, you can close it.

extra bits

create a letter pp. 54-55

There is an important difference between creating a document from a template and simply opening a template:

- When you create a document from a template, you make a copy of the template that can be saved as a regular Word document.

- When you open a template, however, you open the original template and any changes you make will be saved in the template.

turn on proofing pp. 56-57

- You don't have to use both the spelling and grammar checkers. I personally don't like Word's grammar checker and normally keep it turned off when creating my documents.

- Word's AutoCorrect feature may automatically correct some spelling and typographical errors as you type. AutoCorrect is an advanced feature of Word that is not covered in this book.

enter text p. 58

- To include blank lines between paragraphs in the body of your letter, just press Enter (Windows) or Return (Mac OS) twice after each paragraph.

resolve spelling and grammar errors pp. 59-60

- Not all words and phrases that Word marks as possible spelling or grammar errors are errors. Word marks words it does not recognize as spelling errors and it marks phrases that do not meet requirements of built-in grammar and style rules as grammar errors.

- Do not add a word to Word's dictionary unless you know for sure that it is spelled correctly. Once a word is added to the dictionary, Word will never mark it as a potential error again.

- If you duplicated my letter but don't see the same green squiggles, it may be because of Writing style options set for the grammar checker. Open the Options or Preferences dialog as instructed on page 56 or 57 and make sure your settings are identical to mine.

finish up p. 61

- Don't get carried away with formatting text in the body of your letter. Too many font style changes can quickly turn a professional-looking document into something that looks very amateurish.

- Give your files descriptive names. For example, I like to name letters with the last name of the addressee followed by the date. Then I know at a glance that the document named Smith-102104 is a letter I wrote to Mr. Smith on October 21, 2004.

5. prepare a résumé

A résumé is probably the most important document you create when you're looking for a new job. This piece of paper is a concise summary of your qualifications and work experience. Like an advertisement for your capabilities, its purpose is to begin convincing the reader that you might be the right candidate for an open position. If properly prepared—and sent to the right person—it can help you get a job interview. Then it's up to you to finish what the résumé started.

In this chapter, we'll create a basic résumé with the kinds of standard formatting you'd find in most résumé documents. To help ensure consistent formatting, we'll use Word's Format Painter feature. Even if the résumé you want to create looks a bit different from this one, you should learn everything you need to know to create a résumé to your specifications.

MARIA LANGER
12345 Main Street, Suite A
Wickenburg, AZ 85390
v. 928/684-1111 f. 928/684-2222
maria@theflyingm.com

OBJECTIVE
To obtain work as a helicopter tour/charter pilot and/or Robinson helicopter ferry pilot.

QUALIFICATIONS
- Over 1,000 helicopter hours as pilot in command
- Extensive flight time in Robinson R22, Robinson R44, and Bell 206L1 helicopters
- Numerous cross-country flights in excess of 300 miles
- All Robinson Helicopter Company requirements for ferrying R22 and R44 helicopters in the southwestern United States.

EMPLOYMENT HISTORY

Papillon Airways, Grand Canyon, AZ   April 2004 to Present
Pilot/Captain
I fly Bell 206L1-C30P helicopters on tours of Grand Canyon in a variety of challenging conditions. As Captain, I have direct responsibility for the operation of my assigned aircraft and the safety of my passengers.

Flying M Air, LLC, Wickenburg, AZ   October 2001 to Present
Owner/Pilot
I fly Robinson R22 and Robinson R44 helicopters on part 91 tours of the Wickenburg area. As owner/operator of the company, I am responsible for all aspects of the business, including finances, maintenance arrangements, regulation compliance, and day-to-day operations.

Flying M Productions, Wickenburg, AZ   May 1990 to Present
Freelance Writer
I am the author of over 50 technical books and over 100 articles for computer magazines. I have also written about helicopters and aviation for Sport Aviation, SW Aviator, and America's Flyways.

Automatic Data Processing, Roseland, NJ   August 1987 to May 1990
Senior Financial Analyst
Worked on special projects to help management analyze business performance and trends. Created automated analysis applications with Lotus 1-2-3.

New York City Comptroller's Office, New York, NY   July 1982 to August 1987
Field Audit Supervisor
Worked my way up from starting position as an auditor to supervisor in less than two years. Supervised a staff of 13 auditors working throughout New York City.

EDUCATION

Papillon Airways, Grand Canyon, AZ   April 2004
Turbine Transition Training for Bell 206L1-C30P

Robinson Helicopter Company, Torrance, CA   October 2002
Factory Safety Course

Hofstra University, Hempstead, NY   September 1978 to May 1982
BBA with Highest Honors in Accounting

65

create a document

There are two ways to create a new document for a résumé.

If you have already created a letterhead template, as discussed in Chapter 3, you can use that as your starting document. Follow the instructions on page 54 or 55 to create a new document based on that template. Then select all the placeholder text and press Backspace (Windows) or Delete (Mac OS) to delete it. If your letterhead includes a logo and you want to exclude it from the résumé, click the logo to select it and press Backspace (Windows) or Delete (Mac OS).

If you don't want to use your letterhead—perhaps you want a more personal touch—you can follow the instructions on pages 40–43 to create a blank new document and enter your contact information at the top of the page. Then use techniques in Chapter 2 to format this information.

When you're finished, you should have a new document with just your contact information at the top of the page, like this. This example uses the Gill Sans font in various sizes. I applied bold and small caps font formatting to my name to make it stand out.

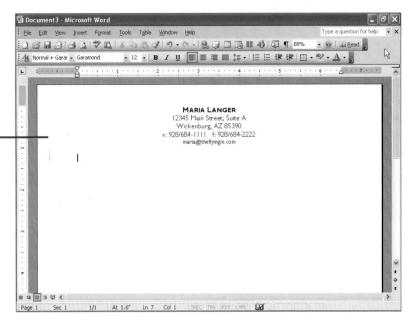

enter objective

This résumé starts with an Objective—what you want to achieve.

1 Position the insertion point on the second blank line. ————————

> **MARIA LANGER**
> 12345 Main Street, Suite A
> Wickenburg, AZ 85390
> v: 928/684-1111 f: 928/684-2222
> maria@theflyingm.com

> **MARIA LANGER**
> 12345 Main Street, Suite A
> Wickenburg, AZ 85390
> v: 928/684-1111 f: 928/684-2222
> maria@theflyingm.com

2 Type Objective. ———————— Objective

3 Press Enter (Windows) or Return (Mac OS).

4 Type the text of your objective.

5 Press Enter (Windows) or Return (Mac OS).

Here's what the Objective section might look like when you're done.

> **MARIA LANGER**
> 12345 Main Street, Suite A
> Wickenburg, AZ 85390
> v: 928/684-1111 f: 928/684-2222
> maria@theflyingm.com
>
> Objective
> To obtain work as a helicopter tour/charter pilot and/or Robinson helicopter ferry pilot

enter qualifications

The Qualifications section lists a few of the most important qualifications you have for the job. You can enter this information in narrative form (a paragraph) or as a list. In this example, we'll enter a list.

1 Position the insertion point on the first blank line after the Objective section. —————

Objective
To obtain work as a helicopter tour/charter pilot and/or Robinson helicopter ferry pilot.
I

2 Type Qualifications.

3 Press Enter (Windows) or Return (Mac OS). —————

Objective
To obtain work as a helicopter tour/charter pilot and/or Robinson helicopter ferry pilot.
Qualifications
I

4 Click the Bullets button on the Formatting toolbar (Windows; left) or the Bullets button in the Bullets and Numbering section of the Formatting Palette (Mac OS; right).

A bullet automatically appears at the beginning of the line.

Objective
To obtain work as a helicopter tour/charter pilot and/or Robinson helicopter ferry pilot.
Qualifications
• I

5 Type the text for a qualification.

6 Press Enter (Windows) or Return (Mac OS). A bullet appears at the new line.

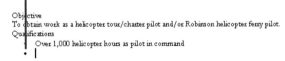

Objective
To obtain work as a helicopter tour/charter pilot and/or Robinson helicopter ferry pilot.
Qualifications
    Over 1,000 helicopter hours as pilot in command
• I

7 Repeat steps 5 and 6 for each qualification you want to list.

8 Click the Bullets button again to "turn off" bullet formatting.

Here's what the Qualifications section might look like when you're done.

Qualifications
• Over 1,000 helicopter hours as pilot in command
• Extensive flight time in Robinson R22, Robinson R44, and Bell 206L1 helicopters
• Numerous cross-country flights in excess of 300 miles
• All Robinson Helicopter Company requirements for ferrying R22 and R44 helicopters in southwestern United States
I

prepare a résumé

enter job history

The Employment History section lists your most recent or pertinent jobs, including company name, dates of employment, job title, and responsibilities.

1 Position the insertion point on the first blank line after the Qualifications section.

2 Type Employment History.

3 Press Enter (Windows) or Return (Mac OS).

Employment History

4 Type the name of the company you worked for, followed by the city and state the company is in.

5 Press the Tab key.

6 Type the dates you worked for that company.

Employment History
Papillon Airways, Grand Canyon, AZ April 2004 to Present

7 Press Enter (Windows) or Return (Mac OS).

8 Type your job title.

9 Press Enter (Windows) or Return (Mac OS).

10 Type two or three sentences describing your responsibilities in that position.

Employment History
Papillon Airways, Grand Canyon, AZ April 2004 to Present
Pilot/Captain
I fly Bell 206L1-C30P helicopters on tours of Grand Canyon in a variety of challenging conditions. As Captain, I have direct responsibility for the operation of my assigned aircraft and the safety of my passengers.

11 Press Enter (Windows) or Return (Mac OS).

12 Repeat steps 4–11 for each job you want to list.

Here's what the Employment History section might look like when you're done.

Employment History
Papillon Airways, Grand Canyon, AZ April 2004 to Present
Pilot/Captain
I fly Bell 206L1-C30P helicopters on tours of Grand Canyon in a variety of challenging conditions. As Captain, I have direct responsibility for the operation of my assigned aircraft and the safety of my passengers.
Flying M Air, LLC, Wickenburg, AZ   October 2001 to Present
Owner/Pilot
I fly Robinson R22 and Robinson R44 helicopters on Part 91 tours of the Wickenburg area. As owner/operator of the company, I am responsible for all aspects of the business, including finances, maintenance arrangements, regulation compliance, and day-to-day operations.
Flying M Productions, Wickenburg, AZ   May 1990 to Present
Freelance Writer
I am the author of over 50 technical books and over 100 articles for computer magazines. I have also written about helicopters and aviation for Sport Aviation, SW Aviator, and America's Flyways.
Automatic Data Processing, Roseland, NJ   August 1987 to May 1990
Senior Financial Analyst
Worked on special projects to help management analyze business performance and trends. Created automated analysis applications with Lotus 1-2-3.
New York City Comptroller's Office, New York, NY July 1982 to August 1987
Field Audit Supervisor
Worked my way up from starting position as auditor to supervisor in less than two years. Supervised staff of 13 auditors working throughout New York City.

enter education

The Education section lists college degrees as well as pertinent training.

1 Position the insertion point on the first blank line after the Employment History section.

2 Type Education.

3 Press Enter (Windows) or Return (Mac OS).

4 Type the name of the school you went to, followed by the city and state the school is in.

5 Press the Tab key.

6 Type the dates you attended school or training.

7 Press Enter (Windows) or Return (Mac OS).

8 Type your degree or the course of study.

9 Press Enter (Windows) or Return (Mac OS).

10 Repeat steps 4–9 for each education item you want to list.

Here's what the Education section might look like when you're done.

Education
Papillon Airways, Grand Canyon, AZ April 2004
Turbine Transition Training for Bell 206L1-C30P
Robinson Helicopter Company, Torrance, CA October 2002
Factory Safety Course
Hofstra University, Hempstead, NY   September 1978 to May 1982
BBA with Highest Honors in Accounting

format headings

We'll make the headings stand out with font and paragraph formatting. We'll use the Format Painter feature to copy formatting options quickly and ensure consistency.

1 Select the first heading (Objective).

Objective
To obtain work as a he

2 Choose Font from the Format menu to display the Font dialog.

3 If necessary, click the Font tab (Windows) or button (Mac OS).

4 Set formatting options as follows:
Font: Gill Sans MT or Gill Sans
Font style: Bold
Size: 14
Effects: Small caps

5 Click OK.

Your settings are applied to the selected text.

OBJECTIVE
To obtain work as a he

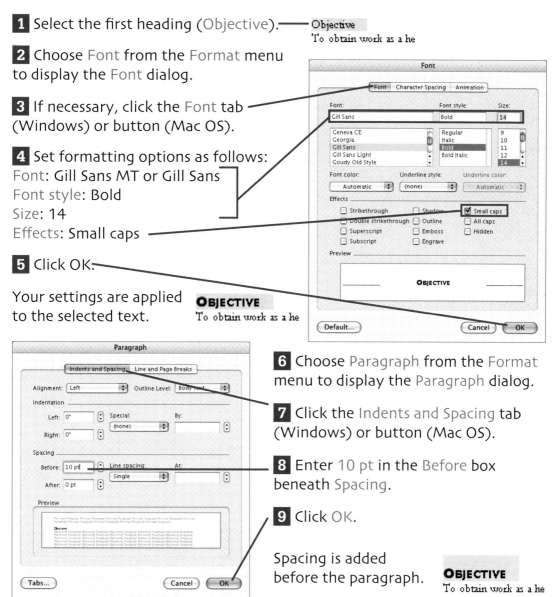

6 Choose Paragraph from the Format menu to display the Paragraph dialog.

7 Click the Indents and Spacing tab (Windows) or button (Mac OS).

8 Enter 10 pt in the Before box beneath Spacing.

9 Click OK.

Spacing is added before the paragraph.

OBJECTIVE
To obtain work as a he

prepare a résumé

71

format headings (cont'd)

10 Double-click the Format Painter button on the Standard toolbar.

Windows

Mac OS

The button becomes selected and the mouse pointer turns into a Format Painter pointer.

In Windows, the Format Painter pointer has a tiny paintbrush.

In Mac OS, the Format Painter pointer has a plus sign.

11 Select the word Qualifications. Its formatting changes to match Objective.

OBJECTIVE
To obtain work as a helicopt

QUALIFICATIONS
- Over 1,000 helicopt

12 Select the remaining headings, one at a time: Employment History and Education. The formatting of both headings changes.

13 Press Esc to turn off the Format Painter feature.

When you're finished, the résumé should look something like this.

MARIA LANGER
12345 Main Street, Suite A
Wickenburg, AZ 85390
v: 928/684-1111 f: 928/684-2222
maria@theflyingm.com

OBJECTIVE
To obtain work as a helicopter tour/charter pilot and/or Robinson helicopter ferry pilot.

QUALIFICATIONS
- Over 1,000 helicopter hours as pilot in command
- Extensive flight time in Robinson R22, Robinson R44, and Bell 206L1 helicopters
- Numerous cross-country flights in excess of 300 miles
- All Robinson Helicopter Company requirements for ferrying R22 and R44 helicopters in the southwestern United States.

EMPLOYMENT HISTORY
Papillon Airways, Grand Canyon, AZ April 2004 to Present
Pilot/Captain
I fly Bell 206L1-C30P helicopters on tours of Grand Canyon in a variety of challenging conditions. As Captain, I have direct responsibility for the operation of my assigned aircraft and the safety of my passengers.
Flying M Air, LLC, Wickenburg, AZ October 2001 to Present
Owner/Pilot
I fly Robinson R22 and Robinson R44 helicopters on part 91 tours of the Wickenburg area. As owner/operator of the company, I am responsible for all aspects of the business, including finances, maintenance arrangements, regulation compliance, and day-to-day operations.
Flying M Productions, Wickenburg, AZ   May 1990 to Present
Freelance Writer
I am the author of over 50 technical books and over 100 articles for computer magazines. I have also written about helicopters and aviation for Sport Aviation, SW Aviator, and America's Flyways.
Automatic Data Processing, Roseland, NJ   August 1987 to May 1990
Senior Financial Analyst
Worked on special projects to help management analyze business performance and trends. Created automated analysis applications with Lotus 1-2-3.
New York City Comptroller's Office, New York, NY July 1982 to August 1987
Field Audit Supervisor
Worked my way up from starting position as an auditor to supervisor in less than two years. Supervised a staff of 13 auditors working throughout New York City.

EDUCATION
Papillon Airways, Grand Canyon, AZ April 2004
Turbine Transition Training for Bell 206L1-C30P
Robinson Helicopter Company, Torrance, CA October 2002
Factory Safety Course
Hofstra University, Hempstead, NY   September 1978 to May 1982
BBA with Highest Honors in Accounting

prepare a résumé

format items

Now, we'll use paragraph and tab formatting for the first line of each item under Employment History and Education. The Format Painter feature will make duplicating the formatting easy.

1 Select the first line under Employment History.

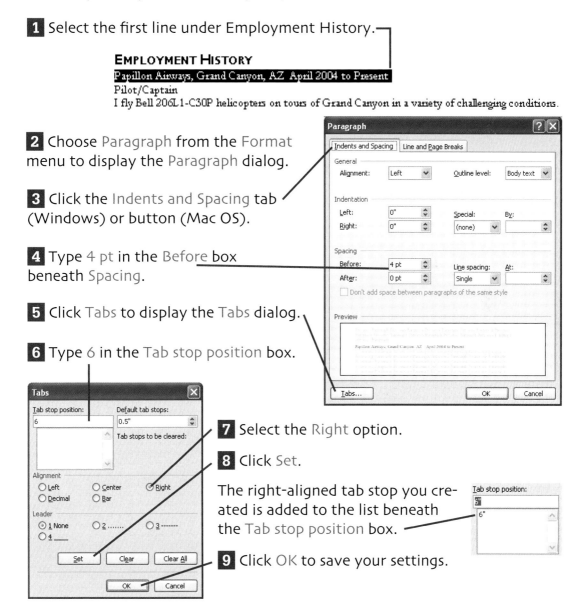

EMPLOYMENT HISTORY
Papillon Airways, Grand Canyon, AZ April 2004 to Present
Pilot/Captain
I fly Bell 206L1-C30P helicopters on tours of Grand Canyon in a variety of challenging conditions.

2 Choose Paragraph from the Format menu to display the Paragraph dialog.

3 Click the Indents and Spacing tab (Windows) or button (Mac OS).

4 Type 4 pt in the Before box beneath Spacing.

5 Click Tabs to display the Tabs dialog.

6 Type 6 in the Tab stop position box.

7 Select the Right option.

8 Click Set.

The right-aligned tab stop you created is added to the list beneath the Tab stop position box.

9 Click OK to save your settings.

format items (cont'd)

The text is shifted down and a right-aligned tab stop shifts the dates to the right.

EMPLOYMENT HISTORY

Papillon Airways, Grand Canyon, AZ	April 2004 to Present

Pilot/Captain
I fly Bell 206L1-C30P helicopters on tours of Grand Canyon in a variety of challenging conditions.

10 Double-click the Format Painter button (see page 72). The mouse pointer turns into a Format Painter pointer.

11 One by one, select each paragraph containing the name of a company under Employment History. The paragraph formatting changes to match the first company.

12 One by one, select each paragraph containing the name of a school or training organization under Education. The paragraph formatting changes to match the companies.

13 Press Esc to turn off the Format Painter feature.

When you're finished, the résumé should look something like this.

MARIA LANGER
12345 Main Street, Suite A
Wickenburg, AZ 85390
v: 928/684-1111 f: 928/684-2222
maria@theflyingm.com

OBJECTIVE
To obtain work as a helicopter tour/charter pilot and/or Robinson helicopter ferry pilot

QUALIFICATIONS
- Over 1,000 helicopter hours as pilot in command
- Extensive flight time in Robinson R22, Robinson R44, and Bell 206L1 helicopters
- Numerous cross-country flights in excess of 300 miles
- All Robinson Helicopter Company requirements for ferrying R22 and R44 helicopters in the southwestern United States.

EMPLOYMENT HISTORY
Papillon Airways, Grand Canyon, AZ   April 2004 to Present
Pilot/Captain
I fly Bell 206L1-C30P helicopters on tours of Grand Canyon in a variety of challenging conditions. As Captain, I have direct responsibility for the operation of my assigned aircraft and the safety of my passengers.
Flying M Air, LLC, Wickenburg, AZ   October 2001 to Present
Owner/Pilot
I fly Robinson R22 and Robinson R44 helicopters on part 91 tours of the Wickenburg area. As owner/operator of the company, I am responsible for all aspects of the business, including finances, maintenance arrangements, regulation compliance, and day-to-day operations.
Flying M Productions, Wickenburg, AZ   May 1990 to Present
Freelance Writer
I am the author of over 50 technical books and over 100 articles for computer magazines. I have also written about helicopters and aviation for Sport Aviation, SW Aviator, and America's Flyways.
Automatic Data Processing, Roseland, NJ   August 1987 to May 1990
Senior Financial Analyst
Worked on special projects to help management analyze business performance and trends. Created automated analysis applications with Lotus 1-2-3.
New York City Comptroller's Office, New York, NY   July 1982 to August 1987
Field Audit Supervisor
Worked my way up from starting position as an auditor to supervisor in less than two years. Supervised a staff of 13 auditors working throughout New York City.

EDUCATION
Papillon Airways, Grand Canyon, AZ   April 2004
Turbine Transition Training for Bell 206L1-C30P
Robinson Helicopter Company, Torrance, CA   October 2002
Factory Safety Course
Hofstra University, Hempstead, NY   September 1978 to May 1982
BBA with Highest Honors in Accounting

prepare a résumé

indent descriptions

We'll indent the descriptive text in the Employment History area using the ruler and the Format Painter.

1 Click to position the blinking insertion point anywhere In the para-graph of descriptive text under the first job's title.

Papillon Airways, Grand Canyon, AZ   April 2004 to Present
Pilot/Captain
I fly Bell 206L1-C30P helicopters on tours of Grand Canyon in a variety of challenging conditions. As Captain, I have direct responsibility for the operation of my assigned aircraft and the safety of my passengers.

2 Drag the left indent marker (the bottom-most of the three left indentation markers on the ruler) about 1/4 inch to the right.

Papillon Airways, Grand Canyon, AZ
Pilot/Captain
I fly Bell 206L1-C30P helicopters on to
As Captain, I have direct responsibility
passengers.

As you drag, a vertical line appears to indicate where the new indentation setting will appear.

When you release the mouse button, each line in the paragraph shifts to the right.

Papillon Airways, Grand Canyon, AZ   April 2004 to Present
Pilot/Captain
    I fly Bell 206L1-C30P helicopters on tours of Grand Canyon in a variety of challenging conditions. As Captain, I have direct responsibility for the operation of my assigned aircraft and the safety of my passengers.

3 Double-click the Format Painter button (see page 72).

4 One by one, click in each paragraph of descriptive text under your job titles. Each paragraph shifts to match the one you for-matted first.

When you're finished indenting paragraphs, the résumé should look something like this.

MARIA LANGER
12345 Main Street, Suite A
Wickenburg AZ 85390
v:928/684-1111 f:928/684-2222
maria@theflyingm.com

OBJECTIVE
To obtain work as a helicopter tour/charter pilot and/or Robinson helicopter ferry pilot

QUALIFICATIONS
• Over 1,000 helicopter hours as pilot in command
• Extensive flight time in Robinson R22, Robinson R44, and Bell 206L1 helicopters
• Numerous cross-country flights in excess of 300 miles
• All Robinson Helicopter Company requirements for ferrying R22 and R44 helicopters in the southwestern United States.

EMPLOYMENT HISTORY
Papillon Airways, Grand Canyon, AZ   April 2004 to Present
Pilot/Captain
    I fly Bell 206L1-C30P helicopters on tours of Grand Canyon in a variety of challenging conditions. As Captain, I have direct responsibility for the operation of my assigned aircraft and the safety of my passengers.
Flying M Air, LLC, Wickenburg, AZ   October 2001 to Present
Owner/Pilot
    I fly Robinson R22 and Robinson R44 helicopters on part 91 tours of the Wickenburg area. As owner/operator of the company, I am responsible for all aspects of the business, including finances, maintenance arrangements, regulation compliance, and day-to-day operations
Flying M Productions, Wickenburg, AZ   May 1990 to Present
Freelance Writer
    I am the author of over 50 technical books and over 100 articles for computer magazines. I have also written about helicopters and aviation for Sport Aviation, SW Aviator, and America's Flyways.
Automatic Data Processing, Roseland, NJ   August 1987 to May 1990
Senior Financial Analyst
    Worked on special projects to help management analyze business performance and trends. Created automated analysis applications with Lotus 1-2-3.
New York City Comptroller's Office, New York, NY   July 1982 to August 1987
Field Audit Supervisor
    Worked my way up from starting position as an auditor to supervisor in less than two years. Supervised a staff of 13 auditors working throughout New York City.

EDUCATION
Papillon Airways, Grand Canyon, AZ   April 2004
Turbine Transition Training for Bell 206L1-C30P
Robinson Helicopter Company, Torrance, CA   October 2002
Factory Safety Course
Hofstra University, Hempstead, NY   September 1978 to May 1982
BBA with Highest Honors in Accounting

finish formatting

The résumé needs a bit more formatting before it's complete. Here are some suggestions.

Select each company name and use the Bold button on the Formatting toolbar (Windows) or Formatting Palette (Mac OS) to make it bold.

Select each school or training organization name and use the Bold button on the Formatting toolbar (Windows) or Formatting Palette (Mac OS) to make it bold.

Select each job title and use the Italic button on the Formatting toolbar (Windows) or Formatting Palette (Mac OS) to make it italic.

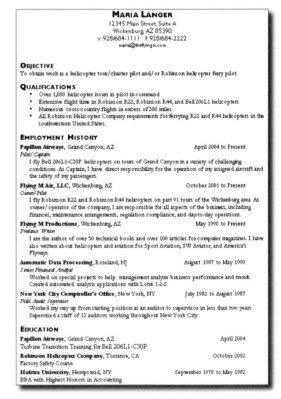

Here's what your résumé might look like when you've finished applying formatting.

justify page

If your résumé is brief, it may look like it's all bunched up at the top of the paper when printed. You can fix this with the page justification feature.

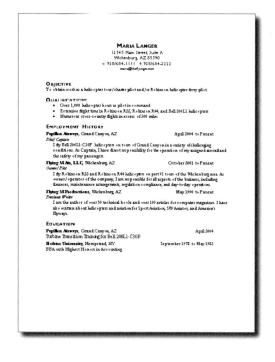

1 In Windows, choose Page Setup from the File menu to display the Page Setup dialog...

...or in Mac OS, choose Document from the Format menu to display the Document dialog.

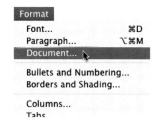

justify page (cont'd)

2 Click the Layout tab (Windows) or button (Mac OS).

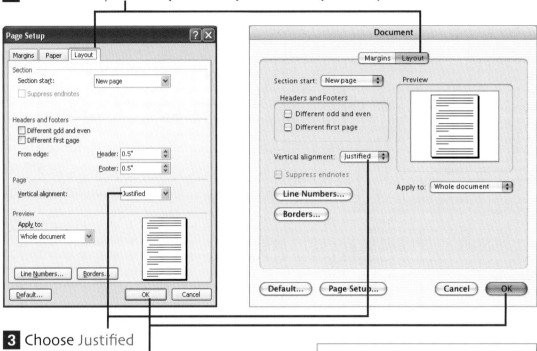

3 Choose Justified from the Vertical alignment drop-down list (Windows) or pop-up menu (Mac OS).

4 Click OK.

The page contents are distributed vertically between the top and bottom margins.

prepare a résumé

insert a page break

If your résumé is very long, it might require two pages to print. Although it's best to limit your résumé to one page, if you can't edit it to make it shorter, you might find it necessary to insert a manual page break to prevent the page break from occurring in the middle of a paragraph or some other undesired location.

1 Position the insertion point at the beginning of the line you want to appear at the top of the second page.

New York City Comptroller's Office, New York, N
Field Audit Supervisor
   Worked my way up from starting position as an au
   Supervised a staff of 13 auditors working through

EDUCATION
Papillon Airways, Grand Canyon, AZ
Turbine Transition Training for Bell 206L1-C30P

In Windows:

2 Choose Break from the Insert menu to display the Break dialog.

3 Select Page break.

4 Click OK.

In Mac OS:

2 Choose Page Break from the Break submenu under the Insert menu.

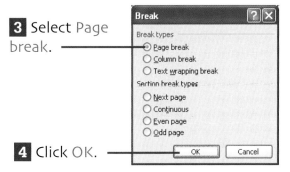

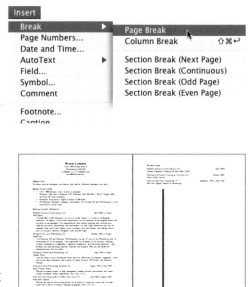

A page break is inserted in the document at the insertion point. The text after it is forced to the next page.

finish up

Once you're satisfied with your résumé, it's time to finish up. For more information about any of these steps, consult Chapter 2.

1 Save the résumé. When you use the Save command, Word displays the Save As dialog. Be sure to save the document in your My Documents (Windows) or Documents (Mac OS) folder or some other location where you can easily find it.

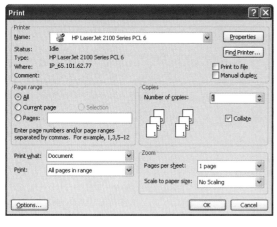

2 Print the résumé. Use the Print command to print out a copy. Use good quality paper and make sure your printer has a good toner or ink jet cartridge so print quality is good.

3 Close the document file. If you're done working with the résumé, close it.

extra bits

enter qualifications p. 68

- When entering qualifications, don't get carried away. Limit yourself to 4 or 5 items.
- Use parallel constructions when composing list items. For example, if the first item on the list is a full sentence, all items on the list should be a full sentence. If the first item on the list is first person past tense, all items on the list should be first person past tense. Consult a style guide such as "The Elements of Style" for help.

format headings pp. 71-72

- To copy font formatting using the Format Painter, you must select the text with the formatting you want to copy before clicking or double-clicking the Format Painter button.
- Double-clicking the Format Painter button turns it on for multiple uses. If you only wanted to copy a format to one destination, click the Format Painter button once and select the destination text. The cursor returns to normal after one use.

format items pp. 73-74

- To copy paragraph formatting using the Format Painter, you can click anywhere in the paragraph with the formatting you want to copy before clicking or double-clicking the Format Painter button. Selecting the entire paragraph is not required.
- If the dates of employment do not shift to the right as shown on page 74 after setting up the tab stop or using the Format Painter, it's probably because you didn't press the Tab key immediately before the date. Position the insertion point to the left of the date and press the Tab key. The text should shift.

extra bits

indent descriptions p. 75

- If the ruler is not showing, choose Ruler from the View menu to display it.

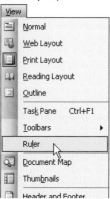

insert a page break p. 79

- You can only insert a manual page break before an automatic one. Inserting a manual page break after an automatic page break will break the document into more pages.
- To delete a page break, position the insertion point right at the beginning of the page and press Backspace (Windows) or Delete (Mac OS).

justify page pp. 77-78

- If your résumé is very short, adjust your margins so they're at least 1.5 inches at the top and bottom. Otherwise, you might wind up with big gaps between lines of text. For more on how to set margins, see Chapter 3.

prepare a résumé

6. create
business cards

Business cards are an important part of anyone's personal marketing toolkit. Not only do they provide a handy way to distribute your contact information to acquaintances and business associates, but they help reinforce your company's business identity.

Word's label feature makes it easy to create business cards on special business card stock. This paper, manufactured by companies such as Avery, enables you to print 10 standard-sized business cards on a single sheet. When the page emerges from your printer, simply tear the cards apart at the perforations.

This chapter explains how to create business cards that include complete contact information and a company logo.

open the labels dialog

You use the Labels tab of the Envelopes and Labels dialog (Windows) or the Labels dialog (Mac OS) to create a business card document.

In Windows:

1 Choose Envelopes and Labels from the Letters and Mailings submenu under the Tools menu.

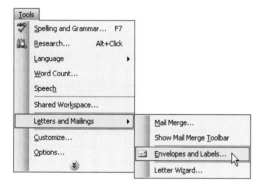

2 In the Envelopes and Labels dialog that appears, click the Labels tab to display its options.

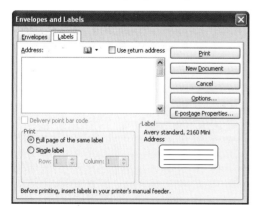

In Mac OS:

Choose Labels from the Tools menu.

The Labels dialog appears.

create business cards

select card product

The first task is to select the type of paper you will be using for your business cards. In this example, I'm using Avery product number 5371.

1 Click the Options button in the Labels tab of the Envelopes and Labels dialog (Windows) or the Labels dialog (Mac OS).

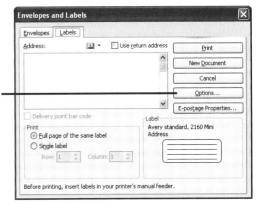

The Label Options dialog appears.

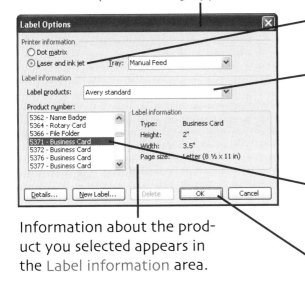

Information about the product you selected appears in the Label information area.

2 Select the Laser and ink jet option.

3 Choose the name of the business card paper manufacturer from the Label products drop-down list (Windows) or pop-up menu (Mac OS).

4 Select the business card paper's product name or code from the Product number scrolling list.

5 Click OK to return to the Envelopes and Labels (Windows) or Labels (Mac OS) dialog.

The name of the product you selected should appear in the Label area.

enter card text

Now, enter the text you want to appear on every card.

1 Position the blinking insertion point in the Address box of
the Labels tab of the Envelopes
and Labels dialog (Windows) or
Labels dialog (Mac OS).

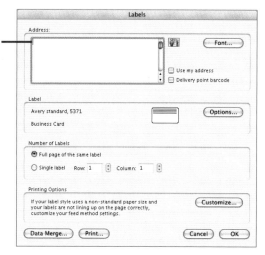

2 Type in all the contact
information you want to
appear on the card. Press Enter
(Windows) or Return (Mac
OS) at the end of each line.

As shown here, I included
my name, title, company
name, address, phone
numbers, e-mail address,
and Web site.

create the document

When you save your settings in the Envelopes and Labels dialog (Windows) or Labels dialog (Mac OS), Word creates the business card document.

In Windows, click the New Document button In the Labels tab of the Envelopes and Labels dialog.

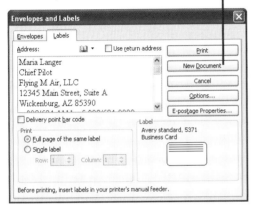

In Mac OS, click the OK button in the Labels dialog.

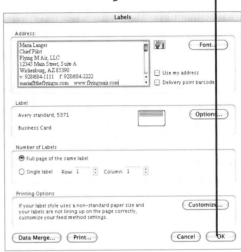

Word creates a new document that uses its table feature to lay out the ten business cards.

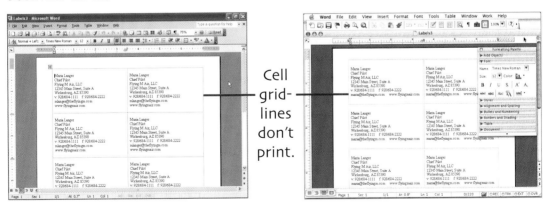

Cell grid-lines don't print.

Windows

Mac OS

format the text

You may want to format the business card text with a different font, size, and style. Just apply formatting to one card; you'll be copying that card to replace the other cards before printing.

1 Select the text you want to format in the first (top-left) business card on the page.

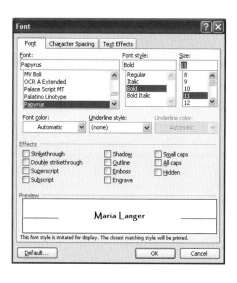

2 Choose Font from the Format menu to display the Font dialog.

3 Set font formatting options as desired. If you need help, refer to Chapter 2.

4 Click OK to save your settings.

5 Repeat steps 1–4 for all the text you want to format in the first card.

Here's what my card looks like so far. I applied 11 pt bold Papyrus font to my name, 12 pt Gill Sans font to my company name, and 10 pt Gill Sans font to the remaining text.

create business cards

6 Select all the text on the first card.

7 Click the Center button on the Formatting toolbar (Windows) or the Align Center button in the Alignment and Spacing area of the Formatting Palette (Mac OS).

The text is centered.

insert an image

Inserting a small image or logo helps reinforce your company identity.

1 Position the insertion point to the left of the first letter in the first card.

2 Choose From File from the Picture submenu under the Insert menu.

3 Use the Insert Picture (Windows) or Choose a Picture (Mac OS) dialog that appears to locate and select the image you want to insert. If you need help using this dialog, consult Chapter 2.

4 Click Insert.

The image is inserted in the first card.

5 Press Enter (Windows) or Return (Mac OS) to place the image in its own paragraph.

6 If necessary, follow the instructions on page 49 to resize the image.

When you're done, the first card might look something like this.

create business cards

duplicate the card

When the first card on the page looks the way you want it to, duplicate it to replace the other cards, which are acting as placeholders, on the page.

1 Position the mouse pointer near the bottom-right corner of the first card.

2 Triple-click the mouse button. The entire card becomes selected.

3 Choose Copy from the Edit menu. The first card is copied to the clipboard.

4 Press the Tab key to select the next card.

5 Choose Paste Cells from the Edit menu.

The selected card is replaced with a copy of the first card.

6 Repeat steps 4 and 5 to replace the remaining cards with the finished card.

When you're finished, the document should look like the one on the next page.

finish your cards

When the document is complete, you can save, print, and close it.

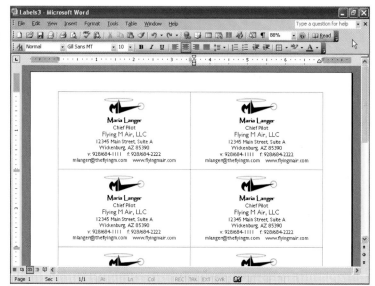

1 Save the business cards. Be sure to save the business card document in your My Documents (Windows) or Documents (Mac OS) folder or some other location where you can easily find it.

2 Print the business cards. Insert the business card paper into your printer's print tray or manual feeder and use the Print command to print a sheet of business cards. You can then tear along the perforations to separate the sheet of cards into ten individual cards.

3 Close the document file. If you're done working with the business cards, close the document.

create business cards

extra bits

open the labels dialog p. 84

- You must have at least one document open to use the Envelopes and Labels (Windows) or Labels (Mac OS) command. If no documents are open, click the New Blank Document button on the standard toolbar to create one. You can then choose the Labels command.

select card product p. 85

- You can get the name of the business card paper manufacturer and the product number from the package the business card paper comes in.

enter card text p. 86

- The Use return address (Windows) or Use my address (Mac OS) check box must be turned off to enter custom text in the Address box in the Labels tab of the Envelopes and Labels dialog (Windows) or Labels dialog (Mac OS).

- For best results, don't enter more than 7 or 8 lines of text in your business card. If you enter more, you won't be able to fit a logo or other graphic.

- The Mac OS version of Word enables you to format business card (or label) text right inside the Labels dialog. Just click the Font button to display the Font dialog and format selected text in the Address box.

create the document p. 87

- If the gray table gridlines do not appear, choose Show Gridlines from the Table menu.

duplicate the card p. 91

- Do not press the Tab key after pasting in the last card on the page. Doing so will create a new row in the table and mess up the document. If you do this by mistake (oops!), choose Undo Next Cell from the Edit menu.

create business cards

7. produce a flyer

Flyers are a great way to spread the word about a product or event. Not only can they summarize all the important information you need to share, but they're easy to create and inexpensive to reproduce in quantity.

In this chapter, we'll produce a flyer like the one shown here to advertise a special, limited-time offer. The flyer will include page borders, formatted text, and a positioned graphic. As you work through this project, you'll learn plenty of techniques to help you create your own flyers and single-page brochures.

Special Offer
this August only

SUNRISE HELICOPTER TOURS

- See the desert come to life in the early morning light.

- Enjoy cool air and a smooth, turbulence-free flight.

- Flights depart at 5:30 AM
  30 minutes: $79/person
  60 minutes: $159/person

Call for Reservations:
Flying M Air
684-1111

prepare a document

Start by creating a new document and changing the view.

1 Click the New Blank Document button on the Standard toolbar to create a new document.

2 Click the Print Layout View button (Windows) or Page Layout View button (Mac OS) at the bottom of the document window. This switches you to a layout view where you can see the document the way it will print.

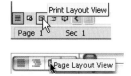

3 Choose Whole Page from the Zoom drop-down list on the Standard toolbar.

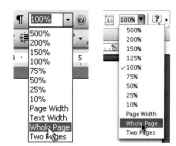

The view changes so you can see the entire page at once.

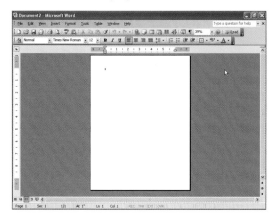 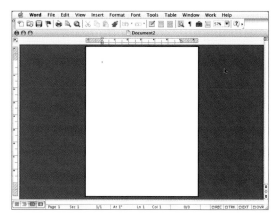

set page options

Next, set the margins and other page layout options.

1 In Windows, choose Page Setup from the File menu...

...or in Mac OS, choose Document from the Format menu.

2 In the Page Setup (Windows) or Document (Mac OS) dialog that appears, click the Margins tab (Windows) or button (Mac OS).

3 Type .75 in the Top, Bottom, Left, and Right boxes.

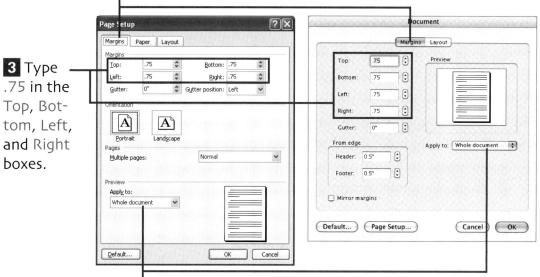

4 Choose Whole document from the Apply to drop-down list (Windows) or pop-up menu (Mac OS).

set page options (cont'd)

5 Click the Layout tab (Windows) or button (Mac OS) to display layout options.

6 Choose Center from the Vertical alignment drop-down list (Windows) or pop-up menu (Mac OS).

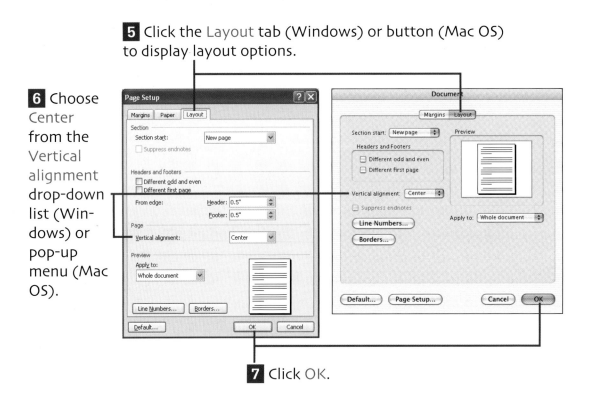

7 Click OK.

produce a flyer

set default formats

Because the text on this flyer will be large and we're working with it in a reduced view, we'll set a default font and font size now. We'll also add some spacing before each paragraph to separate the paragraphs a bit. This will make the text easy to read while we work and give us an idea of how much text will fit on the page.

1 Choose Font from the Format menu.

2 Click the Font tab (Windows) or button (Mac OS) in the Font dialog that appears.

3 Set font options as follows:
Font: Arial Rounded MT Bold
Font style: Bold
Size: 18

4 Click OK.

5 Choose Paragraph from the Format menu.

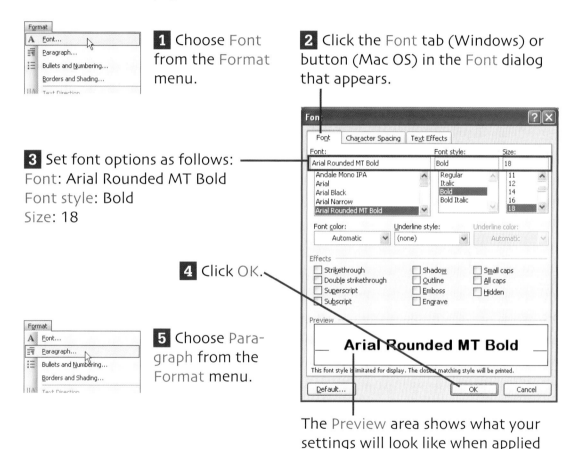

The Preview area shows what your settings will look like when applied to text.

set default formats (cont'd)

6 Click the Indents and Spacing tab (Windows) or button (Mac OS).

7 Choose Left from the Alignment drop-down list (Windows) or pop-up menu (Mac OS).

8 Type 24 pt in the Before box in the Spacing area.

9 Click OK.

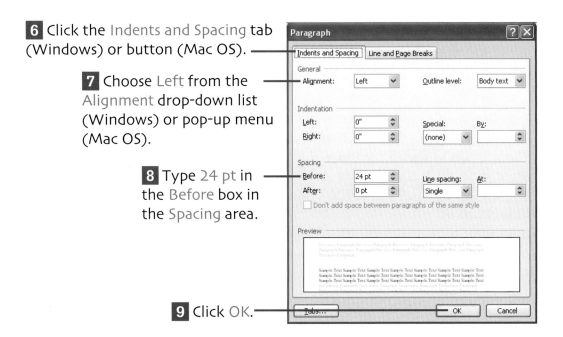

At this point, you should see a blink-ing insertion point half-way down the page near the left margin of the document window.

produce a flyer

add a page border

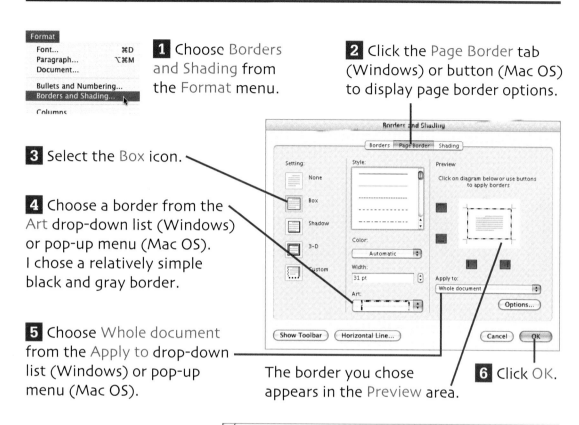

1 Choose Borders and Shading from the Format menu.

2 Click the Page Border tab (Windows) or button (Mac OS) to display page border options.

3 Select the Box icon.

4 Choose a border from the Art drop-down list (Windows) or pop-up menu (Mac OS). I chose a relatively simple black and gray border.

5 Choose Whole document from the Apply to drop-down list (Windows) or pop-up menu (Mac OS).

The border you chose appears in the Preview area.

6 Click OK.

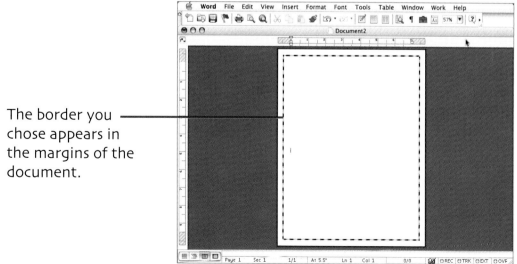

The border you chose appears in the margins of the document.

enter text

The next step is to enter the text you want to appear on the flyer.

Type the text in, using text entry techniques discussed in Chapter 2.

When you're finished, it might
look something like this.

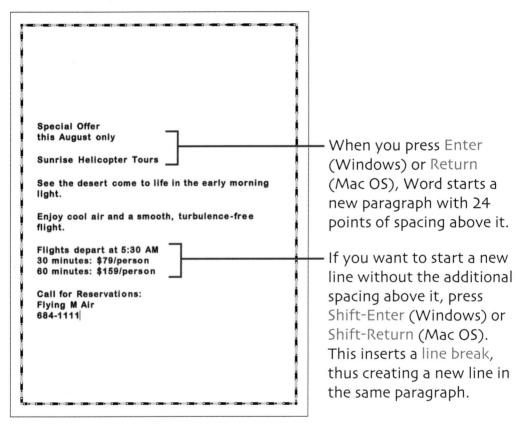

**Special Offer
this August only**

Sunrise Helicopter Tours

**See the desert come to life in the early morning
light.**

**Enjoy cool air and a smooth, turbulence-free
flight.**

**Flights depart at 5:30 AM
30 minutes: $79/person
60 minutes: $159/person**

**Call for Reservations:
Flying M Air
684-1111**

When you press Enter
(Windows) or Return
(Mac OS), Word starts a
new paragraph with 24
points of spacing above it.

If you want to start a new
line without the additional
spacing above it, press
Shift-Enter (Windows) or
Shift-Return (Mac OS).
This inserts a line break,
thus creating a new line in
the same paragraph.

produce a flyer

format text

Once you have all the text you want on the flyer and can see how it fits, you can go back and format specific text to make it larger or smaller. You can also change fonts, styles, and colors. You do all this with the Font dialog.

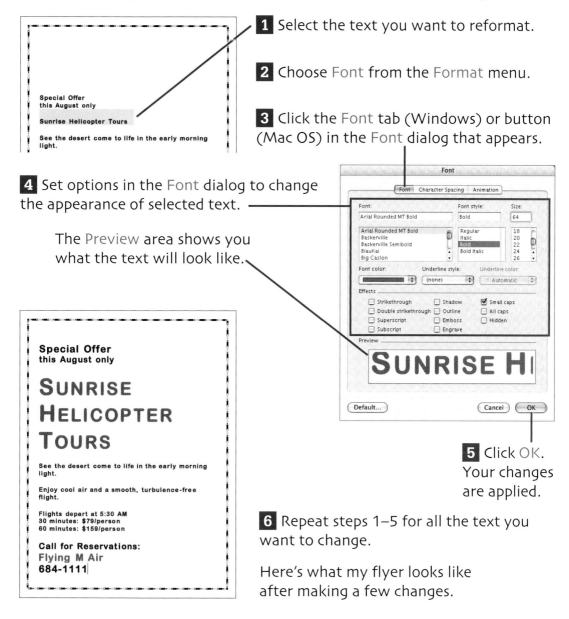

1 Select the text you want to reformat.

2 Choose Font from the Format menu.

3 Click the Font tab (Windows) or button (Mac OS) in the Font dialog that appears.

4 Set options in the Font dialog to change the appearance of selected text.

The Preview area shows you what the text will look like.

5 Click OK. Your changes are applied.

6 Repeat steps 1–5 for all the text you want to change.

Here's what my flyer looks like after making a few changes.

add a bulleted list

If your flyer includes a list of items, you can format them with bullets so they're easily recognized as a list.

1 Select the paragraphs that you want to format as a list.

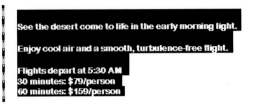

2 Click the Bullets button on the Standard toolbar (Windows) or the Bullets button in the Bullets and Numbering area of the Formatting Palette (Mac OS).

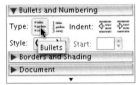

The paragraphs you selected are formatted as a bulleted list.

position an image

You can include an image in your flyer and position it exactly where you want it to appear.

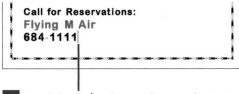

1 Position the insertion point at the end of the document.

2 Follow the instructions on pages 47–48 to insert an image file into the document.

3 If your image needs to be resized, follow the instructions on page 49 to resize it.

At this point, your document might look like this. As you can see, inserting the image caused a second page to be added to my document. I'll fix that when I move the image.

4 Double-click the image to display the Format Picture dialog.

5 Click the Layout tab (Windows) or button (Mac OS).

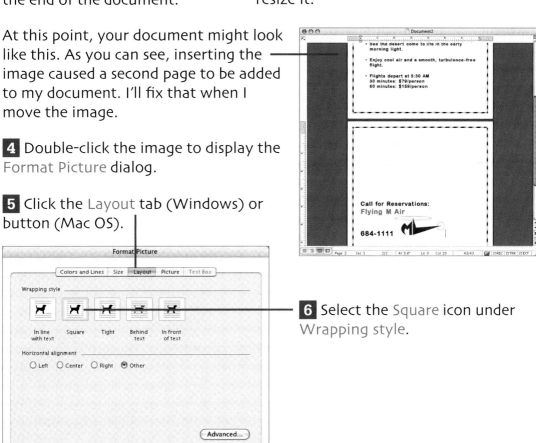

6 Select the Square icon under Wrapping style.

7 Click OK.

position an image (cont'd)

The image shifts and circles (Windows) or boxes (Mac OS) appear at its corners and sides.

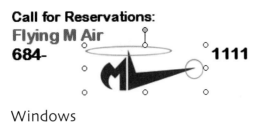

Windows

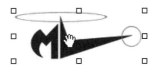

Call for Reservations:
Flying M Air
684-1111

Mac OS

8 Position the mouse pointer in the middle of the image.

In Windows, the mouse pointer turns into a pointer with a four-headed arrow.

In Mac OS, the mouse pointer turns into a hand.

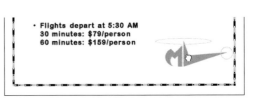

9 Drag the image to the bottom-right corner of the first page of the document. In Windows, a box representing the image's outline moves as you drag it. In Mac OS, a shadow of the image moves as you drag it, as shown here.

When you release the mouse button, the image appears in its new position. Any text that would be hidden shifts so it wraps around the image.

produce a flyer

print in color (Windows)

If you have a color printer and have included color in your flyer, you should print it in color.

1 Choose Print from the File menu to display the Print dialog.

2 Choose your color printer from the Name drop-down list.

3 Click the Properties button to display the Properties dialog for your printer.

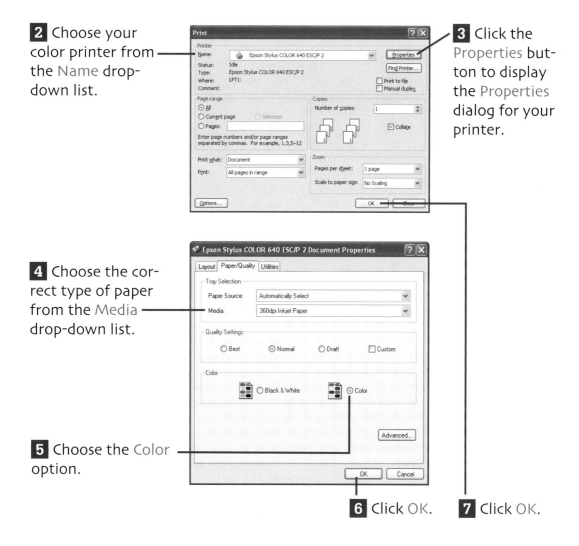

4 Choose the correct type of paper from the Media drop-down list.

5 Choose the Color option.

6 Click OK.   **7** Click OK.

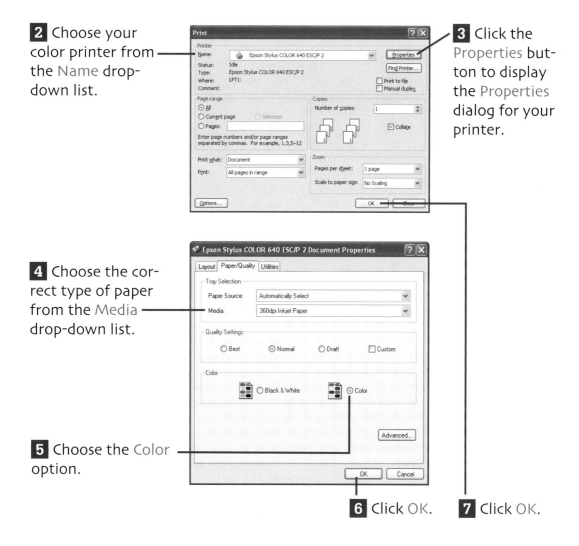

produce a flyer

print in color (Mac OS)

If you have a color printer and have included color in your flyer, you should print it in color.

1 Choose Print from the File menu to display the Print dialog.

2 Choose your color printer from the Printer pop-up menu.

3 Choose Print Settings from the third pop-up menu to display settings for your printer.

4 Choose the correct type of paper from the Media Type pop-up menu.

5 Choose Color from the Ink pop-up menu.

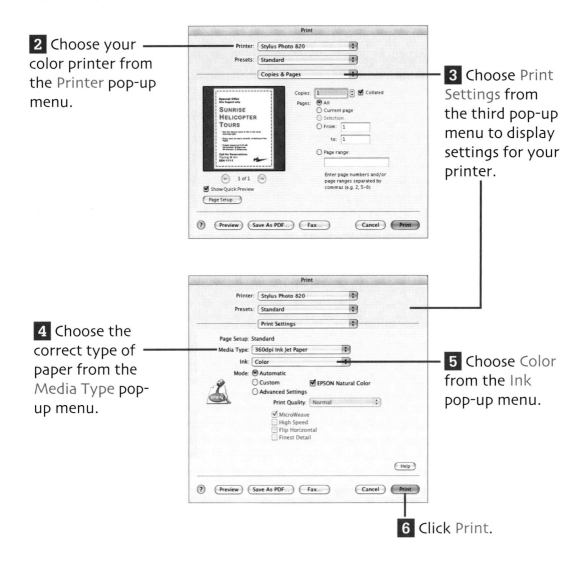

6 Click Print.

produce a flyer

finish your flyer

When you're finished creating and printing your flyer, you can save and close it.

1 Save the flyer. Be sure to save the document in your My Documents (Windows) or Documents (Mac OS) folder or some other location where you can easily find it.

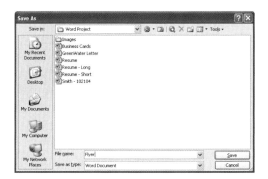

2 Close the document file. If you're done working with the flyer, close the document.

extra bits

set page options pp. 97-98

- Some printers do not allow small margins. If you set margins smaller than that allowed by your printer, a dialog like the one shown here will appear. Click Fix to tell Microsoft Word to adjust the margins to the smallest allowed measurement.

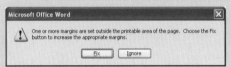

add a page border p. 101

- The first time you use the Art drop-down list in Word for Windows, a dialog may appear, telling you that the feature is not installed. Click the Yes button in that dialog and follow the instructions that appear onscreen to install border art.

enter text p. 102
format text p. 103
add a bulleted list p. 104

- The trick to entering and formatting text on a flyer is to make sure all the text appears on a single page. If your text stretches to two pages, you can get it back down to one page by editing out unnecessary text or making font sizes smaller.

position an image pp. 105-106

- When you set the Wrapping style option to Square in the Layout screen of the Format Picture dialog, you place the image on its own graphic layer so it can be moved anywhere on a page.

print in color pp. 107-108

- The Properties dialog (Windows) and Print dialog (Mac OS) may offer different options than those illustrated on pages 107 and 108. If you're not sure how to set these options to print in color, check the documentation that came with your printer.

produce a flyer

8. print an envelope

Microsoft Word has a built-in envelope-printing feature that makes it easy to create professional-looking envelopes for all of your correspondence.

As you'll see in this chapter, Word can automatically address an envelope based on text in a letter or other document. Or you can create an envelope on-the-fly with any address you want to use.

Maria Langer
Flying M Air, LLC
12345 Main Street, Suite A
Wickenburg, AZ 85390

llululululllullululululul
John Smith
Amenities Director
The GreenWater Resort & Casino
12345 Resort Drive
Quartzite, AZ 85344

select an addressee

If you want to print an envelope for a person you've already written a letter to, Word can address the envelope based on the address already typed in the letter. (If you prefer to create an envelope on-the-fly, you can skip this step.)

1 Open the letter to the person you want to print an envelope for. (See Chapter 2 for more information about opening existing Word documents.)

2 Select the address in the document.

Flying M Air, LLC
12345 Main Street, Suite A
Wickenburg, AZ 85390
v: 928/684-1111 f: 928/684-2222
flyingmair@theflyingm.com www.flyingmair.com

October 21, 2004

John Smith
Amenities Director
The GreenWater Resort & Casino
12345 Resort Drive
Quartzite, AZ 85344

Dear Mr. Smith,

My ground crew and I will be in the Quartzite area next Tuesday, October 26, with our **new 2004 Robinson R44 Raven II helicopter.** I'd like the opportunity to show you this ship and take you and one or two members of your staff for a ride. I think you'll agree that our rides would make a *great* activity for resort guests.

print an envelope

open the envelope dialog

You create an envelope with the Envelopes tab of the Envelopes and Labels dialog (Windows) or with the Envelope dialog (Mac OS). (For simplicity's sake, I'll refer to this as simply the Envelope dialog when discussing the Windows and Mac OS versions of this dialog at the same time.)

In Windows:

1 Choose Envelopes and Labels from the Letters and Mailings submenu under the Tools menu to display the Envelopes and Labels dialog.

2 Click the Envelopes tab to display envelope options.

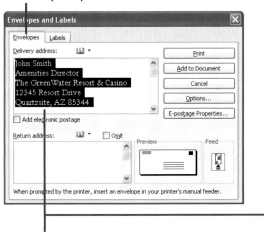

In Mac OS:

Choose Envelopes from the Tools menu.

The Envelope dialog appears.

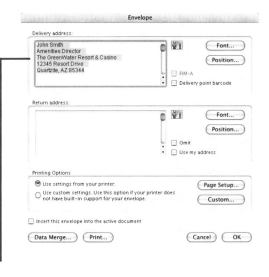

As you can see here, if you selected an addressee before opening the Envelope dialog, the Delivery address box in the dialog is already filled in.

enter addresses

The Envelope dialog has two boxes for envelope addresses: Delivery address and Return address.

1 If the Delivery address box is not already filled in correctly, click in the Delivery address box and type the name and address of the person you want to address the envelope to. Be sure to press Enter (Windows) or Return (Mac OS) after each line.

Jane Jones
1313 Mockingbird Lane
Munster, AL 54236

2 To include a return address on the envelope, click in the Return address box and type in your name and address. Be sure to press Enter (Windows) or Return (Mac OS) after each line.

Maria Langer
Flying M Air, LLC
12345 Main Street, Suite A
Wickenburg, AZ 85390

To omit the return address from the envelope—perhaps you're printing an envelope that already has a return address printed on it—turn on the Omit check box.

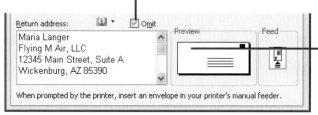

Return address: ☑ Omit
Maria Langer
Flying M Air, LLC
12345 Main Street, Suite A
Wickenburg, AZ 85390

Preview   Feed

When prompted by the printer, insert an envelope in your printer's manual feeder.

In Windows, when you turn on the Omit check box, the Preview area of the Envelopes tab of the Envelopes and Labels dialog changes to show that a return address will not print on the envelope.

set address fonts (Windows)

You can customize the appearance of an envelope by setting font options for the delivery and return addresses.

1 Click the Options button in the Envelopes tab of the Envelopes and Labels dialog.

2 Click the Envelope Options tab in the Envelope Options dialog that appears.

3 Click the Font button in the area for the address you want to format.

A font dialog for the type of address you are formatting appears.

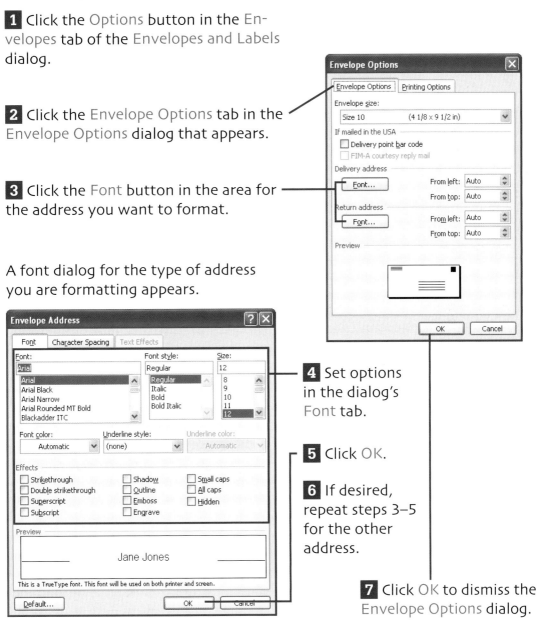

4 Set options in the dialog's Font tab.

5 Click OK.

6 If desired, repeat steps 3–5 for the other address.

7 Click OK to dismiss the Envelope Options dialog.

print an envelope

115

set address fonts (Mac OS)

You can customize the appearance of an envelope by setting font options for the delivery and return addresses.

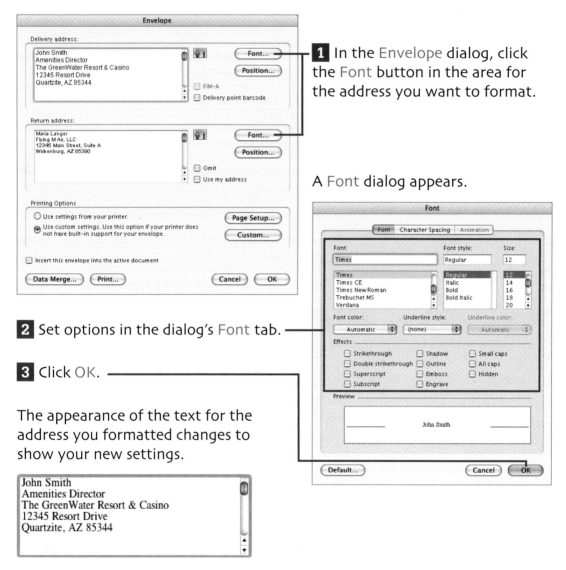

1 In the Envelope dialog, click the Font button in the area for the address you want to format.

A Font dialog appears.

2 Set options in the dialog's Font tab.

3 Click OK.

The appearance of the text for the address you formatted changes to show your new settings.

4 If desired, repeat steps 1–3 for the other address.

print an envelope

include a bar code

You can include a delivery point bar code—also known as a POSTNET bar code—for the delivery address. This special code is used by the post office's routing equipment to read the zip code and speed your letter on its way.

In Windows:

1 Click the Options button in the Envelopes tab of the Envelopes and Labels dialog.

2 Click the Envelope Options tab in the Envelope Options dialog that appears.

3 Turn on the Delivery point bar code check box. ────

The Preview area changes to show a bar code above the delivery address. ────

4 Click OK. ────

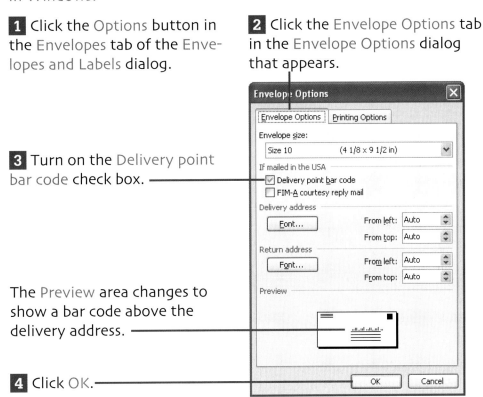

In Mac OS:

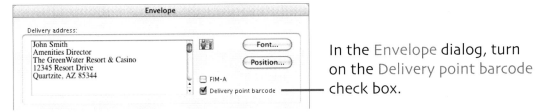

In the Envelope dialog, turn on the Delivery point barcode check box.

set printing options (Windows)

To ensure that your printer prints the envelope correctly the first time, set the envelope size and feed method.

1 Click the Feed button in the Envelopes tab of the Envelopes and Labels dialog.

The Printing Options tab of the Envelope Options dialog appears.

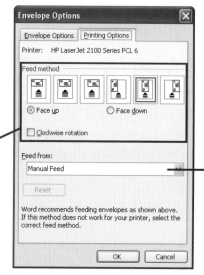

2 Set options in the Feed method area to specify how envelopes are fed into your printer.

Changing the Face up/Face down and Clockwise rotation settings changes the illustrations on the icons, like this:

3 Choose an option from the Feed from drop-down list.

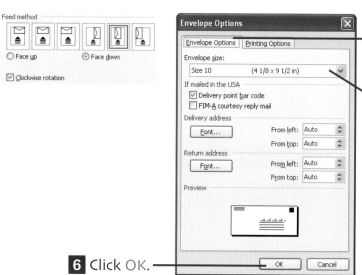

4 Click the Envelope Options tab.

5 Choose an option from the Envelope size drop-down list.

6 Click OK.

print an envelope

set printing options (Mac OS)

To ensure that your printer prints the envelope correctly the first time, set the envelope size and feed method.

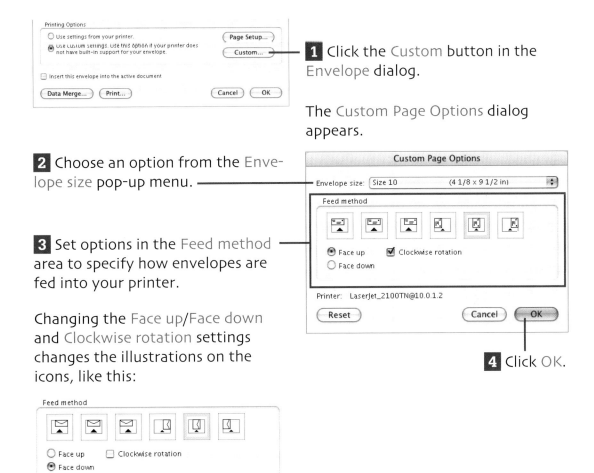

1 Click the Custom button in the Envelope dialog.

The Custom Page Options dialog appears.

2 Choose an option from the Envelope size pop-up menu.

3 Set options in the Feed method area to specify how envelopes are fed into your printer.

Changing the Face up/Face down and Clockwise rotation settings changes the illustrations on the icons, like this:

4 Click OK.

print the envelope

When you're finished setting options in the Envelope dialog, you can print the envelope.

1 Put an envelope in the appropriate feed tray of your printer.

In Windows:

2 Click the Print button in the Envelopes tab of the Envelopes and Labels dialog.

The envelope prints immediately, without displaying a dialog.

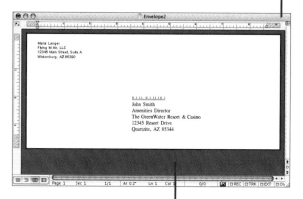

4 Close the envelope document Word created. You don't have to save it.

In Mac OS:

2 Click the Print button in the Envelope dialog.

Word creates an envelope document and displays the Print dialog.

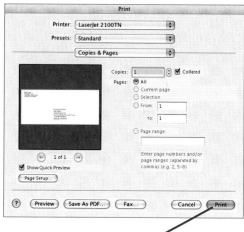

3 Click the Print button. The envelope prints.

print an envelope

extra bits

select an addressee p. 112

- Word is smart. In many cases, it can "guess" which text in a letter document is the address to use for an envelope's delivery address. Try it for yourself! Skip step 2 on page 112 and see what happens when you open the Envelope dialog.

enter addresses p. 114

- If you use Outlook (Windows) or Entourage (Mac OS) to maintain a contacts database, you can click the Address Book button near the Delivery address or Return address box to choose a contact to insert.

- In Word for Macintosh, you can turn on the Use my address check box to insert your name and address in the Return address box.

- You must turn on the Omit check box if you don't want to include a return address on an envelope. If you fail to do so, Word may print placeholder text in the return address area of the envelope when it prints.

- In Windows, if you enter a new return address (one that wasn't already in the Return address box), when you finish printing the envelope Windows will display a dialog asking if you want to save the return address as the default return address. Click Yes if you want that return address to automatically be entered each time you create an envelope.

include a bar code p. 117

- To include a bar code on an envelope, the delivery address must include a zip code.

- Bar codes can only be created for U.S. addresses.

- If you turn on the Delivery point bar code check box option for an envelope, you can also turn on the FIM-A check box. This option, which is designed for courtesy reply envelopes, prints a code that identifies the address side of the envelope.

print an envelope

extra bits

set printing options (Mac OS) p. 119

- If you're not sure how to set printing options, select the Use settings from your printer radio button in the Printing Options area of the Envelope dialog. In most cases, these settings are correct and the envelope will come out fine.

print the envelope p. 120

- In Windows, you can add the envelope to the currently active document as a new page in the document. You can then print the envelope when you print the document. Click the Add to Document button in the Envelopes tab of the Envelopes and Labels dialog.

- In Mac OS, you can save the envelope document Word created as part of the printing process. Just choose Save from the File menu and use the Save As dialog that appears to name and save the envelope. You can then open and print it again another time.

9. create return address labels

Return address labels make it quick and easy to finish off correspondence—whether you're mailing bills or sending out packages to customers. With Word's label feature, you can create professional-looking return address labels in minutes.

But take a moment to think about what return address labels really are. They're preprinted stickers that all say the same thing. If you take that idea a step further, it's easy to imagine using this feature to create stickers you can use to label products, spread your company slogan, or even clearly identify the owner of the books and videos you loan to friends.

This chapter explains how you can create a full page of identical labels that you can use for return addresses or anything else.

open the labels dialog

You use the Labels tab of the Envelopes and Labels dialog (Windows) or the Labels dialog (Mac OS) to create a label document.

In Windows:

1 Choose Envelopes and Labels from the Letters and Mailings submenu under the Tools menu.

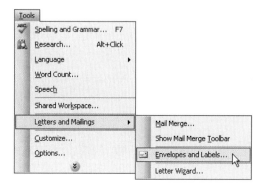

2 In the Envelopes and Labels dialog that appears, click the Labels tab to display its options.

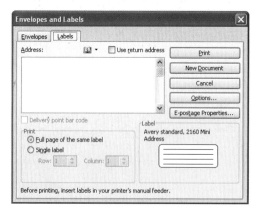

In Mac OS:

Choose Labels from the Tools menu.

The Labels dialog appears.

create return address labels

select label product

The first task is to select the type of labels you will be using.

1 Click the Options button in the Labels tab of the Envelopes and Labels dialog (Windows) or the Labels dialog (Mac OS).

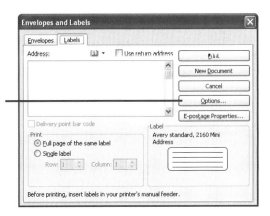

The Label Options dialog appears.

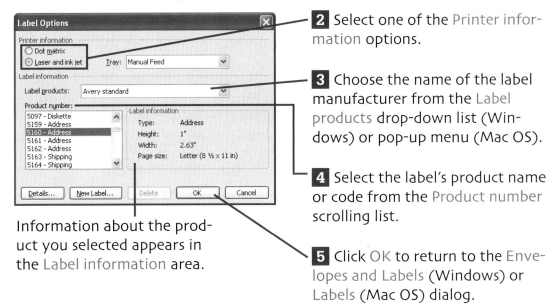

2 Select one of the Printer information options.

3 Choose the name of the label manufacturer from the Label products drop-down list (Windows) or pop-up menu (Mac OS).

4 Select the label's product name or code from the Product number scrolling list.

Information about the product you selected appears in the Label information area.

5 Click OK to return to the Envelopes and Labels (Windows) or Labels (Mac OS) dialog.

create return address labels   **125**

create a custom label

If the labels you're using are not listed in the Label Options dialog, you can create custom settings for a label product. To do this, you'll need a sample of the label sheet and an accurate ruler.

1 Click the Options button in the Labels tab of the Envelopes and Labels dialog (Windows) or the Labels dialog (Mac OS).

2 Select Laser and inkjet in the Printer information area.

3 Click the New Label button.

The Label Options dialog appears.

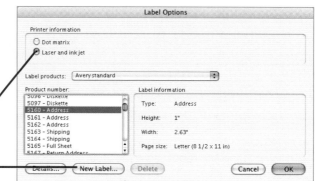

The New Custom laser dialog appears.

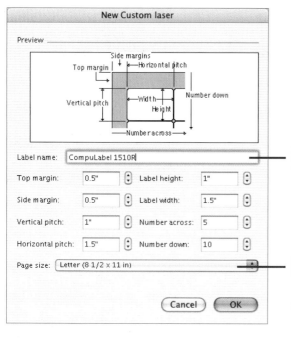

4 Enter a name for your custom label in the Label name box.

5 Choose a size option from the Page size drop-down list (Windows) or pop-up menu (Mac OS).

create return address labels

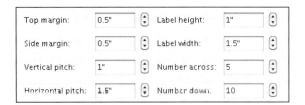

6 Type values into each box in the dialog, as follows:

Top margin is the distance from the top edge of the label sheet to the first label on the sheet.

Side margin is the distance from the left edge of the label sheet to the first label.

Vertical pitch is the distance from the top edge of the first label on the sheet to the top edge of the second label on the sheet. (This may be different from label height!)

Horizontal pitch is the distance from the left edge of the first label on the sheet to the left edge of the label to its right. (This may be different from label width!)

Label height is the distance from the top edge of a label to the bottom edge of the same label.

Label width is the distance from the left edge of a label to the right edge of the same label.

Number across is the number of labels across the page.

Number down is the number of labels down the page.

7 Click OK to save your custom settings.

The label you created appears in the Product number list of the Label Options dialog. Make sure it's selected if you want to use it now. ———

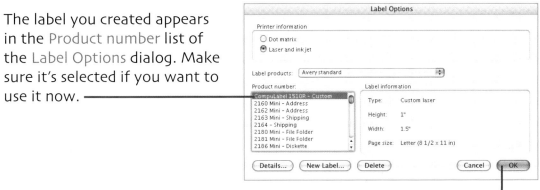

8 Click OK to return to the Labels dialog.

enter text

Now, enter the text you want to appear on every label.

1 Position the blinking insertion point in the Address box of the Labels tab of the Envelopes and Labels dialog (Windows) or Labels dialog (Mac OS).

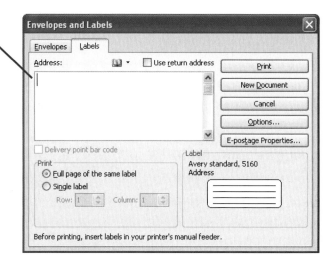

2 Type in all of the information you want to appear on the label. Press Enter (Windows) or Return (Mac OS) at the end of each line.

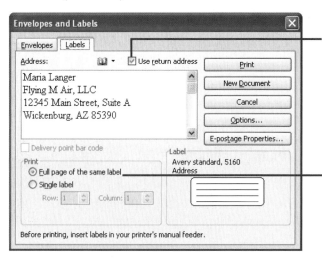

A quick way to enter your return address is to turn on the Use return address (Windows) or Use my address (Mac OS) check box.

3 Select the Full page of the same label option in the Print (Windows) or Number of Labels (Mac OS) area.

create the document

When you save your settings in the Envelopes and Labels dialog (Windows) or Labels dialog (Mac OS), Word creates the label document.

In Windows, click the New Document button in the Labels tab of the Envelopes and Labels dialog.

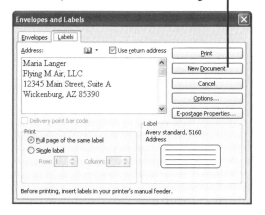

In Mac OS, click the OK button in the Labels dialog.

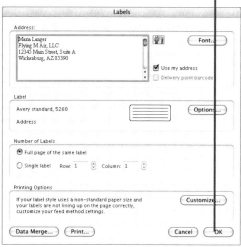

Word creates a new document that uses its table feature to create the labels.

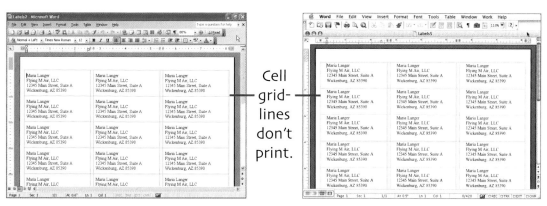

Cell grid-lines don't print.

Windows

Mac OS

finish your labels

When the labels are complete, you can save, print, and close the label document.

1 Save the labels. Use the Save command to display the Save As dialog and save the labels in a place where they'll be easy to find. Saving the label document makes it even quicker and easier to create labels. The next time you want to print labels, just open the document and print it.

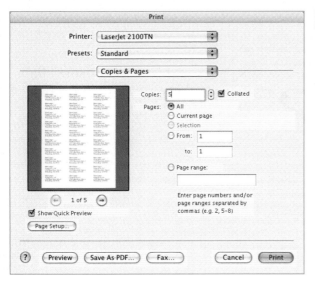

2 Print the labels. Insert the label stock into your printer's print tray or manual feeder and use the Print command to print them. Enter a value in the Number of copies (Windows) or Copies (Mac OS) box to print as many sheets of labels as you like.

3 Close the document file. If you're done working with the labels, close the document.

extra bits

open the labels dialog p. 124

- You must have at least one document open to use the Envelopes and Labels (Windows) or Labels (Mac OS) command. If no documents are open, click the New Blank Document button on the Standard toolbar to create one. You can then choose the Labels command.

select label product p. 125

- You can get the name of the label manufacturer and the product number from the package the labels come in.

enter text p. 128

- The Use return address (Windows) or Use my address (Mac OS) check box must be turned off to enter custom text in the Address box in the Labels tab of the Envelopes and Labels dialog (Windows) or Labels dialog (Mac OS).

create the document p. 129

- If you want to format the text of your labels, do so after the document has been created. Simply select the text you want to format and apply font and paragraph formatting. Consult Chapter 2 for more information about formatting text.

- If you don't want to create a label document—perhaps you just want to print labels quickly without saving them for future use—click the Print button in the Labels tab of the Envelopes and Labels dialog (Windows) or the Labels dialog (Mac OS). In Windows, the labels are sent right to the printer; in Mac OS, use the Print dialog that appears to send the labels to the printer.

index

index

index

index

index

index

Ready to Learn More?

*Full-color projects
from the folks
who bring you
Visual QuickStart
Guides...*

Visual QuickProject

Creating
Spreadsheets and Charts
in Excel

MARIA LANGER

creating spreadsheets
and charts in Excel

Visual QuickProject Guide

by Maria Langer

Peachpit
Press

Visual QuickProject Guide
Creating Spreadsheets and Charts in Excel
Maria Langer

Peachpit Press

1249 Eighth Street
Berkeley, CA 94710
510/524-2178
800/283-9444
510/524-2221 (fax)

Find us on the World Wide Web at: www.peachpit.com
To report errors, please send a note to errata@peachpit.com
Peachpit Press is a division of Pearson Education

Editor: Nancy Davis
Production Editors: Connie Jeung-Mills, Lisa Brazieal
Proofreader: Ted Waitt
Compositor: Maria Langer
Indexer: Julie Bess
Cover design: Peachpit Press / Aren Howell
Interior design: Elizabeth Castro
Cover photo credit: PictureQuest

Notice of Rights

Notice of Liability

Trademarks

ISBN 0-321-25582-8

Printed and bound in the United States of America

To Timothy Clam,
for making my summer
so memorable

Special Thanks to...

Nancy Davis, for thinking of me for the Visual QuickProject series. And for remaining somewhat calm when I missed deadlines (sorry!) and pressure began to build.

Ted Waitt, for making sure I dotted my i's and crossed my t's.

Connie Jeung-Mills and Lisa Brazieal, for helping me fine-tune the book's layout and appearance.

Julie Bess, for delivering yet another great index on short notice.

Microsoft Corporation, for continuing to improve the world's best spreadsheet program for Windows and Macintosh users.

To Mike, for the usual things.

contents

contents

3. build the budget worksheet (cont'd)

4. duplicate the worksheet   49

5. consolidate the results   59

6. format worksheets   69

contents

introduction

This Visual QuickProject Guide offers a unique way to learn about new technologies. Instead of drowning you in theoretical possibilities and lengthy explanations, this Visual QuickProject Guide uses big, color illustrations coupled with clear, concise step-by-step instructions to show you how to complete a specific project in a matter of hours.

Our project in this book is to create an Excel workbook file that compares actual to budgeted income and expenses for three months, consolidates the results, and illustrates consolidated expenses as a pie chart. Although our example uses income and expense items for a fictional business, you can easily customize the worksheets for your own business or personal use. For example, you can create a worksheet that compares your personal budgeted and actual expenditures to see how well you're keeping to your budget. Or use the skills you'll learn throughout this book to keep track of your business's customer invoices and payments.

As you work through the project, you'll learn how to build worksheet files from the ground up, enter data and formulas, and copy formulas to save time. You'll see how powerful and flexible Excel is by working through examples that show off its most commonly used features. You'll try out Excel's consolidation feature and create and "explode" a colorful, three-dimensional chart. You'll also fine-tune the appearance of your worksheet files by applying all kinds of formatting. Along the way, you'll get plenty of ideas for how you can use Excel to crunch the numbers in your life.

what you'll create

Create a worksheet file that compares budgeted to actual income and expenses for a full month.

Item Name	Budget	Actual	Difference	% Diff
Income Items				
Sales	8200	9103	903	0.11012195
Interest Income	100	83	-17	-0.17
Other Income	200	115	-85	-0.425
Total Income	8500	9301	801	0.09423529
Expense Items				
Automobile	150	182	32	0.21333333
Bank Fees	25	25	0	0
Contributions	30	50	20	0.66666667
Depreciation	300	300	0	0
Insurance	120	120	0	0
Interest Expense	75	94	19	0.25333333
Office Supplies	200	215	15	0.075
Postage	360	427	67	0.18611111
Professional Fees	180	180	0	0
Rent	1200	1200	0	0
Repairs	120	245	125	1.04166667
Taxes	360	365	5	0.01388889
Telephone	275	209	-66	-0.24
Travel & Entertainment				
Entertainment	500	412	-88	-0.176
Meals	250	342	92	0.368
Travel	600	269	-331	-0.5516667
Utilities	800	741	-59	-0.07375
Other Expenses	150	248	98	0.65333333
Total Expenses	5695	5624	-71	-0.0124671
Net Income	2805	3677	872	0.31087344

Duplicate the worksheet and modify the duplicates for two other months.

Item Name	Budget	Actual	Difference	% Diff
Income Items				
Sales	8500	9458	958	0.11270588
Interest Income	100	94	-6	-0.06
Other Income	200	354	154	0.77
Total Income	8800	9906	1106	0.12568182
Expense Items				
Automobile	200	194	-6	-0.03
Bank Fees	25	25	0	0
Contributions	100	80	-20	-0.2
Depreciation	300	300	0	0
Insurance	280	280	0	0
Interest Expense	75	121	46	0.61333333
Office Supplies	300	274	-26	-0.0866667
Postage	400	412	12	0.03
Professional Fees	200	400	200	1
Rent	1200	1200	0	0
Repairs	120	348	228	1.9
Taxes	360	410	50	0.13888889
Telephone	275	419	144	0.52363636
Travel & Entertainment				
Entertainment	400	319	-81	-0.2025
Annual Party	1800	2513	713	0.39611111
Meals	100	98	-2	-0.02
Travel	300	278	-22	-0.0733333
Utilities	1000	1348	348	0.348
Other Expenses	150	684	534	3.56
Total Expenses	7595	9703	2118	0.27892533
Net Income	1215	203	-1012	-0.8329218

Item Name	Budget	Actual	Difference	% Diff
Income Items				
Sales	10500	9751	-749	-0.0713333
Interest Income	250	194	-56	-0.224
Other Income	300	27	-273	-0.91
Total Income	11050	9972	-1078	-0.0975566
Expense Items				
Automobile	240	284	44	0.18333333
Bank Fees	25	37	12	0.48
Contributions	100	250	150	1.5
Depreciation	300	300	0	0
Insurance	120	120	0	0
Interest Expense	100	128	28	0.28
Office Supplies	500	617	117	0.234
Postage	480	584	104	0.21666667
Professional Fees	350	650	300	0.85714286
Rent	1200	1200	0	0
Repairs	210	548	338	1.60952381
Taxes	360	360	0	0
Telephone	300	541	241	0.80333333
Travel & Entertainment				
Entertainment	500	486	-14	-0.028
Meals	250	347	97	0.388
Travel	600	247	-353	-0.5883333
Utilities	1000	1341	341	0.341
Total Expenses	6635	8040	1405	0.21175584
Net Income	4415	1932	-2483	-0.5624009

Create a consolidation that combines all information with live links to the source data.

	Budget	Actual	Difference	% Diff
Income Items				
Sales	27200	28312	1112	0.04088235
Interest Income	450	371	-79	-0.1755556
Other Income	700	496	-204	-0.2914286
Total Income	28350	29179	829	0.02924162
Expense Items				
Automobile	590	660	70	0.11864407
Bank Fees	75	87	12	0.16
Contributions	230	380	150	0.65217391
Depreciation	900	900	0	0
Insurance	520	520	0	0
Interest Expense	250	343	93	0.372
Office Supplies	1000	1106	106	0.106
Postage	1240	1423	183	0.14758065
Professional Fees	730	1230	500	0.68493151
Rent	3600	3600	0	0
Repairs	450	1141	691	1.53555556
Taxes	1080	1135	55	0.05092593
Telephone	850	1169	319	0.37529412
Travel & Entertainment				
Entertainment	1400	1217	-183	-0.1307143
Annual Party	1800	2513	713	0.39611111
Meals	600	787	187	0.31166667
Travel	1500	794	-706	-0.4706667
Utilities	2800	3430	630	0.225
Other Expenses	300	932	632	2.10666667
Total Expenses	19915	23367	3452	0.17333668
Net Income	8435	5812	-2623	-0.3109662

Format the worksheets so they look great when printed.

Print your worksheets, with custom headers and footers.

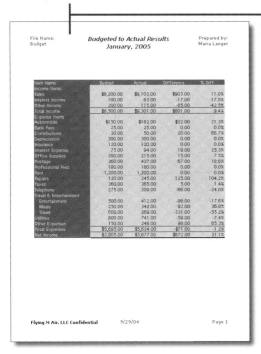

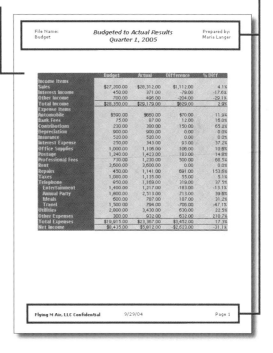

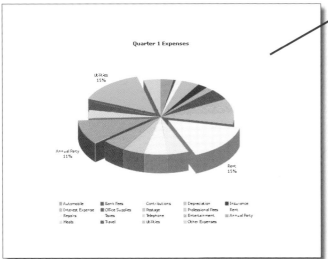

Create a colorful, "exploded" pie chart of consolidated expenses.

how this book works

The title of each section explains what is covered on that page.

Captions explain what you're seeing and why. They also point to relevant parts of Excel's interface.

An introductory sentence or paragraph summarizes what you'll do.

Numbered steps explain actions to perform in a specific order.

Important terms, names of interface elements, and text you should type exactly as shown appear in orange.

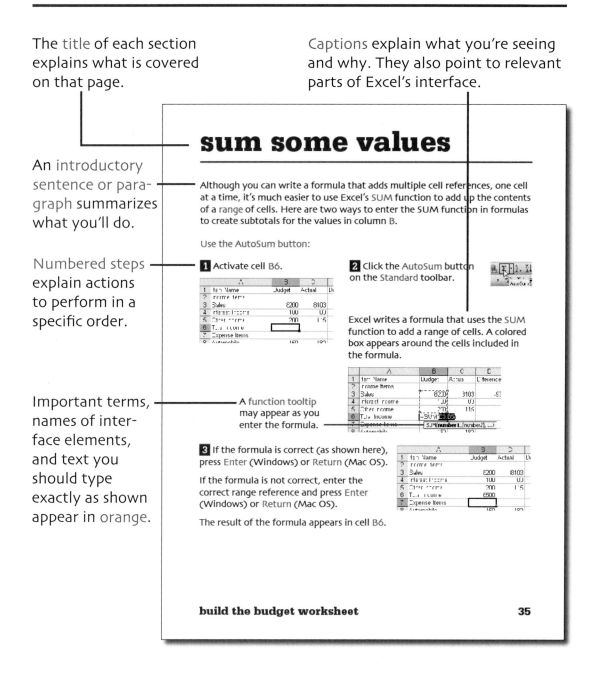

sum some values

Although you can write a formula that adds multiple cell references, one cell at a time, it's much easier to use Excel's SUM function to add up the contents of a range of cells. Here are two ways to enter the SUM function in formulas to create subtotals for the values in column B.

Use the AutoSum button:

1 Activate cell B6.

2 Click the AutoSum button on the Standard toolbar.

Excel writes a formula that uses the SUM function to add a range of cells. A colored box appears around the cells included in the formula.

A function tooltip may appear as you enter the formula.

3 If the formula is correct (as shown here), press Enter (Windows) or Return (Mac OS).

If the formula is not correct, enter the correct range reference and press Enter (Windows) or Return (Mac OS).

The result of the formula appears in cell B6.

build the budget worksheet 35

The extra bits section at the end of each chapter contains additional tips and tricks that you might like to know—but that aren't absolutely necessary.

enter values

The heading for each group of tips matches the section title.

extra bits

name the sheet p. 24

- As you'll see in Chapter 8, you can instruct Excel to automatically display a sheet name in a printed report's header or footer. That's a good reason to give a sheet an appropriate name.

activate a cell p. 27

- When you use the point-and-click method for activating a cell, you must click. If you don't click, the cell pointer won't move and the cell you're pointing to won't be activated.

enter row headings p. 28

- When you enter text in a cell, Excel's AutoComplete feature may suggest entries based on previous entries in the column.

To accept an entry, press Enter (Windows) or Return (Mac OS) when it appears. Otherwise, just keep typing what you want to enter. The AutoComplete suggestion will eventually go away.

make a column wider p. 30

- You can't change the width of a single cell. You must change the width of the entire column the cell is in.

enter values pp. 31–32

- You can enter any values you like in this step. But if you enter the same values I do, you can later compare the results of your formulas to mine to make sure the formulas you enter in the next step are correct.

- Do not include currency symbols or commas when entering values. Doing so will apply number formatting. I explain how to format cell contents, including values, in Chapter 6.

- If you use the arrow keys to move from one cell to the next, the selection area disappears. Although you can enter values without a selection area, using a selection area makes it easier to move from one cell to another.

- If, after entering values, you discover that one of the values is incorrect, activate the cell with the incorrect value, enter the correct value, and press Return or Enter to save it.

The page number(s) next to the heading makes it easy to refer back to the main content.

44   **build the budget worksheet**

the web site

Find this book's companion Web site at:
http://www.langerbooks.com/excelquickproject/.

Content is up-
dated regularly
with news, tips,
and more.

Read timely
articles about
getting the most
out of Excel.

Access a database
of frequently
asked questions.

Download
sample files
used in the
book.

Access excerpts
from the book.

Share your com-
ments and tips with
other site visitors.

the next step

While this Visual QuickProject Guide will walk you through all of the steps required to create and format worksheets and charts, there's more to learn about Excel. After you complete this project, consider picking up one of my books about Excel— Microsoft Office Excel 2003 for Windows: Visual QuickStart Guide or Microsoft Excel X for Macintosh: Visual QuickStart Guide—as a handy, in-depth reference.

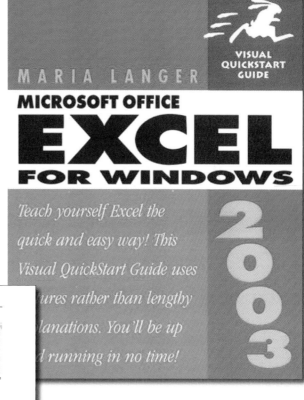

Both books include more advanced information about using Excel to create worksheets, lists, and charts. They tell you about all the options you see in Excel dialogs, explain how to customize Excel so it works the way you need it to, and provide detailed, step-by-step instructions for using basic, intermediate, and advanced Excel features.

1. meet microsoft excel

Microsoft Excel is a full-featured spread-sheet program that you can use to create worksheets and charts like the ones you'll create with this book.

As you work with Excel, you'll see that it has a lot of the same interface elements you're familiar with from using your other Windows or Mac OS programs: windows, menus, dialogs, and buttons. And, as you work your way through this book you'll see that the Windows and Mac OS versions of Excel are remarkably similar—so similar that instructions for one version of the program usually work for the other.

In this chapter, I introduce you to Excel's interface elements and tell you about the techniques you'll need to know to use Excel. If this project is your first hands-on experience with Excel or your computer, be sure to read through this chapter!

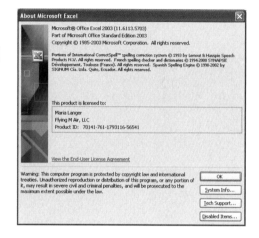

This book covers Excel 2003 for Windows...

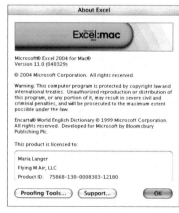

...and Excel 2004 for Macintosh.

But if you have an earlier version of Excel, you should still be able to follow most of the instructions in this book.

learn the lingo

Before you start working with Excel, let me review a few of the terms I'll use throughout this book. If you've been working with your computer for a while, this may seem a bit basic, but I do want to make sure we're on the same page (so to speak) as we work through this project.

An icon is a graphical representation of a file.

EXCEL   Microsoft Excel

Here's what the Excel program icons look like in Windows (left) and Mac OS X (right).

Budget   Budget

And here's what an Excel document icon looks like in Windows (left) and Mac OS X (right).

Windows Explorer is the Windows program that you use to work with files.

If you need to learn more about using Windows, be sure to check out Windows XP: Visual QuickStart Guide by Chris Fehily.

Finder is the Mac OS program that you use to work with files.

If you need to learn how to use Mac OS X, check out Mac OS X Panther: Visual Quick-Start Guide by Maria Langer. (Yes, that's me.)

meet microsoft excel

mouse around

The white (Windows) or black (Mac OS) arrow that appears on your screen is the mouse pointer. Move your mouse and the mouse pointer moves.

Point means to position the tip of the mouse pointer on something. For example, you can point to a menu,...   ...or point to a button.

The mouse pointer can also change its appearance when you point to other things. For example, if you point to a cell in an Excel worksheet window, it changes into a cross pointer...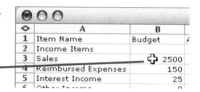

...and if you point to a column heading in an Excel worksheet window, it changes to an arrow pointing down.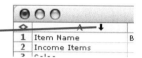

You use the button(s) on your mouse to click, double-click, and drag.

Click means to press and release the left button on a Windows mouse or the only button on a Mac OS mouse.

Right-click means to press and release the right button on a Windows mouse. (You can't right-click on a Mac unless your Mac has a two-button mouse.)

Double-click means to click twice fast—without moving the mouse between clicks.

Drag means to point to something, hold the mouse button down, and move the mouse. You use this technique to move icons, select text, and perform other tasks.

A typical Windows mouse has two buttons.

A standard Mac OS mouse has only one button. On the Apple Pro Mouse shown here, the whole top of the mouse is a button.

start or open excel

In Windows, you start a program. In Mac OS, you open a program. To keep things simple, I'll use the word start for both platforms.

In Windows:

1 Click Start to display the Start menu.

2 Click All Programs.

3 Click Microsoft Office.

4 Click Microsoft Office Excel 2003.

Excel starts and an untitled workbook window appears, as shown on page 5.

In Mac OS:

1 Double-click your hard disk icon to open its window.

2 Double-click Applications.

3 Double-click Microsoft Office 2004.

4 Double-click Microsoft Excel.

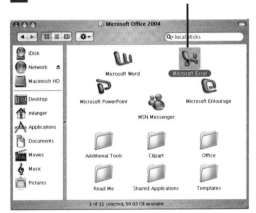

Excel starts. If a Project Gallery window appears, click Cancel to dismiss it. An untitled workbook window appears, as shown on page 6.

meet microsoft excel

look at excel (Windows)

Here are some of the important interface elements in Excel for Windows.

title bar   menu bar   Standard toolbar   Formatting toolbar

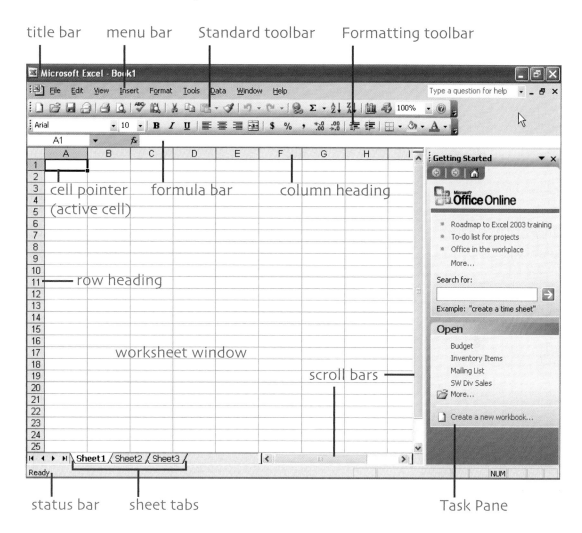

cell pointer (active cell)   formula bar   column heading

row heading

worksheet window

scroll bars

status bar   sheet tabs   Task Pane

look at excel (Mac OS)

Here are some of the important interface elements in Excel for Mac OS X.

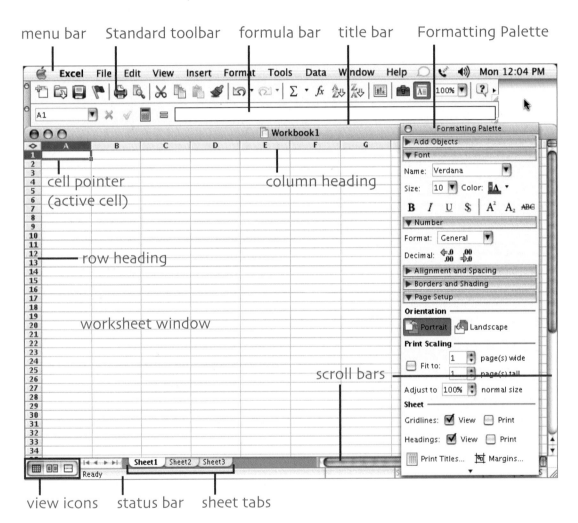

menu bar · Standard toolbar · formula bar · title bar · Formatting Palette

cell pointer (active cell)

column heading

row heading

worksheet window

scroll bars

view icons · status bar · sheet tabs

change the view

Excel for Windows has two views: Normal and Page Break Preview.

Excel for Mac OS has three views: Normal, Page Layout, and Page Break Preview.

You can change a window's view by choosing the name of the view you want from the View menu...

...or, in Excel 2004 for Macintosh, by clicking one of the View buttons at the bottom of the window. As shown here, you can point to a button to determine which view it's for.

Throughout this book, we'll stick to Normal view, which is illustrated on pages 5 and 6.

scroll a window

Scroll bars on a window make it possible to shift window contents up or down (or sideways) to see hidden contents.

A Windows scroll bar.

A Mac OS scroll bar.

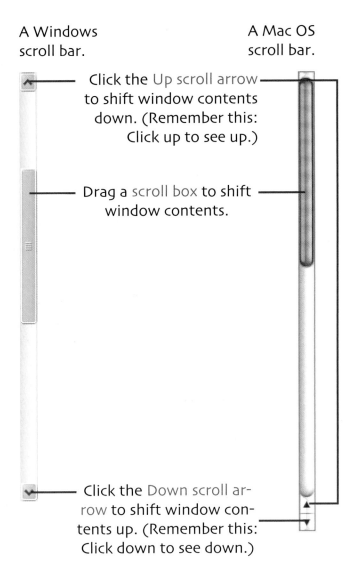

Click the Up scroll arrow to shift window contents down. (Remember this: Click up to see up.)

Drag a scroll box to shift window contents.

Click the Down scroll arrow to shift window contents up. (Remember this: Click down to see down.)

meet microsoft excel

choose from a menu

A menu is a list of commands that can be accessed from the menu bar at the top of the program window (Windows) or screen (Mac OS).

To display a menu, click its name.

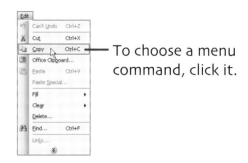

To choose a menu command, click it.

A submenu is a menu that pops out of another menu when you select it.

To choose a submenu command, display the submenu and click the command.

A contextual menu appears when you right-click something (Windows) or hold down the Control key while clicking something (Mac OS).

To choose a contextual menu command, display the menu and click the command.

use a toolbar

Excel has a number of toolbars with buttons you can click to access commands quickly.

In Excel for Windows, two toolbars appear automatically: the Standard toolbar and the Formatting toolbar.

In Excel for Mac OS, one toolbar and a palette appear automatically: the Standard toolbar and the Formatting Palette.

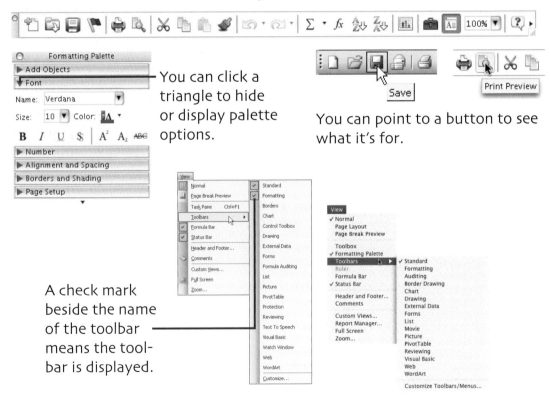

You can click a triangle to hide or display palette options.

You can point to a button to see what it's for.

A check mark beside the name of the toolbar means the toolbar is displayed.

To display a toolbar, choose its name from the Toolbars submenu under the View menu.

have a dialog

A dialog (or dialog box) is a window that appears onscreen when your computer needs to communicate with you.

When a dialog offers options for you to complete a task, it can display the options in a number of ways.

Tabs or buttons let you switch from one group of settings to another.

Scrolling lists offer multiple options in a list.

Check boxes are for turning an option on or off. Click a check box to toggle its setting.

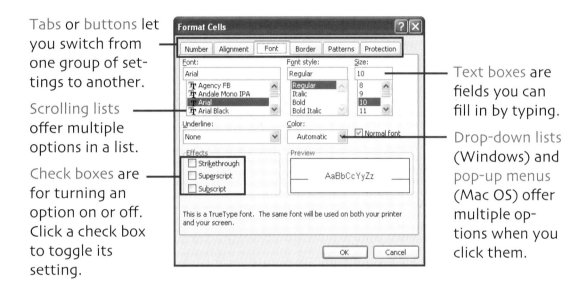

Text boxes are fields you can fill in by typing.

Drop-down lists (Windows) and pop-up menus (Mac OS) offer multiple options when you click them.

Option buttons (Windows) or radio buttons (Mac OS) let you select one option in a group.

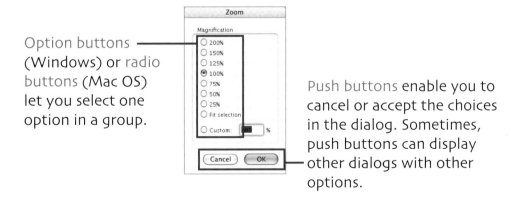

Push buttons enable you to cancel or accept the choices in the dialog. Sometimes, push buttons can display other dialogs with other options.

exit or quit excel

When you're finished using Excel, you should exit or quit it.

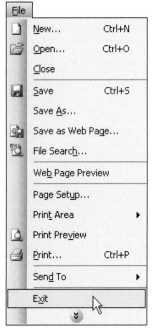

In Windows: Choose Exit from the File menu.

In Mac OS: Choose Quit Excel from the Excel menu.

If a document with unsaved changes is open, Excel displays a dialog that gives you a chance to save the document. (I tell you how to save documents in Chapter 2.)

extra bits

mouse around p. 3

- It is possible to get a multiple-button mouse for your Macintosh. But this book assumes you have a standard mouse with only one button.

- It's also possible to get a three-button mouse for your Windows PC. Frankly, I think two buttons are confusing enough, so I'll assume that's all your mouse has.

- You can also get a mouse with a roller—for Windows or Mac OS. (It's pretty common on Windows mice.) You can use the roller to scroll an active window. Since this feature doesn't work consistently, I don't bother talking about it in this book.

start or open excel p. 4

- These instructions assume you have installed the entire Microsoft Office suite of products, including Excel, Word, PowerPoint, and Outlook (or Entourage). If you have installed just Excel on your computer, consult the manual that came with it for instructions on how to start it.

- If you have a version of Excel other than Excel 2003 for Windows or Excel 2004 for Mac OS, you might have to follow a different procedure for starting Excel. Check the documentation that came with your version of Excel to learn how to start it.

- Chances are, your Start menu won't look exactly like mine. But if you follow the instructions, you should be able to find and start Excel using your Start menu.

- There are lots of ways to start Excel in Windows and Mac OS. If you have a method you prefer, go for it!

extra bits

look at excel (Mac OS) p. 6

- When you first launch Excel 2004 for Mac OS, it may display a worksheet window in Page Layout view. You can switch to Normal view shown here by clicking the Normal View icon at the bottom-left corner of the window. I tell you more about views on page 7.

- If the formula bar does not appear, choose Formula Bar from the View menu to display it.

scroll a window p. 8

- You can customize Mac OS X so the scroll arrows are at either end of the scroll bars. Choose System Preferences from the Apple menu and click the Appearance tab to get started.

choose from a menu p. 9

- Contextual menus are sometimes known as shortcut menus.

- If a menu command has a shortcut key, it appears on the menu beside the command. For example, the Save command has a shortcut key of Ctrl-S (in Windows) or Command-S (in Mac OS). Pressing that key combination invokes the Save command without displaying the File menu.

use a toolbar p. 10

- In Windows, the Standard and Formatting toolbars sometimes appear on the same line. If so, not all buttons may appear. You can display the toolbars on separate lines by dragging the move handle of either toolbar down until it appears on its own line.

have a dialog p. 11

- You can select any number of check boxes in a group, but you can select only one option or radio button in a group.

2. create the workbook file

Excel documents are called workbook files. A workbook can include multiple sheets of information.

Excel supports two kinds of sheets for working with data:

• Worksheets, which are also known as spreadsheets, are for recording text and numerical information and performing calculations. Our project will use worksheets for the monthly budget information and the consolidation.

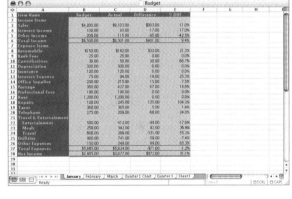

• Chart sheets are for displaying worksheet information as graphs or charts. Excel supports many types of charts, including the pie chart that's part of our project.

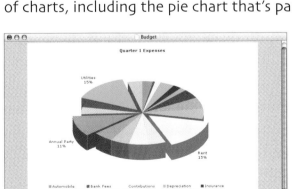

You can think of Excel sheets as pages in an Excel book—that's what I do. Then, when you create a workbook for a project—like our monthly budget with consolidation and chart—you can fill it with the sheets that apply to that project to keep everything together.

In this chapter, we'll create and save the workbook file we'll use to build our project.

create the workbook

Excel offers a number of ways to create a blank workbook file. The quickest and easiest way is with the New button.

1 Click the New button on the Standard toolbar.

Windows

Mac OS

A new workbook document appears. It displays a worksheet window, like the ones on pages 5 and 6.

2 In Mac OS, click the Normal View button at the bottom of the window to switch to Normal view.

set view options (Windows)

You can set view options to determine which screen elements appear while you're working with Excel. It's a good idea to display the tools you'll need to complete this project before you start creating worksheets.

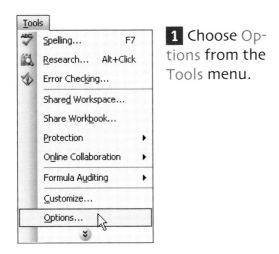

1 Choose Options from the Tools menu.

2 In the Options dialog that appears, click the View tab.

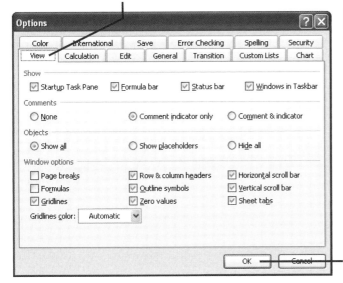

3 Make sure the following check boxes are turned on:

- Formula bar
- Gridlines
- Row & column headers
- Outline symbols
- Zero values
- Horizontal scroll bar
- Vertical scroll bar
- Sheet tabs

4 Click OK.

set view prefs (Mac OS)

You can set view preferences to determine which screen elements appear while you're working with Excel. It's a good idea to display the tools you'll need to complete this project before you start creating worksheets.

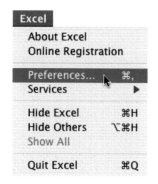

1 Choose Preferences from the Excel menu.

2 In the Preferences dialog that appears, click View.

3 Make sure the following check boxes are turned on:

- Formula bar
- Gridlines
- Row & column headers
- Outline symbols
- Zero values
- Horizontal scroll bar
- Vertical scroll bar
- Sheet tabs

4 Click OK.

create the workbook file

save the workbook (Windows)

You can save a workbook file to keep a record of it on disk or to open and work with it at a later date. For this project, we'll save the workbook in the My Documents folder.

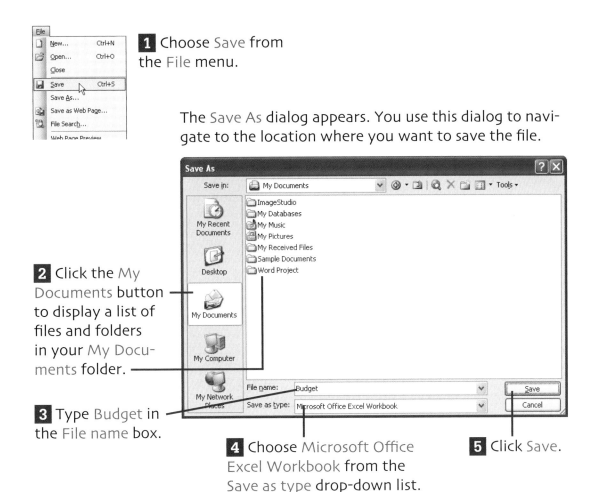

1 Choose Save from the File menu.

The Save As dialog appears. You use this dialog to navigate to the location where you want to save the file.

2 Click the My Documents button to display a list of files and folders in your My Documents folder.

3 Type Budget in the File name box.

4 Choose Microsoft Office Excel Workbook from the Save as type drop-down list.

5 Click Save.

The document is saved in your My Documents folder. Its name appears in the title bar.

Microsoft Excel - Budget

create the workbook file

save the workbook (Mac OS)

You can save a document to keep a record of it on disk or to open and work with it at a later date. For this project, we'll save the workbook in the Documents folder inside your Home folder.

1 Choose Save from the File menu.

The Save As dialog appears. You use this dialog to navigate to the location where you want to save the file.

Click this button to display files in a list as shown here.

2 Type Budget in the Save As box.

Click this button to expand the dialog and show the file list.

3 Click Documents in the dialog's Sidebar to display a list of files and folders in your Documents folder.

4 Choose Excel Workbook from the Format pop-up menu.

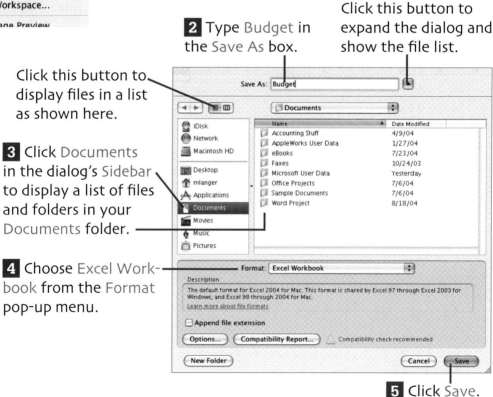

5 Click Save.

The document is saved in your Documents folder. Its name appears in the title bar.

create the workbook file

extra bits

create the workbook p. 16

- In Mac OS, you can set preferences so new workbooks always appear in Normal view and the Formula bar appears automatically when you start Excel. Choose Preferences from the Excel menu and click View in the Preferences dialog that appears. In the Show area, turn on the Formula bar check box and choose Normal from the pop-up menu. Click OK to save your settings.

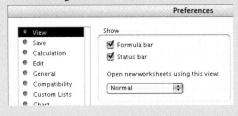

save the workbook pp. 19-20

- It's a good idea to save your workbook file occasionally as you build it. Just choose Save from the File menu or click the Save button on the Standard toolbar. Excel saves the current version of the file without displaying a dialog.

- To save a file with a different name or in a different disk location, choose Save As from the File menu. Then set options in the Save As dialog that appears to save the file. Remember that the original version of the file remains on disk but is not updated with any changes that you made since you saved it.

save the workbook (Mac OS) p. 20

- If you plan to share your workbook file with a Windows user, turn on the Append file extension check box in the Save As dialog. This adds the .xls file extension to the file so it is recognized by Windows as an Excel workbook file.

3. build the budget worksheet

The primary element of our project is the monthly budget worksheet. This worksheet lists all of the income and expense categories with columns for budgeted amounts, actual amounts, dollar difference, and percent difference. It also includes subtotals and totals.

As you can see, an Excel worksheet window closely resembles an accountant's paper worksheet. It includes columns and rows that intersect at cells. To build our budget worksheet, we'll enter information into cells.

In this chapter, we'll create the budget worksheet as shown here. (We'll apply formatting to the worksheet so it looks more presentable later in this project.)

	A	B	C	D	E
1	Item Name	Budget	Actual	Difference	% Diff
2	Income Items				
3	Sales	8200	9103	903	0.11012195
4	Interest Income	100	83	-17	-0.17
5	Other Income	200	115	-85	-0.425
6	Total Income	8500	9301	801	0.09423529
7	Expense Items				
8	Automobile	150	182	32	0.21333333
9	Bank Fees	25	25	0	0
10	Contributions	30	50	20	0.66666667
11	Depreciation	300	300	0	0
12	Insurance	120	120	0	0
13	Interest Expense	75	94	19	0.25333333
14	Office Supplies	200	215	15	0.075
15	Postage	360	427	67	0.18611111
16	Professional Fees	180	180	0	0
17	Rent	1200	1200	0	0
18	Repairs	120	245	125	1.04166667
19	Taxes	360	365	5	0.01388889
20	Telephone	275	209	-66	-0.24
21	Travel & Entertainment				
22	Entertainment	500	412	-88	-0.176
23	Meals	250	342	92	0.368
24	Travel	600	269	-331	-0.5516667
25	Utilities	800	741	-59	-0.07375
26	Other Expenses	150	248	98	0.65333333
27	Total Expenses	5695	5624	-71	-0.0124671
28	Net Income	2805	3677	872	0.31087344
29					

name the sheet

The sheet tabs at the bottom of the worksheet window enable you to identify the active sheet. Each new workbook file includes three worksheets named Sheet1, Sheet2, and Sheet3. You can change the name of a sheet to make it more descriptive.

It's easy to identify the active sheet. Its sheet tab is white and the sheet name appears in bold text. And, if you have sharp eyes, you may notice that the active sheet's tab seems to appear on top of the other tabs.

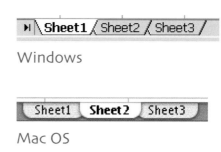

Windows

Mac OS

1 Double-click the Sheet1 sheet tab. The name of the tab becomes selected.

2 Type January. The text you type overwrites the selected sheet name.

3 Press Enter (Windows) or Return (Mac OS). The new name is saved.

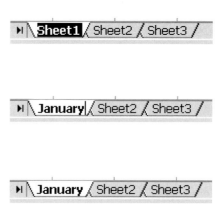

build the budget worksheet

understand references

The concept of references or addressing is important when working with spreadsheets. A reference or address identifies the part of the worksheet that you are working with.

Columns are referred to with letters.

For example, this is column F.

Rows are referred to with numbers.

For example, this is row 10.

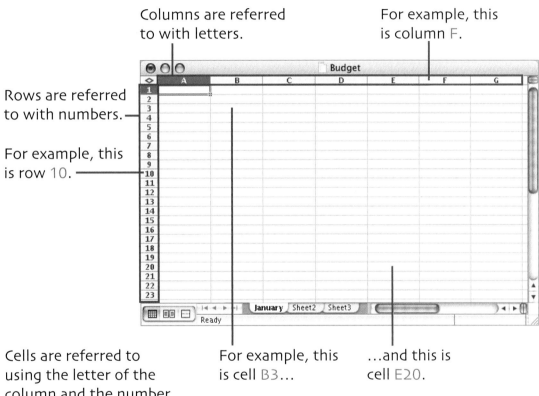

Cells are referred to using the letter of the column and the number of the row.

For example, this is cell B3...

...and this is cell E20.

enter information

To build the budget worksheet, you'll enter three kinds of information into Excel worksheet cells:

• Labels (shown here in orange) are text entries that are used to identify information in the worksheet. For example, the word Budget is a label that will appear at the top of the column containing budget information.

• Values (shown here in green) are numbers, dates, or times. Values differ from labels in that you can perform mathematical calculations on them. In our budget worksheet, you'll enter numbers as values for budget and actual information.

	A	B	C	D	E
1	Item Name	Budget	Actual	Difference	% Diff
2	Income Items				
3	Sales	8200	9103	903	0.11012195
4	Interest Income	100	83	-17	-0.17
5	Other Income	200	115	-85	-0.425
6	Total Income	8500	9301	801	0.09423529
7	Expense Items				
8	Automobile	150	182	32	0.21333333
9	Bank Fees	25	25	0	0
10	Contributions	30	50	20	0.66666667
11	Depreciation	300	300	0	0
12	Insurance	120	120	0	0
13	Interest Expense	75	94	19	0.25333333
14	Office Supplies	200	215	15	0.075
15	Postage	360	427	67	0.18611111
16	Professional Fees	180	180	0	0
17	Rent	1200	1200	0	0
18	Repairs	120	245	125	1.04166667
19	Taxes	360	365	5	0.01388889
20	Telephone	275	209	-66	-0.24
21	Travel & Entertainment				
22	Entertainment	500	412	-88	-0.176
23	Meals	250	342	92	0.368
24	Travel	600	269	-331	-0.5516667
25	Utilities	800	741	-59	-0.07375
26	Other Expenses	150	248	98	0.65333333
27	Total Expenses	5695	5624	-71	-0.0124671
28	Net Income	2805	3677	872	0.31087344
29					

• Formulas (shown here in yellow) are calculations written in a special notation that Excel can understand. When you enter a formula in a cell, Excel displays the result of the formula, not the formula itself. Formulas are a powerful feature of spreadsheet programs because they can perform all kinds of simple and complex calculations for you. In our budget worksheet, we'll use formulas to calculate the difference between budget and actual information in dollars and percents and to calculate column subtotals and totals.

build the budget worksheet

activate a cell

To enter information into a cell, you must activate it. That means moving the cell pointer to the cell in which you want to enter a label, value, or formula.

There are lots of ways to move the cell pointer, but rather than bombard you with a lot of unnecessary options, I'll tell you the two ways I use most.

Point and click:

1 Move the mouse pointer, which looks like a cross, over the cell you want to activate.

2 Press the mouse button once. The cell pointer moves to the cell you pointed to.

Use the arrow keys:

On the keyboard, press the arrow key corresponding to the direction you want the cell pointer to move.

For example, in this illustration, if I wanted to move the cell pointer from cell C8 to cell D6...

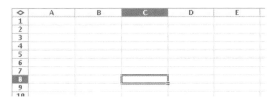

...I'd press the right arrow key once... ...and the up arrow key twice.

enter row headings

The row headings in our budget worksheet will identify the categories of income and expenses and label the subtotals and net income.

1 Activate cell A1 (the first cell in the worksheet).

2 Type Item Name.

3 Press Enter (Windows) or Return (Mac OS). The cell pointer moves down one cell.

4 Repeat steps 2 and 3 for the following labels:

Income Items	Professional Fees
Sales	Rent
Interest Income	Repairs
Other Income	Taxes
Total Income	Telephone
Expense Items	Travel & Entertainment
Automobile	Entertainment
Bank Fees	Meals
Contributions	Travel
Depreciation	Utilities
Insurance	Other Expenses
Interest Expense	Total Expenses
Office Supplies	Net Income
Postage	

When you're finished, the worksheet should look like this.

	A	B
1	Item Name	
2	Income Items	
3	Sales	
4	Interest Income	
5	Other Income	
6	Total Income	
7	Expense Items	
8	Automobile	
9	Bank Fees	
10	Contributions	
11	Depreciation	
12	Insurance	
13	Interest Expense	
14	Office Supplies	
15	Postage	
16	Professional Fees	
17	Rent	
18	Repairs	
19	Taxes	
20	Telephone	
21	Travel & Entertainment	
22	Entertainment	
23	Meals	
24	Travel	
25	Utilities	
26	Other Expenses	
27	Total Expenses	
28	Net Income	
29		
30		

build the budget worksheet

enter column headings

Our budget worksheet includes several columns of data and calculations. We'll use column headings to identify them.

1 Activate cell B1 (the one to the right of where you entered Item Name).

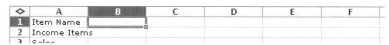

2 Type Budget.

3 Press Tab. The cell pointer moves one cell to the right.

4 Repeat steps 2 and 3 for the following labels:

Actual
Difference
% Diff

When you're finished, the worksheet should look like this.

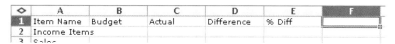

make a column wider

If the text in a cell has too many characters to fit in that cell, part of the cell's contents may appear truncated when you enter information in the cell to its right.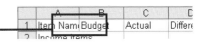

All the information you entered is still there; it's just hidden because the column it's in is too narrow. You can use Excel's AutoWidth feature to quickly make a column wider.

1 Position the mouse pointer on the right border of column A. The mouse pointer turns into a bar with two arrows coming out of it.

2 Double-click. The column automatically widens to accommodate the widest text in the column.

Have you been saving your work?

Now is a good time to click the Save button on the Standard toolbar to save your work up to this point.

build the budget worksheet

enter values

The whole purpose of the worksheet is to compare budgeted to actual amounts. It's time to enter those amounts. Since we need to enter values in two columns, we'll use an entry selection area.

1 Position the mouse pointer over cell B3.

◇	A	B	C	D	E
1	Item Name	Budget	Actual	Difference	% Diff
2	Income Items				
3	Sales	✛			
4	Interest Income				
5	Other Income				

2 Press the mouse button down and drag down and to the right to cell C26. All cells between B3 and C26 are enclosed in a selection box, but cell B3 remains the active cell.

◇	A	B	C	D	E
1	Item Name	Budget	Actual	Difference	% Diff
2	Income Items				
3	Sales				
4	Interest Income				
5	Other Income				
6	Total Income				
7	Expense Items				
8	Automobile				
9	Bank Fees				
10	Contributions				
11	Depreciation				
12	Insurance				
13	Interest Expense				
14	Office Supplies				
15	Postage				
16	Professional Fees				
17	Rent				
18	Repairs				
19	Taxes				
20	Telephone				
21	Travel & Entertainment				
22	Entertainment				
23	Meals				
24	Travel				
25	Utilities				
26	Other Expenses		✛		
27	Total Expenses				
28	Net Income				
29					

3 Type 8200.
It appears in cell B3.

◇	A	B	C	D
1	Item Name	Budget	Actual	D
2	Income Items			
3	Sales	8200		
4	Interest Income			
5	Other Income			
6	Total Income			

4 Press Enter (Windows) or Return (Mac OS). Cell B4 becomes the active cell.

◇	A	B	C	D
1	Item Name	Budget	Actual	D
2	Income Items			
3	Sales	8200		
4	Interest Income			
5	Other Income			
6	Total Income			

enter values (cont'd)

5 Repeat steps 3 and 4 for the remaining values in column B shown here. When a cell that should remain blank becomes active, just press Enter or Return again to make the next cell active. After entering the last value in the column, when you press Enter or Return, cell C3 becomes active.

	A	B	C	D
1	Item Name	Budget	Actual	
2	Income Items			
3	Sales	8200		
4	Interest Income	100		
5	Other Income	200		
6	Total Income			
7	Expense Items			
8	Automobile	150		
9	Bank Fees	25		
10	Contributions	30		
11	Depreciation	300		
12	Insurance	120		
13	Interest Expense	75		
14	Office Supplies	200		
15	Postage	360		
16	Professional Fees	180		
17	Rent	1200		
18	Repairs	120		
19	Taxes	360		
20	Telephone	275		
21	Travel & Entertainment			
22	Entertainment	500		
23	Meals	250		
24	Travel	600		
25	Utilities	800		
26	Other Expenses	150		
27	Total Expenses			
28	Net Income			

6 Repeat steps 3 and 4 for the values in column C shown here. When a cell that should remain blank becomes active, just press Enter or Return again to make the next cell active. After entering the last value in the column, when you press Return or Enter, cell B3 becomes active again.

	A	B	C	D
1	Item Name	Budget	Actual	
2	Income Items			
3	Sales	8200	8103	
4	Interest Income	100	83	
5	Other Income	200	115	
6	Total Income			
7	Expense Items			
8	Automobile	150	182	
9	Bank Fees	25	25	
10	Contributions	30	50	
11	Depreciation	300	300	
12	Insurance	120	120	
13	Interest Expense	75	94	
14	Office Supplies	200	215	
15	Postage	360	427	
16	Professional Fees	180	180	
17	Rent	1200	1200	
18	Repairs	120	245	
19	Taxes	360	365	
20	Telephone	275	209	
21	Travel & Entertainment			
22	Entertainment	500	412	
23	Meals	250	342	
24	Travel	600	269	
25	Utilities	800	741	
26	Other Expenses	150	248	
27	Total Expenses			
28	Net Income			

7 Click anywhere in the worksheet window to deselect the selected cells.

build the budget worksheet

calculate a difference

Column D, which will display the difference between budgeted and actual amounts, will contain simple formulas that subtract one cell's contents from another's using cell references. In this step, we'll write the first formula. Later, we'll copy the formula to other cells in the column.

	A	B	C	D	
1	Item Name	Budget	Actual	Difference	%
2	Income Items				
3	Sales	8200	8103		
4	Interest Income	100	83		
5	Other Income	200	115		

1 Activate cell D3.

	A	B	C	D	
1	Item Name	Budget	Actual	Difference	%
2	Income Items				
3	Sales	8200	8103	=	
4	Interest Income	100	83		
5	Other Income	200	115		

2 Type =.

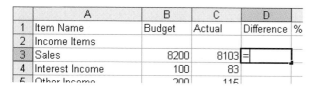

	A	B	C	D	
1	Item Name	Budget	Actual	Difference	%
2	Income Items				
3	Sales	8200	8103	=C3	
4	Interest Income	100	83		
5	Other Income	200	115		

3 Click in cell C3.

Its cell reference appears in cell D3.

	A	B	C	D	
1	Item Name	Budget	Actual	Difference	%
2	Income Items				
3	Sales	8200	8103	=C3-	
4	Interest Income	100	83		
5	Other Income	200	115		

4 Type −.

	A	B	C	D	
1	Item Name	Budget	Actual	Difference	%
2	Income Items				
3	Sales	8200	8103	=C3-B3	
4	Interest Income	100	83		
5	Other Income	200	115		

5 Click in cell B3.

Its cell reference is appended to the formula in cell D3.

	A	B	C	D	
1	Item Name	Budget	Actual	Difference	%
2	Income Items				
3	Sales	8200	8103	-97	
4	Interest Income	100	83		
5	Other Income	200	115		

6 Press Enter (Windows) or Return (Mac OS).

The result of the formula you entered appears in cell D3.

calculate a percent diff

Column E calculates the percent difference between the budgeted and actual amounts. The percentage is based on the budgeted amount. We'll write the first formula now and copy it to other cells in column E later.

	A	B	C	D	E
1	Item Name	Budget	Actual	Difference	% Diff
2	Income Items				
3	Sales	8200	8103	-97	
4	Interest Income	100	83		
5	Other Income	200	115		

1 Activate cell E3.

	A	B	C	D	E
1	Item Name	Budget	Actual	Difference	% Diff
2	Income Items				
3	Sales	8200	8103	-97	=
4	Interest Income	100	83		
5	Other Income	200	115		

2 Type =.

	A	B	C	D	E
1	Item Name	Budget	Actual	Difference	% Diff
2	Income Items				
3	Sales	8200	8103	-97	=D3
4	Interest Income	100	83		
5	Other Income	200	115		

3 Click in cell D3.

Its cell reference appears in cell E3.

	A	B	C	D	E
1	Item Name	Budget	Actual	Difference	% Diff
2	Income Items				
3	Sales	8200	8103	-97	=D3/
4	Interest Income	100	83		
5	Other Income	200	115		

4 Type /.

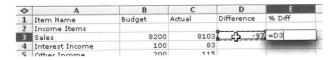

5 Click in cell B3.

Its cell reference is appended to the formula in cell E3.

The formula in cell E3 now reads =D3/B3.

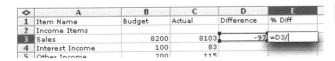

6 Press Enter (Windows) or Return (Mac OS).

The result of the formula you entered appears in cell E3.

Result row: Sales | 8200 | 8103 | -97 | -0.0118293

build the budget worksheet

sum some values

Although you can write a formula that adds multiple cell references, one cell at a time, it's much easier to use Excel's SUM function to add up the contents of a range of cells. Here are two ways to enter the SUM function in formulas to create subtotals for the values in column B.

Use the AutoSum button:

1 Activate cell B6.

	A	B	C	
1	Item Name	Budget	Actual	Di
2	Income Items			
3	Sales	8200	8103	
4	Interest Income	100	83	
5	Other Income	200	115	
6	Total Income			
7	Expense Items			
8	Automobile	150	182	

2 Click the AutoSum button on the Standard toolbar.

Excel writes a formula that uses the SUM function to add a range of cells. A colored box appears around the cells included in the formula.

A function tooltip may appear as you enter the formula.

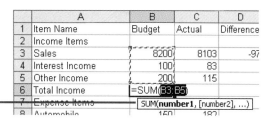

	A	B	C	D
1	Item Name	Budget	Actual	Difference
2	Income Items			
3	Sales	8200	8103	-97
4	Interest Income	100	83	
5	Other Income	200	115	
6	Total Income	=SUM(B3:B5)		
7	Expense Items	SUM(**number1**, [number2], ...)		
8	Automobile	150	182	

3 If the formula is correct (as shown here), press Enter (Windows) or Return (Mac OS).

If the formula is not correct, enter the correct range reference and press Enter (Windows) or Return (Mac OS).

The result of the formula appears in cell B6.

	A	B	C	
1	Item Name	Budget	Actual	Di
2	Income Items			
3	Sales	8200	8103	
4	Interest Income	100	83	
5	Other Income	200	115	
6	Total Income	8500		
7	Expense Items			
8	Automobile	150	182	

sum some values (cont'd)

Type and drag:

1 Activate cell B27.

◇	A	B	C	
1	Item Name	Budget	Actual	D
2	Income Items			
3	Sales	8200	8103	
4	Interest Income	100	83	
5	Other Income	200	115	
6	Total Income	8500		
7	Expense Items			
8	Automobile	150	182	
9	Bank Fees	25	25	
10	Contributions	30	50	
11	Depreciation	300	300	
12	Insurance	120	120	
13	Interest Expense	75	94	
14	Office Supplies	200	215	
15	Postage	360	427	
16	Professional Fees	180	180	
17	Rent	1200	1200	
18	Repairs	120	245	
19	Taxes	360	365	
20	Telephone	275	209	
21	Travel & Entertainment			
22	Entertainment	500	412	
23	Meals	250	342	
24	Travel	600	269	
25	Utilities	800	741	
26	Other Expenses	150	248	
27	Total Expenses			
28	Net Income			
29				

2 Type =SUM(.

25	Utilities	800	741
26	Other Expenses	150	248
27	Total Expenses	=SUM(	
28	Net Income	SUM(**number1**, [number2], ...)	
29			

A function tooltip may appear as you enter the formula.

3 Position the mouse pointer on cell B8.

◇	A	B	C	
1	Item Name	Budget	Actual	Diff
2	Income Items			
3	Sales	8200	8103	
4	Interest Income	100	83	
5	Other Income	200	115	
6	Total Income	8500		
7	Expense Items			
8	Automobile	✛ 150	182	
9	Bank Fees	25	25	B8
10	Contributions	30	50	
11	Depreciation	300	300	
12	Insurance	120	120	

4 Press the mouse button and drag down to cell B26. All cells you dragged over are selected and referenced in the formula in cell B27.

6	Total Income	8500	
7	Expense Items		
8	Automobile	150	182
9	Bank Fees	25	25
10	Contributions	30	50
11	Depreciation	300	300
12	Insurance	120	120
13	Interest Expense	75	94
14	Office Supplies	200	215
15	Postage	360	427
16	Professional Fees	180	180
17	Rent	1200	1200
18	Repairs	120	245
19	Taxes	360	365
20	Telephone	275	209
21	Travel & Entertainment		
22	Entertainment	500	412
23	Meals	250	342
24	Travel	600	269
25	Utilities	800	741
26	Other Expenses	✛ 150	248
27	Total Expenses	=SUM(B8:B26	19R x 1C
28	Net Income	SUM(**number1**, [number2], ...)	
29			

5 Type).

6	Total Income	8500	
7	Expense Items		
8	Automobile	150	182
9	Bank Fees	25	25
10	Contributions	30	50
11	Depreciation	300	300
12	Insurance	120	120
13	Interest Expense	75	94
14	Office Supplies	200	215
15	Postage	360	427
16	Professional Fees	180	180
17	Rent	1200	1200
18	Repairs	120	245
19	Taxes	360	365
20	Telephone	275	209
21	Travel & Entertainment		
22	Entertainment	500	412
23	Meals	250	342
24	Travel	600	269
25	Utilities	800	741
26	Other Expenses	150	248
27	Total Expenses	=SUM(B8:B26)	
28	Net Income		
29			

6 Press Enter (Windows) or Return (Mac OS). The result of the formula appears in cell B27.

25	Utilities	800	741
26	Other Expenses	150	248
27	Total Expenses	5695	
28	Net Income		
29			

build the budget worksheet

calculate net income

The final row of the worksheet contains cells to calculate the net income: total income minus total expenses. Here's how to enter that final formula.

1 Activate cell B28.

26	Other Expenses	150
27	Total Expenses	5695
28	Net Income	
29		

2 Type =.

26	Other Expenses	150
27	Total Expenses	5695
28	Net Income	=
29		

3 Click cell B6. Its reference appears in the formula in cell B28.

	A	B
1	Item Name	Budget A
2	Income Items	
3	Sales	8200
4	Interest Income	100
5	Other Income	200
6	Total Income	8500
7	Expense Items	
8	Automobile	150
9	Bank Fees	25
10	Contributions	30
11	Depreciation	300
12	Insurance	120
13	Interest Expense	75
14	Office Supplies	200
15	Postage	360
16	Professional Fees	180
17	Rent	1200
18	Repairs	120
19	Taxes	360
20	Telephone	275
21	Travel & Entertainment	
22	Entertainment	500
23	Meals	250
24	Travel	600
25	Utilities	800
26	Other Expenses	150
27	Total Expenses	5695
28	Net Income	=B6

4 Type −.

	A	B
1	Item Name	Budget A
2	Income Items	
3	Sales	8200
4	Interest Income	100
5	Other Income	200
6	Total Income	8500
7	Expense Items	
8	Automobile	150
9	Bank Fees	25
10	Contributions	30
11	Depreciation	300
12	Insurance	120
13	Interest Expense	75
14	Office Supplies	200
15	Postage	360
16	Professional Fees	180
17	Rent	1200
18	Repairs	120
19	Taxes	360
20	Telephone	275
21	Travel & Entertainment	
22	Entertainment	500
23	Meals	250
24	Travel	600
25	Utilities	800
26	Other Expenses	150
27	Total Expenses	5695
28	Net Income	=B6-

5 Click cell B27. Its reference appears in the formula in cell B28.

	A	B
1	Item Name	Budget A
2	Income Items	
3	Sales	8200
4	Interest Income	100
5	Other Income	200
6	Total Income	8500
7	Expense Items	
8	Automobile	150
9	Bank Fees	25
10	Contributions	30
11	Depreciation	300
12	Insurance	120
13	Interest Expense	75
14	Office Supplies	200
15	Postage	360
16	Professional Fees	180
17	Rent	1200
18	Repairs	120
19	Taxes	360
20	Telephone	275
21	Travel & Entertainment	
22	Entertainment	500
23	Meals	250
24	Travel	600
25	Utilities	800
26	Other Expenses	150
27	Total Expenses	5695
28	Net Income	=B6-B27

6 Press Enter (Windows) or Return (Mac OS). The result of the formula appears in cell B28.

26	Other Expenses	150
27	Total Expenses	5695
28	Net Income	2805
29		

Have you been saving your work?

Now is a good time to click the Save button on the Standard toolbar to save your work up to this point.

Microsoft Exc

File Edit

Save

build the budget worksheet

copy formulas

Excel lets you copy a formula in one cell to another cell that needs a similar formula. This can save a lot of time when building a worksheet with multiple columns or rows that need similar formulas.

For example, you can copy the formula in cell B6 (total income for budgeted amounts) to cell C6 (total income for actual amounts).

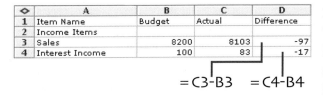

	A	B	C
1	Item Name	Budget	Actual
2	Income Items		
3	Sales	8200	8103
4	Interest Income	100	83
5	Other Income	200	115
6	Total Income	8500	8301

$= SUM(B3:B5)$
$= SUM(C3:C5)$

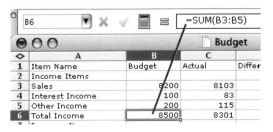

	A	B	C	D
1	Item Name	Budget	Actual	Difference
2	Income Items			
3	Sales	8200	8103	-97
4	Interest Income	100	83	-17

$= C3-B3$ $= C4-B4$

Similarly, you can copy the formula in cell D3 (difference between budgeted and actual sales) to D4 (difference between budgeted and actual interest income).

Excel automatically rewrites the cell references so they refer to the correct cells. You can view a cell's formula by activating the cell and looking in the formula bar near the top of the window.

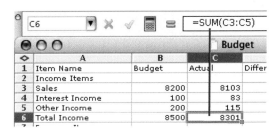

build the budget worksheet

copy and paste

One way to copy formulas is with the Copy and Paste commands.

1 Drag to select cells D3 and E3.

	A	B	C	D	E
1	Item Name	Budget	Actual	Difference	% Diff
2	Income Items				
3	Sales	8200	8103	-97	-0.0∢83
4	Interest Income	100	83		

2 Choose Copy from the Edit menu.

A marquee appears around selected cells.

	D	E
	Difference	% Diff
3	-97	-0.01183

Edit
- Can't Undo   Ctrl+Z
- Cut
- Copy   Ctrl+X / Ctrl+C
- Office Clipboard...
- Paste   Ctrl+V
- Paste Special...
- Fill

3 Activate cell D8.

	A	B	C	D	E
1	Item Name	Budget	Actual	Difference	% Diff
2	Income Items				
3	Sales	8200	8103	-97	-0.01183
4	Interest Income	100	83		
5	Other Income	200	115		
6	Total Income	8500			
7	Expense Items				
8	Automobile	150	182		
9	Bank Fees	25	25		

4 Choose Paste from the Edit menu.

Edit
- Can't Undo   Ctrl+Z
- Cut   Ctrl+X
- Copy   Ctrl+C
- Office Clipboard...
- Paste   Ctrl+V
- Paste Special...
- Fill

The formulas in cells D3 and E3 are copied to cells D8 and E8. The marquee remains around the originally selected cells, indicating that they can be pasted elsewhere.

	A	B	C	D	E
1	Item Name	Budget	Actual	Difference	% Diff
2	Income Items				
3	Sales	8200	8103	-97	-0.01183
4	Interest Income	100	83		
5	Other Income	200	115		
6	Total Income	8500			
7	Expense Items				
8	Automobile	150	182	32	0.213333
9	Bank Fees	25	25		
10	Contributions	30	50		

5 Activate cell D22.

	A	B	C	D	E
1	Item Name	Budget	Actual	Difference	% Diff
2	Income Items				
3	Sales	8200	8103	-97	-0.01183
4	Interest Income	100	83		
5	Other Income	200	115		
6	Total Income	8500			
7	Expense Items				
8	Automobile	150	182	32	0.213333
9	Bank Fees	25	25		
10	Contributions	30	50		
11	Depreciation	300	300		
12	Insurance	120	120		
13	Interest Expense	75	94		
14	Office Supplies	200	215		
15	Postage	360	427		
16	Professional Fees	180	180		
17	Rent	1200	1200		
18	Repairs	120	245		
19	Taxes	360	365		
20	Telephone	275	209		
21	Travel & Entertainment				
22	Entertainment	500	412		

6 Press Enter. The formulas are copied to cells D22 and E22. The marquee disappears, indicating the selection can no longer be pasted elsewhere.

	A	B	C	D	E
1	Item Name	Budget	Actual	Difference	% Diff
2	Income Items				
3	Sales	8200	8103	-97	-0.01183
4	Interest Income	100	83		
5	Other Income	200	115		
6	Total Income	8500			
7	Expense Items				
8	Automobile	150	182	32	0.213333
9	Bank Fees	25	25		
10	Contributions	30	50		
11	Depreciation	300	300		
12	Insurance	120	120		
13	Interest Expense	75	94		
14	Office Supplies	200	215		
15	Postage	360	427		
16	Professional Fees	180	180		
17	Rent	1200	1200		
18	Repairs	120	245		
19	Taxes	360	365		
20	Telephone	275	209		
21	Travel & Entertainment				
22	Entertainment	500	412	-88	-0.176

Paste Options button
(see extra bits)

use the fill handle

A quick way to copy the contents of one cell to one or more adjacent cells is with the fill handle. We'll use the fill handle to finish up the worksheet entries.

1 Activate cell B6.

◇	A	B	C	
1	Item Name	Budget	Actual	
2	Income Items			
3	Sales	8200	8103	
4	Interest Income	100	83	
5	Other Income	200	115	
6	Total Income	8500		
7	Expense Items			
8	Automobile	150	182	

— Fill handle

2 Position the mouse pointer on the selection's fill handle—a tiny square in the bottom-right corner of the selection box. The mouse pointer turns into a black cross.

◇	A	B	C	
1	Item Name	Budget	Actual	
2	Income Items			
3	Sales	8200	8103	
4	Interest Income	100	83	
5	Other Income	200	115	
6	Total Income	8500		
7	Expense Items			
8	Automobile	150	182	

3 Press the mouse button and drag to the right. As you drag, the mouse pointer may change and a black or gray border stretches over the cells you pass over.

◇	A	B	C	
1	Item Name	Budget	Actual	
2	Income Items			
3	Sales	8200	8103	
4	Interest Income	100	83	
5	Other Income	200	115	
6	Total Income	8500		
7	Expense Items			
8	Automobile	150	182	

In Mac OS, the pointer changes.

4 When the border surrounds cells B6 and C6, release the mouse button. The formula in cell B6 is copied to cell C6.

◇	A	B	C	
1	Item Name	Budget	Actual	Diffe
2	Income Items			
3	Sales	8200	8103	
4	Interest Income	100	83	
5	Other Income	200	115	
6	Total Income	8500	8301	
7	Expense Items			
8	Automobile	150	182	

Auto Fill Options button ⌐
(see extra bits)

build the budget worksheet

5 Repeat steps 1–4 for cell B27 to copy its formula to C27 and for cell B28 to copy its formula to cell C28. When you're finished, the worksheet should look like this.

	A	B	C	D	E
1	Item Name	Budget	Actual	Difference	% Diff
2	Income Items				
3	Sales	8200	8103	-97	-0.0118293
4	Interest Income	100	83		
5	Other Income	200	115		
6	Total Income	8500	8301		
7	Expense Items				
8	Automobile	150	182	32	0.21333333
9	Bank Fees	25	25		
10	Contributions	30	50		
11	Depreciation	300	300		
12	Insurance	120	120		
13	Interest Expense	75	94		
14	Office Supplies	200	215		
15	Postage	360	427		
16	Professional Fees	180	180		
17	Rent	1200	1200		
18	Repairs	120	245		
19	Taxes	360	365		
20	Telephone	275	209		
21	Travel & Entertainment				
22	Entertainment	500	412	-88	-0.176
23	Meals	250	342		
24	Travel	600	269		
25	Utilities	800	741		
26	Other Expenses	150	248		
27	Total Expenses	5695	5624		
28	Net Income	2805	2677		
29					

6 Drag to select cells D3 and E3.

	A	B	C	D	E
1	Item Name	Budget	Actual	Difference	% Diff
2	Income Items				
3	Sales	8200	8103	-97	-0.0118293
4	Interest Income	100	83		
5	Other Income	200	115		
6	Total Income	8500	8301		
7	Expense Items				

7 Position the mouse pointer on the selection's fill handle.

8 Press the mouse button down and drag so the border completely surrounds cells D3 through E6.

	A	B	C	D	E
1	Item Name	Budget	Actual	Difference	% Diff
2	Income Items				
3	Sales	8200	8103	-97	-0.0118293
4	Interest Income	100	83		
5	Other Income	200	115		
6	Total Income	8500	8301		
7	Expense Items				

9 Release the mouse button. The two formulas are copied down to the cells you dragged over.

	A	B	C	D	E
1	Item Name	Budget	Actual	Difference	% Diff
2	Income Items				
3	Sales	8200	8103	-97	-0.0118293
4	Interest Income	100	83	-17	-0.17
5	Other Income	200	115	-85	-0.425
6	Total Income	8500	8301	-199	-0.0234118
7	Expense Items				
8	Automobile	150	182	32	0.21333333

build the budget worksheet

use the fill handle (cont'd)

10 Repeat steps 6–9 to copy cells D8 and E8 to the range beneath it (shown here) and cells D22 and E22 to the range beneath it.

◇	A	B	C	D	E
1	Item Name	Budget	Actual	Difference	% Diff
2	Income Items				
3	Sales	8200	8103	-97	-0.0118293
4	Interest Income	100	83	-17	-0.17
5	Other Income	200	115	-85	-0.425
6	Total Income	8500	9301	801	0.09423529
7	Expense Items				
8	Automobile	150	182	32	0.21333333
9	Bank Fees	25	25		
10	Contributions	30	50		
11	Depreciation	300	300		
12	Insurance	120	120		
13	Interest Expense	75	94		
14	Office Supplies	200	215		
15	Postage	360	427		
16	Professional Fees	180	180		
17	Rent	1200	1200		
18	Repairs	120	245		
19	Taxes	360	365		
20	Telephone	275	209		
21	Travel & Entertainment				

When you're finished, the worksheet should look like this.

◇	A	B	C	D	E
1	Item Name	Budget	Actual	Difference	% Diff
2	Income Items				
3	Sales	8200	8103	-97	-0.0118293
4	Interest Income	100	83	-17	-0.17
5	Other Income	200	115	-85	-0.425
6	Total Income	8500	9301	801	0.09423529
7	Expense Items				
8	Automobile	150	182	32	0.21333333
9	Bank Fees	25	25	0	0
10	Contributions	30	50	20	0.66666667
11	Depreciation	300	300	0	0
12	Insurance	120	120	0	0
13	Interest Expense	75	94	19	0.25333333
14	Office Supplies	200	215	15	0.075
15	Postage	360	427	67	0.18611111
16	Professional Fees	180	180	0	0
17	Rent	1200	1200	0	0
18	Repairs	120	245	125	1.04166667
19	Taxes	360	365	5	0.01388889
20	Telephone	275	209	-66	-0.24
21	Travel & Entertainment				
22	Entertainment	500	412	-88	-0.176
23	Meals	250	342	92	0.368
24	Travel	600	269	-331	-0.5516667
25	Utilities	800	741	-59	-0.07375
26	Other Expenses	150	248	98	0.65333333
27	Total Expenses	5420	5415	-5	-0.0009225
28	Net Income	3080	2886	-194	-0.062987
29					

Have you been saving your work?

Now is a good time to click the Save button on the Standard toolbar to save your work up to this point.

build the budget worksheet

change a value

In reviewing this worksheet, I realize that we made an error when entering values. The actual sales amount for the month wasn't 8103 as we entered. It was really 9103! Better enter the correct value now.

1 Activate cell C3.

	A	B	C	D	E
1	Item Name	Budget	Actual	Difference	% Diff
2	Income Items				
3	Sales	8200	8103	-97	-0.01183
4	Interest Income	100	83	-17	-0.17
5	Other Income	200	115	85	0.425

2 Type 9103. This new value overwrites the value already entered.

	A	B	C	D	E
1	Item Name	Budget	Actual	Difference	% Diff
2	Income Items				
3	Sales	8200	9103	-97	-0.01183
4	Interest Income	100	83	-17	-0.17
5	Other Income	200	115	85	0.425

3 Press Enter (Windows) or Return (Mac OS).

The value changes, but what's more important is that all of the formulas that referenced that value, either directly or indirectly, also change. Compare the orange highlighted cells in this illustration with the same cells in the illustration on the previous page to see for yourself.

This is the reason we use spreadsheet programs!

	A	B	C	D	E
1	Item Name	Budget	Actual	Difference	% Diff
2	Income Items				
3	Sales	8200	9103	903	0.110122
4	Interest Income	100	83	-17	-0.17
5	Other Income	200	115	-85	-0.425
6	Total Income	8500	9301	801	0.094235
7	Expense Items				
8	Automobile	150	182	32	0.213333
9	Bank Fees	25	25	0	0
10	Contributions	30	50	20	0.666667
11	Depreciation	300	300	0	0
12	Insurance	120	120	0	0
13	Interest Expense	75	94	19	0.253333
14	Office Supplies	200	215	15	0.075
15	Postage	360	427	67	0.186111
16	Professional Fees	180	180	0	0
17	Rent	1200	1200	0	0
18	Repairs	120	245	125	1.041667
19	Taxes	360	365	5	0.013889
20	Telephone	275	209	-66	-0.24
21	Travel & Entertainment				
22	Entertainment	500	412	-88	-0.176
23	Meals	250	342	92	0.368
24	Travel	600	269	-331	-0.55167
25	Utilities	800	741	-59	-0.07375
26	Other Expenses	150	248	98	0.653333
27	Total Expenses	5695	5624	-71	-0.01247
28	Net Income	2805	3677	872	0.310873
29					

extra bits

name the sheet p. 24

- As you'll see in Chapter 8, you can instruct Excel to automatically display a sheet name in a printed report's header or footer. That's a good reason to give a sheet an appropriate name.

activate a cell p. 27

- When you use the point-and-click method for activating a cell, you must click. If you don't click, the cell pointer won't move and the cell you're pointing to won't be activated.

enter row headings p. 28

- When you enter text in a cell, Excel's AutoComplete feature may suggest entries based on previous entries in the column.

  To accept an entry, press Enter (Windows) or Return (Mac OS) when it appears. Otherwise, just keep typing what you want to enter. The AutoComplete suggestion will eventually go away.

make a column wider p. 30

- You can't change the width of a single cell. You must change the width of the entire column the cell is in.

enter values pp. 31–32

- You can enter any values you like in this step. But if you enter the same values I do, you can later compare the results of your formulas to mine to make sure the formulas you enter in the next step are correct.

- Do not include currency symbols or commas when entering values. Doing so will apply number formatting. I explain how to format cell contents, including values, in Chapter 6.

- If you use the arrow keys to move from one cell to the next, the selection area disappears. Although you can enter values without a selection area, using a selection area makes it easier to move from one cell to another.

- If, after entering values, you discover that one of the values is incorrect, activate the cell with the incorrect value, enter the correct value, and press Return or Enter to save it.

- A dialog like the one shown below may appear when entering values in a worksheet. Clicking Yes in this dialog converts the worksheet into an Excel list. Click No to dismiss the dialog without making the conversion.

calculate a difference p. 33

- In Excel, all formulas begin with an equals sign (=).
- Although you can write a formula that subtracts one number from another, using cell references in the formula ensures that the formula's results remain correct, even if referenced cells' values change.
- As our formula is written, if the actual amount is lower than the budgeted amount, the difference appears as a negative number. You can make this appear as a positive number by switching the order of the cell references so the formula is =B3-C3.

calculate a percent diff p. 34

- The number of decimal places that appear in the results of the formula depends on the width of the column the formula is in.
- Don't worry that the percentages Excel calculates don't look like percentages. Later, in Chapter 6, we'll format the worksheet so the numbers look like percentages.
- If the budgeted amount in a cell is 0, the formula for the percent difference will display the error message #DIV/0! Enter this formula in cell E3 to prevent that error: =IF(ISERR(D3/B3),0,D3/B3) This rather complex formula uses logic to determine whether the formula results in an error and, if it does, results in 0.

sum some values pp. 35–36

- The SUM function is probably Excel's most used function. It can be used to add up any range of values.
- Excel is not case-sensitive when evaluating functions. You can type SUM, sum, Sum, or even sUm when you write the formula and Excel will understand.

extra bits

- Excel 2004 for Mac OS includes a background error-checking feature that may mark cell B27 with a green error indicator. Activate the cell and click the button that appears to display a menu of error-checking options.

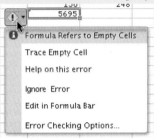

  Since this formula is not in error, choose Ignore Error to remove the error indicator.

copy and paste p. 39

- On Mac OS, you must press the Enter key (as opposed to the Return key) to paste to a selected cell. The Enter key is commonly found on the numeric keypad of a keyboard but may be located elsewhere, especially on PowerBook and iBook keyboards. Pressing Return merely moves the cell pointer down one cell.

- The Paste Options button appears when you use the Paste command. Clicking this button displays a menu of options you can use immediately after pasting one or more cells.

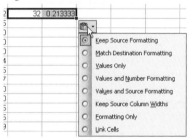

use the fill handle pp. 40–42

- The Auto Fill Options button appears when you use the fill handle to copy formulas. Clicking this button displays a menu of options you can use immediately after filling cells.

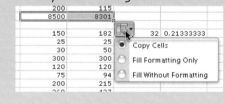

build the budget worksheet

change a value p. 43

- You can use this technique to change any label, value, or formula in a worksheet cell.

- To delete the contents of a cell, activate the cell, press Backspace (Windows) or Delete (Mac OS), and press Enter (Windows) or Return (Mac OS). Don't use the Spacebar to delete a cell's contents; this merely replaces its contents with a space character.

4. duplicate the worksheet

So far, we've created a budget worksheet for one month. Our project, however, includes budget worksheets for three months.

While you could simply repeat the steps in Chapter 3 twice to create two more worksheets, there is a better—and quicker—way. You can duplicate the January worksheet, clear out the values you entered, and enter new values for February. You can then do the same thing for March.

In this chapter, we'll do just that. But just to make things interesting, we'll add and remove a couple of expense categories. As you'll see, this will make the consolidation process in Chapter 5 a bit more challenging.

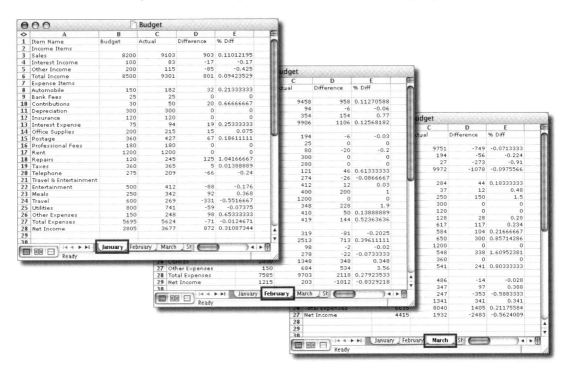

copy the sheet

Excel offers several ways to copy a worksheet. The quickest and easiest way is to drag the sheet tab.

1 Click the tab for the sheet you want to duplicate—in this case, the one we named January— to activate it.

2 Position the mouse pointer on the sheet tab.

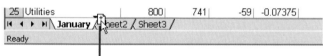

3 Hold down the Ctrl (Windows) or Option (Mac OS) key and drag the sheet tab to the right.

| 25 | Utilities | | 800 | 741 | -59 | -0.07375 |

As you drag, a tiny page icon with a plus sign in it appears at the mouse pointer and a triangle appears to indicate where the duplicate sheet will appear among the sheet tabs.

4 When the triangle appears between the sheets named January and Sheet2, release the mouse button.

A new sheet named January (2) appears.

5 Repeat steps 1–4 to duplicate the worksheet again, placing the copy between January (2) and Sheet2. The new copy is named January (3).

6 Follow the instructions on page 24 to rename January (2) to February and January (3) to March.

duplicate the worksheet

clear the values

At this point, all three sheets are identical except for their names. We need to clear out the values in the February and March sheets, leaving the labels and formulas, so we can enter new values. Because the two sheets are identical and the values are in the same cells in both sheets, we can clear the values in both sheets at the same time.

1 Click the February tab to activate that sheet.

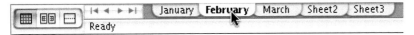

2 Hold down the Ctrl (Windows) or Command (Mac OS) key and click the March tab.

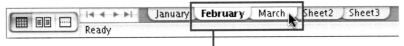

Both tabs become selected (they turn white)…

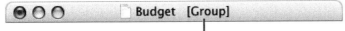

…and [Group] appears beside the workbook name in the title bar.

3 Position the mouse pointer on cell B3, press the mouse button, and drag down to cell C5 to select all of the cells with income values.

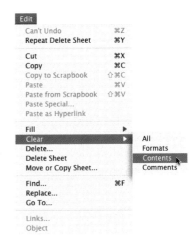

◇	A	B	C	D	E
1	Item Name	Budget	Actual	Difference	% Diff
2	Income Items				
3	Sales	8200	9203	1003	0.12231707
4	Interest Income	100	83	-17	-0.17
5	Other Income	200	115	-85	-0.425
6	Total Income	8500	9401	901	0.106
7	Expense Items				
8	Automobile	150	182	32	0.21333333

4 Choose Contents from the Clear submenu under the Edit menu.

duplicate the worksheet   **51**

clear the values (cont'd)

The cells' contents are removed.

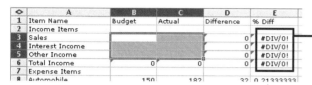

◇	A	B	C	D	E
1	Item Name	Budget	Actual	Difference	% Diff
2	Income Items				
3	Sales			0	#DIV/0!
4	Interest Income			0	#DIV/0!
5	Other Income			0	#DIV/0!
6	Total Income	0	0	0	#DIV/0!
7	Expense Items				
8	Automobile	150	182	32	0.21333333

Don't worry about these errors; they'll go away when you fill in new values.

5 Position the mouse pointer on cell B8, press the mouse button, and drag down to cell C26 to select all of the cells with expense values.

◇	A	B	C	D	E
1	Item Name	Budget	Actual	Difference	% Diff
2	Income Items				
3	Sales	8200	9103	903	0.11012195
4	Interest Income	100	83	-17	-0.17
5	Other Income	200	115	-85	-0.425
6	Total Income	8500	9301	801	0.09423529
7	Expense Items				
8	Automobile	150	182	32	0.21333333
9	Bank Fees	25	25	0	0
10	Contributions	30	50	20	0.66666667
11	Depreciation	300	300	0	0
12	Insurance	120	120	0	0
13	Interest Expense	75	94	19	0.25333333
14	Office Supplies	200	215	15	0.075
15	Postage	360	427	67	0.18611111
16	Professional Fees	180	180	0	0
17	Rent	1200	1200	0	0
18	Repairs	120	245	125	1.04166667
19	Taxes	360	365	5	0.01388889
20	Telephone	275	209	-66	-0.24
21	Travel & Entertainment				
22	Entertainment	500	412	-88	-0.176
23	Meals	250	342	92	0.368
24	Travel	600	269	-331	-0.5516667
25	Utilities	800	741	-59	-0.07375
26	Other Expenses	150	248	98	0.65333333
27	Total Expenses	5695	5624	-71	-0.0124671
28	Net Income	2805	3677	872	0.31087344

6 Choose Contents from the Clear submenu under the Edit menu (shown on previous page).

The cells' contents are removed.

◇	A	B	C	D	E
1	Item Name	Budget	Actual	Difference	% Diff
2	Income Items				
3	Sales			0	#DIV/0!
4	Interest Income			0	#DIV/0!
5	Other Income			0	#DIV/0!
6	Total Income	0	0	0	#DIV/0!
7	Expense Items				
8	Automobile			0	#DIV/0!
9	Bank Fees			0	#DIV/0!
10	Contributions			0	#DIV/0!
11	Depreciation			0	#DIV/0!
12	Insurance			0	#DIV/0!
13	Interest Expense			0	#DIV/0!
14	Office Supplies			0	#DIV/0!
15	Postage			0	#DIV/0!
16	Professional Fees			0	#DIV/0!
17	Rent			0	#DIV/0!
18	Repairs			0	#DIV/0!
19	Taxes			0	#DIV/0!
20	Telephone				
21	Travel & Entertainment				
22	Entertainment			0	#DIV/0!
23	Meals			0	#DIV/0!
24	Travel			0	#DIV/0!
25	Utilities			0	#DIV/0!
26	Other Expenses			0	#DIV/0!
27	Total Expenses	0	0	0	#DIV/0!
28	Net Income	0	0	0	#DIV/0!

7 Click the January tab to clear the group selection. You can then click the February tab to work with just that worksheet.

duplicate the worksheet

insert a row

February is the month when the big company party is held. Although expenses for this party are part of Entertainment expenses, we want to track the party's budgeted and actual expenses on a separate line. To do this, we need to insert a new row between rows 22 and 23 (Entertainment and Meals).

1 Click the February sheet tab to activate that sheet.

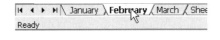

2 Position the mouse pointer on the row heading for row 23. It turns into an arrow pointing to the right.

20	Telephone
21	Travel & Entertainment
22	Entertainment
23	Meals
24	Travel
25	Utilities

3 Click once. The entire row becomes selected.

20	Telephone	0	#DIV/0!
21	Travel & Entertainment		
22	Entertainment	0	#DIV/0!
23	Meals	0	#DIV/0!
24	Travel	0	#DIV/0!
25	Utilities	0	#DIV/0!

4 Choose Rows from the Insert menu.

A new row is inserted beneath row 22 and all the rows beneath it shift down.

20	Telephone	0	#DIV/0!
21	Travel & Entertainment		
22	Entertainment	0	#DIV/0!
23			
24	Meals	0	#DIV/0!
25	Travel	0	#DIV/0!

5 Make sure cell A23 is active—if it isn't, click it.

6 Type Annual Party and press Enter (Windows) or Return (Mac OS).

20	Telephone	0	#DIV/0!
21	Travel & Entertainment		
22	Entertainment	0	#DIV/0!
23	Annual Party		
24	Meals	0	#DIV/0!
25	Travel	0	#DIV/0!

duplicate the worksheet 53

delete a row

The accountant has laid down the law. No more categorizing expenses as Other Expenses. Starting in March, he wants all expenses properly categorized in one of the other existing expense categories. That means we need to delete the row for Other Expenses.

1 Click the March sheet tab to activate that sheet.

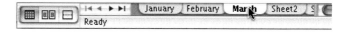

2 Position the mouse pointer on the row heading for row 26. It turns into an arrow pointing to the right.

3 Click once. The entire row becomes selected.

23	Meals			0	#DIV/0!
24	Travel			0	#DIV/0!
25	Utilities			0	#DIV/0!
➡26	Other Expenses			0	#DIV/0!
27	Total Expenses	0	0	0	#DIV/0!
28	Net Income	0	0	0	#DIV/0!
29					

4 Choose Delete from the Edit menu.

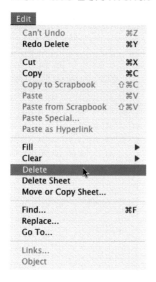

The selected row is deleted and all the rows beneath it shift up.

23	Meals			0	#DIV/0!
24	Travel			0	#DIV/0!
25	Utilities			0	#DIV/0!
26	Total Expenses	0	0	0	#DIV/0!
27	Net Income	0	0	0	#DIV/0!
28					
29					

duplicate the worksheet

enter new values

The February and March worksheets are ready for their values. We'll follow the same basic steps on pages 31–32 to create entry areas and enter the data. To prevent ourselves from accidentally overwriting the formulas in cells B6 and C6, we'll create two separate entry areas for each worksheet.

1 Click the February sheet tab to activate that sheet.

2 Drag from cell B8 to C27 to select that range of cells.

3 Hold down the Ctrl (Windows) or Command (Mac OS) key and drag from cell B3 to C5 to add that range to the selection.

Note that the active cell is the first cell in the second selection.

	A	B	C	D	E
1	Item Name	Budget	Actual	Difference	% Diff
2	Income Items				
3	Sales			0	#DIV/0!
4	Interest Income			0	#DIV/0!
5	Other Income			0	#DIV/0!
6	Total Income	0	0	0	#DIV/0!
7	Expense Items				
8	Automobile			0	#DIV/0!
9	Bank Fees			0	#DIV/0!
10	Contributions			0	#DIV/0!
11	Depreciation			0	#DIV/0!
12	Insurance			0	#DIV/0!
13	Interest Expense			0	#DIV/0!
14	Office Supplies			0	#DIV/0!
15	Postage			0	#DIV/0!
16	Professional Fees			0	#DIV/0!
17	Rent			0	#DIV/0!
18	Repairs			0	#DIV/0!
19	Taxes			0	#DIV/0!
20	Telephone			0	#DIV/0!
21	Travel & Entertainment				
22	Entertainment			0	#DIV/0!
23	Annual Party				
24	Meals			0	#DIV/0!
25	Travel			0	#DIV/0!
26	Utilities			0	#DIV/0!
27	Other Expenses			0	#DIV/0!
28	Total Expenses	0	0	0	#DIV/0!
29	Net Income	0	0	0	#DIV/0!

4 Enter the values shown here in each cell. Be sure to press Enter (Windows) or Return (Mac OS) to advance from one cell to the next. Pay attention; Excel will go through the cells in the top selection before it begins activating cells in the bottom selection.

	A	B	C	D	E
1	Item Name	Budget	Actual	Difference	% Diff
2	Income Items				
3	Sales	8500	9458	958	0.112706
4	Interest Income	100	94	-6	-0.06
5	Other Income	200	354	154	0.77
6	Total Income	8800	9906	1106	0.125682
7	Expense Items				
8	Automobile	200	194	-6	-0.03
9	Bank Fees	25	25	0	0
10	Contributions	100	80	-20	-0.2
11	Depreciation	300	300	0	0
12	Insurance	280	280	0	0
13	Interest Expense	75	121	46	0.613333
14	Office Supplies	300	274	-26	-0.08667
15	Postage	400	412	12	0.03
16	Professional Fees	200	400	200	1
17	Rent	1200	1200	0	0
18	Repairs	120	348	228	1.9
19	Taxes	360	410	50	0.138889
20	Telephone	275	419	144	0.523636
21	Travel & Entertainment				
22	Entertainment	400	319	-81	-0.2025
23	Annual Party	1800	2513	713	0.396111
24	Meals	100	98	-2	-0.02
25	Travel	300	278	-22	-0.07333
26	Utilities	1000	1348	348	0.348
27	Other Expenses	150	684	534	3.56
28	Total Expenses	7585	9703	2118	0.279235
29	Net Income	1215	203	-1012	-0.83292

Excel automatically copies formulas to the blank row when you enter values into it.

enter new values (cont'd)

5 Click the March sheet tab to activate that sheet.

6 Repeat steps 2-4 for cells B8 to C25 and B3 to C5, entering the values shown here.

	A	B	C	D	E
1	Item Name	Budget	Actual	Difference	% Diff
2	Income Items				
3	Sales	10500	9751	-749	-0.07133
4	Interest Income	250	194	-56	-0.224
5	Other Income	300	27	-273	-0.91
6	Total Income	11050	9972	-1078	-0.09756
7	Expense Items				
8	Automobile	240	284	44	0.183333
9	Bank Fees	25	37	12	0.48
10	Contributions	100	250	150	1.5
11	Depreciation	300	300	0	0
12	Insurance	120	120	0	0
13	Interest Expense	100	128	28	0.28
14	Office Supplies	500	617	117	0.234
15	Postage	480	584	104	0.216667
16	Professional Fees	350	650	300	0.857143
17	Rent	1200	1200	0	0
18	Repairs	210	548	338	1.609524
19	Taxes	360	360	0	0
20	Telephone	300	541	241	0.803333
21	Travel & Entertainment				
22	Entertainment	500	486	-14	-0.028
23	Meals	250	347	97	0.388
24	Travel	600	247	-353	-0.58833
25	Utilities	1000	1341	341	0.341
26	Total Expenses	6635	8040	1405	0.211756
27	Net Income	4415	1932	-2483	-0.5624

Have you been saving your work?

Now is a good time to click the Save button on the Standard toolbar to save your work up to this point.

duplicate the worksheet

extra bits

copy the sheet p. 50

- I explain how to identify the sheet tab for an active sheet on page 24.

- If you drag a sheet tab without holding down the Ctrl (Windows) or Option (Mac OS) key, you'll change the sheet's position among the sheet tabs rather than copy it.

clear the values pp. 51–52

- In Excel 2004 for Mac OS, when you clear out the values, you may see green markers in the corners of cells that reference those values. That's Excel's automatic error-checking feature. Ignore them; they will disappear when you enter new values.

- Don't believe that you cleared out the contents of two worksheets at once? Click the sheet tabs for February and March to see for yourself!

- It's important to remove the group sheet selection as instructed in step 6 before entering new values in the February worksheet. Otherwise, you'll enter the same values in both the February and March worksheets.

insert a row p. 53

- The Rows command under the Insert menu inserts as many rows as you have selected above the selected row(s). So if you select three rows and use this command, it will insert three rows above the first selected row.

- If you select a column by clicking on its column heading, you can use the Columns command on the Insert menu to insert a column to the left of it.

- Excel automatically rewrites formulas as necessary when you insert a row or column.

delete a row p. 54

- If you select a column by clicking on its column heading, you can use the Delete command on the Edit menu to delete it.

- Excel automatically rewrites formulas as necessary when you delete a row or column.

duplicate the worksheet   **57**

5. consolidate the results

We now have three worksheets full of budget and actual information. Our next step is to consolidate this information into one summary worksheet for the quarter. We'll do that with Excel's consolidation feature.

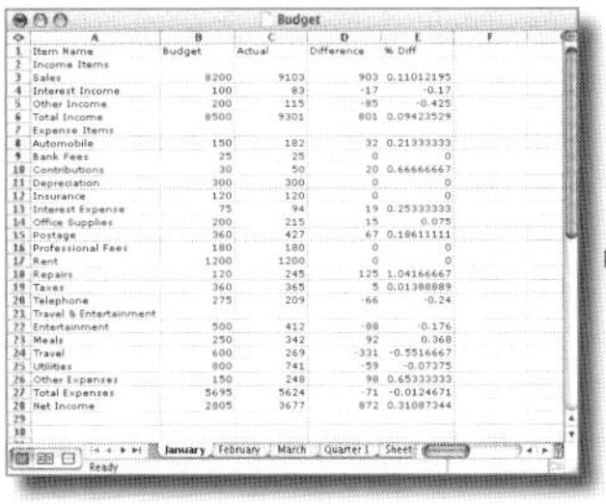

+

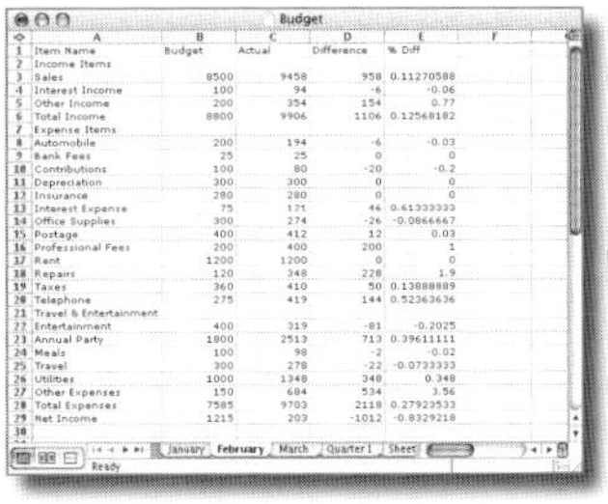

+

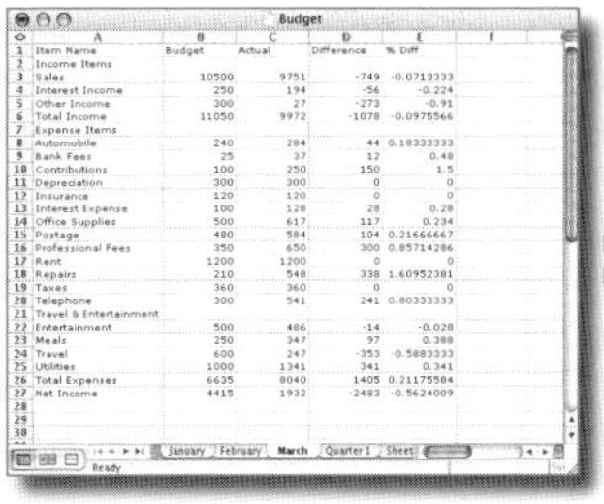

=

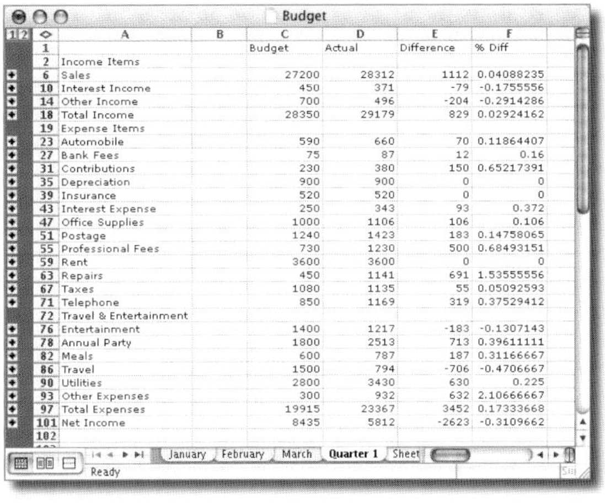

	A	B	C	D	E	F
1			Budget	Actual	Difference	% Diff
2	Income Items					
6	Sales		27200	28312	1112	0.04088235
10	Interest Income		450	371	-79	-0.1755556
14	Other Income		700	496	-204	-0.2914286
18	Total Income		28350	29179	829	0.02924162
19	Expense Items					
23	Automobile		590	660	70	0.11864407
27	Bank Fees		75	87	12	0.16
31	Contributions		230	380	150	0.65217391
35	Depreciation		900	900	0	0
39	Insurance		520	520	0	0
43	Interest Expense		250	343	93	0.372
47	Office Supplies		1000	1106	106	0.106
51	Postage		1240	1423	183	0.14758065
55	Professional Fees		730	1230	500	0.68493151
59	Rent		3600	3600	0	0
63	Repairs		450	1141	691	1.53555556
67	Taxes		1080	1135	55	0.05092593
71	Telephone		850	1169	319	0.37529412
72	Travel & Entertainment					
76	Entertainment		1400	1217	-183	-0.1307143
78	Annual Party		1800	2513	713	0.39611111
82	Meals		600	787	187	0.31166667
86	Travel		1500	794	-706	-0.4706667
90	Utilities		2800	3430	630	0.225
93	Other Expenses		300	932	632	2.10666667
97	Total Expenses		19915	23367	3452	0.17333668
101	Net Income		8435	5812	-2623	-0.3109662
102						

prepare the sheet

The consolidated information will go on its own sheet. We can prepare the sheet by activating it, renaming it, and activating the first cell of the consolidation range.

1 Click the sheet tab for Sheet2 to activate it.

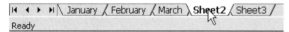

2 Follow the instructions on page 24 to name the sheet tab Quarter 1.

3 Activate cell A1.

consolidate

Excel's consolidation feature uses the Consolidate dialog to collect your consolidation settings, including the worksheet ranges you want to include in the consolidation and the type of consolidation you want to perform.

1 Choose Consolidate from the Data menu.

The Consolidate dialog appears.

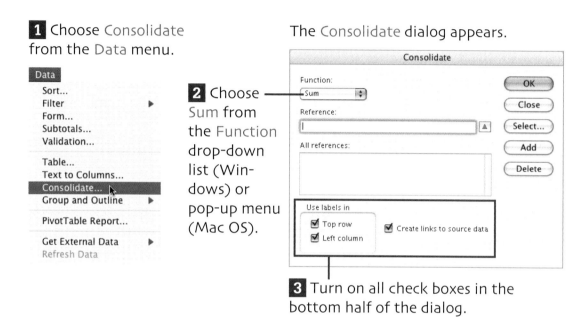

2 Choose Sum from the Function drop-down list (Windows) or pop-up menu (Mac OS).

3 Turn on all check boxes in the bottom half of the dialog.

4 Click the January sheet tab so that sheet becomes active behind the dialog. January! appears in the Reference box.

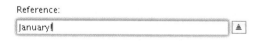

5 Position the mouse pointer on cell A1.

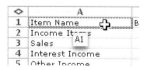

consolidate (cont'd)

6 Press the mouse button and drag down and to the right to select from cell A1 to cell D28. As you drag, the Consolidate dialog collapses so you can see what you're doing and a selection marquee appears around the cells you drag over.

selection marquee

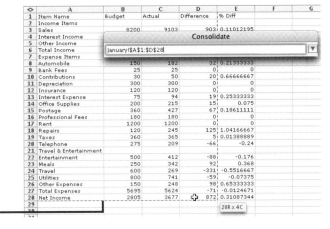

7 Release the mouse button. The range you selected appears in the Reference box.

8 Click Add. The reference is copied to the All references box.

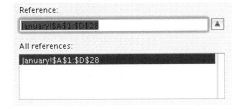

9 Click the February sheet tab to activate that sheet. February!$A$1:$D$28 appears in the Reference box and a selection marquee in the worksheet behind the dialog indicates that range of cells.

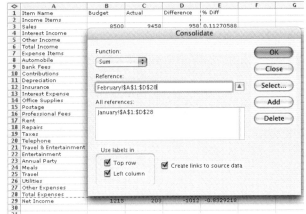

10 Position the mouse pointer on cell A1.

consolidate the results

11 Press the mouse button and drag down and to the right to select from cell A1 to cell D29. As you drag, the Consolidate dialog collapses.

12 Release the mouse button. The range you selected appears in the Reference box.

13 Click Add. The reference is copied to the All references box.

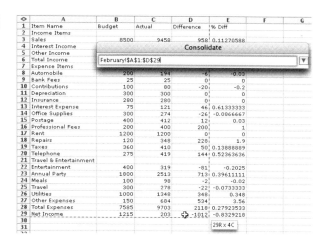

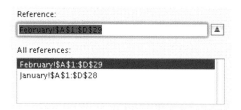

Reference:
February!$A$1:$D$29

All references:
February!$A$1:$D$29
January!$A$1:$D$28

14 Click the March sheet tab so that sheet becomes active. March!$A$1:$D$29 appears in the Reference box and a selection marquee in the worksheet indicates that range of cells.

15 Position the mouse pointer on cell A1.

16 Press the mouse button and drag down and to the right to select from cell A1 to cell D27. As you drag, the Consolidate dialog collapses.

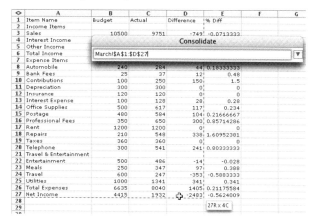

consolidate the results 63

consolidate (cont'd)

17 Release the mouse button. The range you selected appears in the Reference box.

18 Click Add. The reference moves to the All references box.

At this point, the Consolidate dialog should look like this.

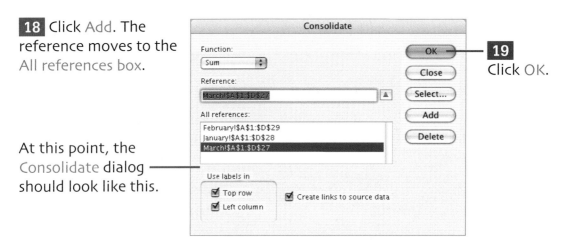

19 Click OK.

Excel creates the consolidation and displays it in the Quarter 1 worksheet.

outline symbols —

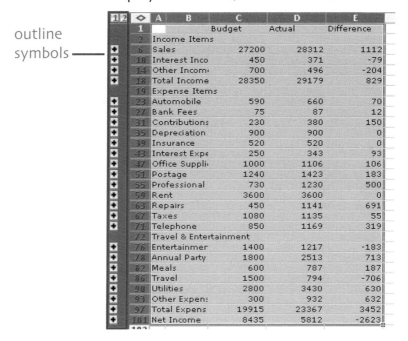

check the consolidation

When you consolidate multiple worksheets as instructed here, you create a new worksheet with "3-D" references to the source worksheets. Because Excel has to display contents from all of the source cells, it automatically displays the consolidation as an outline with the outline collapsed so only the total for each category appears.

Double-click the right border of column A's heading to widen the column.

Click an outline symbol to display or hide rows.

Excel enters the name of the source workbook in column B. In this example, all source data is in Budget.

Activate a cell to see its formula in the formula bar. This example shows a reference to a cell in the February worksheet.

Excel places the category total beneath the detail.

If one of the source worksheets changes, the consolidation automatically changes.

consolidate the results 65

calculate percent diff

When we created our consolidation, we omitted the percent difference calculation on the source worksheets. The reason: Our consolidation used the SUM function to add values in the source worksheets. Adding the percentages would result in incorrect values for the consolidated percent differences. As a result, we need to recreate the percent difference formula in the consolidation worksheet and copy it to the appropriate cells.

1 Click the sheet tab for the Quarter 1 worksheet to activate that sheet.

2 Enter % Diff in cell F1 and press Enter (Windows) or Return (Mac OS).

	A	B	C	D	E	F
1			Budget	Actual	Difference	% Diff
2	Income Items					
6	Sales		27200	28312	1112	
10	Interest Income		450	371	-79	
14	Other Income		700	496	-204	
18	Total Income		28350	29179	829	
19	Expense Items					

3 Enter the formula = E6/C6 in cell F6. You can either type it in or follow the procedure on page 34

	A	B	C	D	E	F
1			Budget	Actual	Difference	% Diff
2	Income Items					
6	Sales		27200	28312	1112	=E6/C6
10	Interest Income		450	371	-79	
14	Other Income		700	496	-204	
18	Total Income		28350	29179	829	
19	Expense Items					

to enter the formula by typing and clicking. (If you do click, be sure to click in the correct cells!) Don't forget to press Enter or Return to complete the formula.

4 Use techniques on pages 39–42 to copy the formula to cells F10 to F18, F23 to F71, and F76 to F101.

When you're finished, it should look like this.

	A	B	C	D	E	F
1			Budget	Actual	Difference	% Diff
2	Income Items					
6	Sales		27200	28312	1112	0.04088235
10	Interest Income		450	371	-79	-0.1755556
14	Other Income		700	496	-204	-0.2914286
18	Total Income		28350	29179	829	0.02924162
19	Expense Items					
23	Automobile		590	660	70	0.11864407
27	Bank Fees		75	87	12	0.16
31	Contributions		230	380	150	0.65217391
35	Depreciation		900	900	0	0
39	Insurance		520	520	0	0
43	Interest Expense		250	343	93	0.372
47	Office Supplies		1000	1106	106	0.106
51	Postage		1240	1423	183	0.14758065
55	Professional Fees		730	1230	500	0.68493151
59	Rent		3600	3600	0	0
63	Repairs		450	1141	691	1.53555556
67	Taxes		1080	1135	55	0.05092593
71	Telephone		850	1169	319	0.37529412
72	Travel & Entertainment					
76	Entertainment		1400	1217	-183	-0.1307143
78	Annual Party		1800	2513	713	0.39611111
82	Meals		600	787	187	0.31166667
86	Travel		1500	794	-706	-0.4706667
90	Utilities		2800	3430	630	0.225
93	Other Expenses		300	932	632	2.10666667
97	Total Expenses		19915	23367	3452	0.17333668
101	Net Income		8435	5812	-2623	-0.3109662
102						

Save your work.

Click the Save button on the Standard toolbar.

consolidate the results

extra bits

consolidate pp.61–64

- Because each worksheet in the consolidation has a slightly different organization—remember, we added a row in one and deleted a row in another—you must turn on the Left column check box to properly consolidate. Doing so tells Excel to sum values based on category name (the row label) rather than row position.

calculate percent diff p.66

- If you use the fill handle to copy the formula in cell F6 to other cells, Excel automatically copies the formula to cells in hidden rows you drag over. This doesn't really matter, though, since we're only interested in the consolidated numbers and will keep the hidden rows hidden.

6. format worksheets

Although the information in our four worksheets is accurate and informative, it doesn't look very good. And in this day and age, looks are almost everything. We need to dress these worksheets up to make them more presentable.

Excel offers many extremely flexible formatting options. Our worksheets can benefit from some font and number formatting, as well as alignment, borders, and color. As shown here, we'll transform our plain Jane worksheets into worksheets that demand attention.

On the following pages, I'll show you how to apply formatting to the January worksheet. You can repeat those steps on your own for the other worksheets in our workbook.

Before

	A	B	C	D	E
1	Item Name	Budget	Actual	Difference	% Diff
2	Income Items				
3	Sales	8200	9103	903	0.11012195
4	Interest Income	100	83	-17	-0.17
5	Other Income	200	115	-85	-0.425
6	Total Income	8500	9301	801	0.09423529
7	Expense Items				
8	Automobile	150	182	32	0.21333333
9	Bank Fees	25	25	0	0
10	Contributions	30	50	20	0.66666667
11	Depreciation	300	300	0	0
12	Insurance	120	120	0	0
13	Interest Expense	75	94	19	0.25333333
14	Office Supplies	200	215	15	0.075
15	Postage	360	427	67	0.18611111
16	Professional Fees	180	180	0	0
17	Rent	1200	1200	0	0
18	Repairs	120	245	125	1.04166667
19	Taxes	360	365	5	0.01388889
20	Telephone	275	209	-66	-0.24
21	Travel & Entertainment				
22	Entertainment	500	412	-88	-0.176
23	Meals	250	342	92	0.368
24	Travel	600	269	-331	-0.5516667
25	Utilities	800	741	-59	-0.07375
26	Other Expenses	150	248	98	0.65333333
27	Total Expenses	5695	5624	-71	-0.0124671
28	Net Income	2805	3677	872	0.31087344

After

	A	B	C	D	E
1	Item Name	Budget	Actual	Difference	% Diff
2	Income Items				
3	Sales	$8,200.00	$9,103.00	$903.00	11.0%
4	Interest Income	100.00	83.00	-17.00	-17.0%
5	Other Income	200.00	115.00	-85.00	-42.5%
6	Total Income	$8,500.00	$9,301.00	$801.00	9.4%
7	Expense Items				
8	Automobile	$150.00	$182.00	$32.00	21.3%
9	Bank Fees	25.00	25.00	0.00	0.0%
10	Contributions	30.00	50.00	20.00	66.7%
11	Depreciation	300.00	300.00	0.00	0.0%
12	Insurance	120.00	120.00	0.00	0.0%
13	Interest Expense	75.00	94.00	19.00	25.3%
14	Office Supplies	200.00	215.00	15.00	7.5%
15	Postage	360.00	427.00	67.00	18.6%
16	Professional Fees	180.00	180.00	0.00	0.0%
17	Rent	1,200.00	1,200.00	0.00	0.0%
18	Repairs	120.00	245.00	125.00	104.2%
19	Taxes	360.00	365.00	5.00	1.4%
20	Telephone	275.00	209.00	-66.00	-24.0%
21	Travel & Entertainment				
22	Entertainment	500.00	412.00	-88.00	-17.6%
23	Meals	250.00	342.00	92.00	36.8%
24	Travel	600.00	269.00	-331.00	-55.2%
25	Utilities	800.00	741.00	-59.00	-7.4%
26	Other Expenses	150.00	248.00	98.00	65.3%
27	Total Expenses	$5,695.00	$5,624.00	-$71.00	-1.2%
28	Net Income	$2,805.00	$3,677.00	$872.00	31.1%

set font formatting

Font formatting changes the way individual characters of text appear. By default, Excel 2003 for Windows uses 10 point Arial font; Excel 2004 for Mac OS uses 10 point Verdana font. You can change the font settings applied to any combination of worksheet cells.

In our worksheets, we'll make the column and row headings bold and larger so they really stand out. We'll also change the font applied to the entire worksheet to something a little more interesting.

1 Drag to select cells A1 to A28.

	A	B	C	D	E
1	Item Name	Budget	Actual	Difference	% Diff
2	Income Items				
3	Sales	8200	9103	903	0.110122
4	Interest Income	100	83	-17	-0.17
5	Other Income	200	115	-85	-0.425
6	Total Income	8500	9301	801	0.094235
7	Expense Items				
8	Automobile	150	182	32	0.213333
9	Bank Fees	25	25	0	0
10	Contributions	30	50	20	0.666667
11	Depreciation	300	300	0	0
12	Insurance	120	120	0	0
13	Interest Expense	75	94	19	0.253333
14	Office Supplies	200	215	15	0.075
15	Postage	360	427	67	0.186111
16	Professional Fees	180	180	0	0
17	Rent	1200	1200	0	0
18	Repairs	120	245	125	1.041667
19	Taxes	360	365	5	0.013889
20	Telephone	275	209	-66	-0.24
21	Travel & Entertainment				
22	Entertainment	500	412	-88	-0.176
23	Meals	250	342	92	0.368
24	Travel	600	269	-331	-0.55167
25	Utilities	800	741	-59	-0.07375
26	Other Expenses	150	248	98	0.653333
27	Total Expenses	5695	5624	-71	-0.01247
28	Net Income	2805	3677	872	0.310873

2 Hold down the Ctrl (Windows) or Command (Mac OS) key and drag to add cells B1 to E1 to the selection.

	A	B	C	D	E
1	Item Name	Budget	Actual	Difference	% Diff
2	Income Items				
3	Sales	8200	9103	903	0.110122
4	Interest Income	100	83	-17	-0.17
5	Other Income	200	115	-85	-0.425
6	Total Income	8500	9301	801	0.094235
7	Expense Items				

3 Click the Bold button on the Formatting toolbar (Windows) or the Formatting Palette (Mac OS).

The text in the selected cells turns bold.

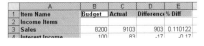

4 Choose 11 from the Font Size drop-down list on the Formatting toolbar (Windows) or Formatting Palette (Mac OS).

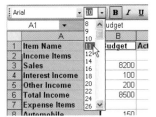

format worksheets

The text in the selected cells gets larger.

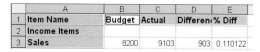

	A	B	C	D	E
1	Item Name	Budget	Actual	Differen	% Diff
2	Income Items				
3	Sales	8200	9103	903	0.110122

6 Choose Lucida Sans from the Font drop-down list on the Formatting toolbar (Windows) or Formatting Palette (Mac OS).

┌─ **5** Click the Select All button in the top corner of the worksheet grid to select all cells in the worksheet.

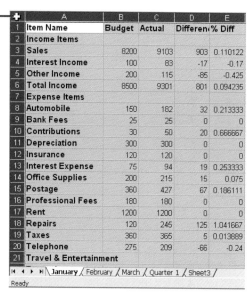

	A	B	C	D	E
1	Item Name	Budget	Actual	Differen	% Diff
2	Income Items				
3	Sales	8200	9103	903	0.110122
4	Interest Income	100	83	-17	-0.17
5	Other Income	200	115	-85	-0.425
6	Total Income	8500	9301	801	0.094235
7	Expense Items				
8	Automobile	150	182	32	0.213333
9	Bank Fees	25	25	0	0
10	Contributions	30	50	20	0.666667
11	Depreciation	300	300	0	0
12	Insurance	120	120	0	0
13	Interest Expense	75	94	19	0.253333
14	Office Supplies	200	215	15	0.075
15	Postage	360	427	67	0.186111
16	Professional Fees	180	180	0	0
17	Rent	1200	1200	0	0
18	Repairs	120	245	125	1.041667
19	Taxes	360	365	5	0.013889
20	Telephone	275	209	-66	-0.24
21	Travel & Entertainment				

|◄ ◄ ► ►|\ January / February / March / Quarter 1 / Sheet3 /
Ready

The text in the selected cells changes to the Lucida Sans font.

	A	B	C	D	E
1	Item Name	Budget	Actual	Differen	% Diff
2	Income Items				
3	Sales	8200	9103	903	0.11012
4	Interest Income	100	83	-17	-0.17
5	Other Income	200	115	-85	-0.425
6	Total Income	8500	9301	801	0.09424
7	Expense Items				
8	Automobile	150	182	32	0.21333
9	Bank Fees	25	25	0	0
10	Contributions	30	50	20	0.66667
11	Depreciation	300	300	0	0
12	Insurance	120	120	0	0
13	Interest Expense	75	94	19	0.25333
14	Office Supplies	200	215	15	0.075
15	Postage	360	427	67	0.18611
16	Professional Fees	180	180	0	0
17	Rent	1200	1200	0	0
18	Repairs	120	245	125	1.04167
19	Taxes	360	365	5	0.01389
20	Telephone	275	209	-66	-0.24
21	Travel & Entertainment				
22	Entertainment	500	412	-88	-0.176

|◄ ◄ ► ►|\ January / February / March / Quarter 1 / Sheet3 /
Ready

format worksheets

format values

The dollar amounts in our worksheets would be a lot easier to read with commas and dollar signs.

1 Drag to select all cells containing numbers in columns B, C, and D.

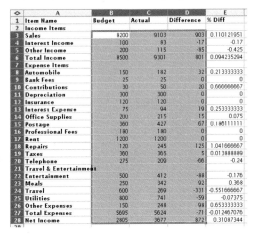

2 In Windows, click the Comma Style button on the Formatting toolbar. Then skip ahead to the top of the next page.

2 In Mac OS, choose Cells from the Format menu.

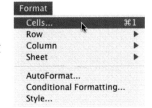

The Format Cells dialog appears.

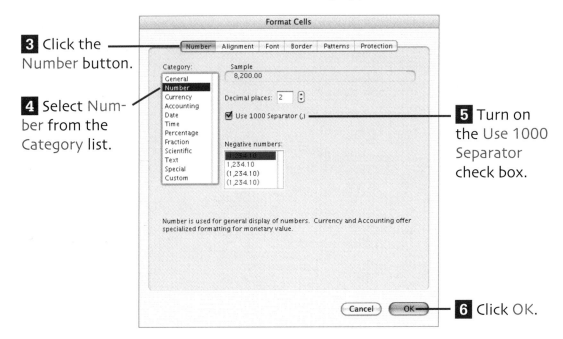

3 Click the Number button.

4 Select Number from the Category list.

5 Turn on the Use 1000 Separator check box.

6 Click OK.

format worksheets

Commas and decimal places appear as appropriate for all values in selected cells.

	A	B	C	D	E
1	Item Name	Budget	Actual	Difference	% Diff
2	Income Items				
3	Sales	8,200.00	9,103.00	903.00	0.110121951
4	Interest Income	100.00	83.00	-17.00	-0.17
5	Other Income	200.00	115.00	-85.00	-0.425
6	Total Income	8,500.00	9,301.00	801.00	0.094235294
7	Expense Items				
8	Automobile	150.00	182.00	32.00	0.213333333
9	Bank Fees	25.00	25.00	0.00	0
10	Contributions	30.00	50.00	20.00	0.666666667
11	Depreciation	300.00	300.00	0.00	0
12	Insurance	120.00	120.00	0.00	0
13	Interest Expense	75.00	94.00	19.00	0.253333333
14	Office Supplies	200.00	215.00	15.00	0.075
15	Postage	360.00	427.00	67.00	0.186111111
16	Professional Fees	180.00	180.00	0.00	0
17	Rent	1,200.00	1,200.00	0.00	0
18	Repairs	120.00	245.00	125.00	1.041666667
19	Taxes	360.00	365.00	5.00	0.013888889
20	Telephone	275.00	209.00	-66.00	-0.24
21	Travel & Entertainment				
22	Entertainment	500.00	412.00	-88.00	-0.176
23	Meals	250.00	342.00	92.00	0.368
24	Travel	600.00	269.00	-331.00	-0.551666667
25	Utilities	800.00	741.00	-59.00	-0.07375
26	Other Expenses	150.00	248.00	98.00	0.653333333
27	Total Expenses	5,695.00	5,624.00	-71.00	-0.012467076
28	Net Income	2,805.00	3,677.00	872.00	0.31087344

7 Drag to select cells B3 to D3, B6 to D6, B8 to D8, and B27 to D28. Remember you must hold down the Ctrl (Windows) or Command (Mac OS) key to select multiple ranges.

	A	B	C	D	E
1	Item Name	Budget	Actual	Difference	% Diff
2	Income Items				
3	Sales	8,200.00	9,103.00	903.00	0.110121951
4	Interest Income	100.00	83.00	-17.00	-0.17
5	Other Income	200.00	115.00	-85.00	-0.425
6	Total Income	8,500.00	9,301.00	801.00	0.094235294
7	Expense Items				
8	Automobile	150.00	182.00	32.00	0.213333333
9	Bank Fees	25.00	25.00	0.00	0
10	Contributions	30.00	50.00	20.00	0.666666667
11	Depreciation	300.00	300.00	0.00	0
12	Insurance	120.00	120.00	0.00	0
13	Interest Expense	75.00	94.00	19.00	0.253333333
14	Office Supplies	200.00	215.00	15.00	0.075
15	Postage	360.00	427.00	67.00	0.186111111
16	Professional Fees	180.00	180.00	0.00	0
17	Rent	1,200.00	1,200.00	0.00	0
18	Repairs	120.00	245.00	125.00	1.041666667
19	Taxes	360.00	365.00	5.00	0.013888889
20	Telephone	275.00	209.00	-66.00	-0.24
21	Travel & Entertainment				
22	Entertainment	500.00	412.00	-88.00	-0.176
23	Meals	250.00	342.00	92.00	0.368
24	Travel	600.00	269.00	-331.00	-0.551666667
25	Utilities	800.00	741.00	-59.00	-0.07375
26	Other Expenses	150.00	248.00	98.00	0.653333333
27	Total Expenses	5,695.00	5,624.00	-71.00	-0.012467076
28	Net Income	2,805.00	3,677.00	872.00	0.31087344

8 Click the Currency Style button in the Formatting toolbar (Windows) or choose Currency from the Format drop-down list in the Formatting Palette (Mac OS).

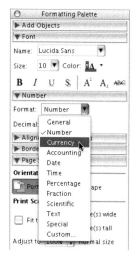

Currency symbols appear beside values in the selected cells.

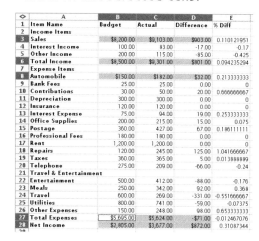

format percentages

We can also use number formatting to format the percentages in column E so they look like percentages.

1 Drag to select all cells containing numbers in column E.

	A	B	C	D	E
1	Item Name	Budget	Actual	Differenc	% Diff
2	Income Items				
3	Sales	$8,200.00	$9,103.00	$ 903.00	0.110122
4	Interest Income	100.00	83.00	(17.00)	-0.17
5	Other Income	200.00	115.00	(85.00)	-0.425
6	Total Income	$8,500.00	$9,301.00	$ 801.00	0.094235
7	Expense Items				
8	Automobile	$ 150.00	$ 182.00	$ 32.00	0.213333
9	Bank Fees	25.00	25.00	-	0
10	Contributions	30.00	50.00	20.00	0.666667
11	Depreciation	300.00	300.00	-	0
12	Insurance	120.00	120.00	-	0
13	Interest Expense	75.00	94.00	19.00	0.253333
14	Office Supplies	200.00	215.00	15.00	0.075
15	Postage	360.00	427.00	67.00	0.186111

2 Click the Percent Style button on the Formatting toolbar (Windows) or choose Percentage from the Format drop-down list on the Formatting Palette (Mac OS).

In Windows, the numbers are formatted as percentages without any decimal places.

	A	B	C	D	E
1	Item Name	Budget	Actual	Differenc	% Diff
2	Income Items				
3	Sales	$8,200.00	$9,103.00	$ 903.00	11%
4	Interest Income	100.00	83.00	(17.00)	-17%
5	Other Income	200.00	115.00	(85.00)	-43%
6	Total Income	$8,500.00	$9,301.00	$ 801.00	9%
7	Expense Items				
8	Automobile	$ 150.00	$ 182.00	$ 32.00	21%
9	Bank Fees	25.00	25.00	-	0%
10	Contributions	30.00	50.00	20.00	67%
11	Depreciation	300.00	300.00	-	0%
12	Insurance	120.00	120.00	-	0%
13	Interest Expense	75.00	94.00	19.00	25%
14	Office Supplies	200.00	215.00	15.00	8%
15	Postage	360.00	427.00	67.00	19%

In Mac OS, the numbers are formatted as percentages with two decimal places.

	A	B	C	D	E
1	Item Name	Budget	Actual	Difference	% Diff
2	Income Items				
3	Sales	$8,200.00	$9,103.00	$903.00	11.01%
4	Interest Income	100.00	83.00	-17.00	-17.00%
5	Other Income	200.00	115.00	-85.00	-42.50%
6	Total Income	$8,500.00	$9,301.00	$801.00	9.42%
7	Expense Items				
8	Automobile	$150.00	$182.00	$32.00	21.33%
9	Bank Fees	25.00	25.00	0.00	0.00%
10	Contributions	30.00	50.00	20.00	66.67%
11	Depreciation	300.00	300.00	0.00	0.00%
12	Insurance	120.00	120.00	0.00	0.00%
13	Interest Expense	75.00	94.00	19.00	25.33%
14	Office Supplies	200.00	215.00	15.00	7.50%
15	Postage	360.00	427.00	67.00	18.61%

(I think Microsoft makes these minor differences between the Windows and Mac OS versions of the software just to drive software book authors crazy.)

3 Click the Increase Decimal button on the Formatting toolbar (Windows) or the Decrease Decimal button on the Formatting Palette (Mac OS).

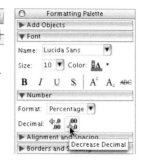

The numbers are reformatted so there's one decimal place.

	A	B	C	D	E
1	Item Name	Budget	Actual	Differenc	% Diff
2	Income Items				
3	Sales	$8,200.00	$9,103.00	$ 903.00	11.0%
4	Interest Income	100.00	83.00	(17.00)	-17.0%
5	Other Income	200.00	115.00	(85.00)	-42.5%
6	Total Income	$8,500.00	$9,301.00	$ 801.00	9.4%
7	Expense Items				
8	Automobile	$ 150.00	$ 182.00	$ 32.00	21.3%
9	Bank Fees	25.00	25.00	-	0.0%
10	Contributions	30.00	50.00	20.00	66.7%
11	Depreciation	300.00	300.00	-	0.0%
12	Insurance	120.00	120.00	-	0.0%
13	Interest Expense	75.00	94.00	19.00	25.3%
14	Office Supplies	200.00	215.00	15.00	7.5%
15	Postage	360.00	427.00	67.00	18.6%

	A	B	C	D	E
1	Item Name	Budget	Actual	Difference	% Diff
2	Income Items				
3	Sales	$8,200.00	$9,103.00	$903.00	11.0%
4	Interest Income	100.00	83.00	-17.00	-17.0%
5	Other Income	200.00	115.00	-85.00	-42.5%
6	Total Income	$8,500.00	$9,301.00	$801.00	9.4%
7	Expense Items				
8	Automobile	$150.00	$182.00	$32.00	21.3%
9	Bank Fees	25.00	25.00	0.00	0.0%
10	Contributions	30.00	50.00	20.00	66.7%
11	Depreciation	300.00	300.00	0.00	0.0%
12	Insurance	120.00	120.00	0.00	0.0%
13	Interest Expense	75.00	94.00	19.00	25.3%
14	Office Supplies	200.00	215.00	15.00	7.5%
15	Postage	360.00	427.00	67.00	18.6%

format worksheets

set column widths

When you create a worksheet, Excel automatically sets a default width for columns. The width of columns in the Windows version of Excel is 8.43 characters (or 64 pixels). The width of columns in the Mac OS version of Excel is 10 characters (or 1.04 inches).

We've already used the AutoFit feature to increase the width of column A so its text fits in the column. And, if you use the Windows version of Excel, you may have noticed that it widened one or two columns to accommodate the number formatting we applied.

Now we'll make column A a little wider again—remember, we increased the text size and applied bold formatting, which make the text take up more space. We'll also set the width of columns B, C, D, and E to a consistent wider setting.

1 Double-click the right border of column A.

	A	B	
1	**Item Name**	**Budget**	A
2	**Income Items**		
3	**Sales**	$ 8,200.00	
4	**Interest Income**	100.00	
5	**Other Income**	200.00	
6	**Total Income**	$ 8,500.00	
7	**Expense Items**		
8	**Automobile**	$ 150.00	
9	**Bank Fees**	25.00	
10	**Contributions**	30.00	
11	**Depreciation**	300.00	
12	**Insurance**	120.00	
13	**Interest Expense**	75.00	
14	**Office Supplies**	200.00	
15	**Postage**	360.00	
16	**Professional Fees**	180.00	
17	**Rent**	1,200.00	
18	**Repairs**	120.00	
19	**Taxes**	360.00	
20	**Telephone**	275.00	
21	**Travel & Entertainment**		
22	**Entertainment**	500.00	
23	**Meals**	250.00	
24	**Travel**	600.00	
25	**Utilities**	800.00	
26	**Other Expenses**	150.00	
27	**Total Expenses**	$ 5,695.00	
28	**Net Income**	$ 2,805.00	
29			

January / February
Ready

The column automatically widens again to accommodate the widest text in the column.

	A	B	
1	**Item Name**	**Budget**	A
2	**Income Items**		
3	**Sales**	$ 8,200.00	
4	**Interest Income**	100.00	
5	**Other Income**	200.00	
6	**Total Income**	$ 8,500.00	
7	**Expense Items**		
8	**Automobile**	$ 150.00	
9	**Bank Fees**	25.00	
10	**Contributions**	30.00	
11	**Depreciation**	300.00	
12	**Insurance**	120.00	
13	**Interest Expense**	75.00	
14	**Office Supplies**	200.00	
15	**Postage**	360.00	
16	**Professional Fees**	180.00	
17	**Rent**	1,200.00	
18	**Repairs**	120.00	
19	**Taxes**	360.00	
20	**Telephone**	275.00	
21	**Travel & Entertainment**		
22	**Entertainment**	500.00	
23	**Meals**	250.00	
24	**Travel**	600.00	
25	**Utilities**	800.00	
26	**Other Expenses**	150.00	
27	**Total Expenses**	$ 5,695.00	
28	**Net Income**	$ 2,805.00	
29			

January / February / Mar
Ready

2 Position the mouse pointer on the column heading for column B. It turns into an arrow pointing down.

B ↓	
Budget	**Act**

format worksheets

3 Press the mouse button and drag to the right to select columns B, C, D, and E.

4 Choose Width from the Column submenu under the Format menu.

	A	B	C	D	E
1	Item Name	Budget	Actual	Differenc	% Diff
2	Income Items				
3	Sales	$8,200.00	$9,103.00	$ 903.00	11.0%
4	Interest Income	100.00	83.00	(17.00)	-17.0%
5	Other Income	200.00	115.00	(85.00)	-42.5%
6	Total Income	$8,500.00	$9,301.00	$ 801.00	9.4%
7	Expense Items				
8	Automobile	$ 150.00	$ 182.00	$ 32.00	21.3%
9	Bank Fees	25.00	25.00	-	0.0%
10	Contributions	30.00	50.00	20.00	66.7%
11	Depreciation	300.00	300.00	-	0.0%
12	Insurance	120.00	120.00	-	0.0%
13	Interest Expense	75.00	94.00	19.00	25.3%
14	Office Supplies	200.00	215.00	15.00	7.5%
15	Postage	360.00	427.00	67.00	18.6%
16	Professional Fees	180.00	180.00	-	0.0%
17	Rent	1,200.00	1,200.00	-	0.0%
18	Repairs	120.00	245.00	125.00	104.2%
19	Taxes	360.00	365.00	5.00	1.4%
20	Telephone	275.00	209.00	(66.00)	-24.0%
21	Travel & Entertainment				

January / February / March / Quarter 1 / Sheet3 /
Ready

The Column Width dialog appears.

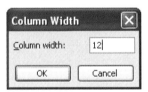

5 In Windows, enter 12 in the text box and click OK...

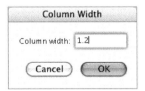

...or in Mac OS, enter 1.2 in the text box and click OK.

	A	B	C	D	E
1	Item Name	Budget	Actual	Difference	% Diff
2	Income Items				
3	Sales	$ 8,200.00	$ 9,103.00	$ 903.00	11.0%
4	Interest Income	100.00	83.00	(17.00)	-17.0%
5	Other Income	200.00	115.00	(85.00)	-42.5%
6	Total Income	$ 8,500.00	$ 9,301.00	$ 801.00	9.4%
7	Expense Items				
8	Automobile	$ 150.00	$ 182.00	$ 32.00	21.3%
9	Bank Fees	25.00	25.00	-	0.0%
10	Contributions	30.00	50.00	20.00	66.7%
11	Depreciation	300.00	300.00	-	0.0%
12	Insurance	120.00	120.00	-	0.0%
13	Interest Expense	75.00	94.00	19.00	25.3%
14	Office Supplies	200.00	215.00	15.00	7.5%
15	Postage	360.00	427.00	67.00	18.6%
16	Professional Fees	180.00	180.00	-	0.0%
17	Rent	1,200.00	1,200.00	-	0.0%
18	Repairs	120.00	245.00	125.00	104.2%
19	Taxes	360.00	365.00	5.00	1.4%
20	Telephone	275.00	209.00	(66.00)	-24.0%
21	Travel & Entertainment				

January / February / March / Quarter 1 / Sheet3 /
Ready   Sum=67056.

The columns widen.

format worksheets

set alignment

By default, text is left-aligned in a cell and a number (including a date or time) is right-aligned in a cell. For our worksheet, the headings at the top of columns B, C, D, and E might look better if they were centered.

1 Drag to select cells B1 through E1.

◇	A	B	C	D	E
1	Item Name	Budget	Actual	Difference	% Diff ✛
2	Income Items				
3	Sales	$8,200.00	$9,103.00	$903.00	11.0%
4	Interest Income	100.00	83.00	-17.00	-17.0%
5	Other Income	200.00	115.00	-85.00	-42.5%

2 Click the Center button on the Formatting toolbar (Windows)...

...or the Align Center button in the Alignment and Spacing area of the Formatting Palette (Mac OS).

You may have to click here to display Alignment and Spacing options.

The cell contents are centered between the cell's left and right boundaries.

◇	A	B	C	D	E
1	Item Name	Budget	Actual	Difference	% Diff
2	Income Items				
3	Sales	$8,200.00	$9,103.00	$903.00	11.0%
4	Interest Income	100.00	83.00	-17.00	-17.0%
5	Other Income	200.00	115.00	-85.00	-42.5%

indent text

Entertainment, Meals, and Travel are three row headings that are part of the major Travel & Entertainment category of expenses. We can make that clear to the people who view the worksheet by indenting those three row headings.

1 Select cells A22 through A24.

2 Click the Increase Indent button on the Formatting toolbar (Windows)…

…or enter 1 in the Indent box in the Alignment and Spacing area of the Formatting Palette and press Return (Mac OS).

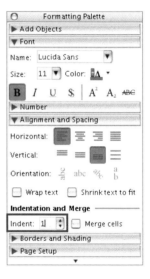

Each cell's contents are shifted to the right.

Save your work.

Click the Save button on the Standard toolbar.

add borders

Borders above and below the totals and net amounts would really help them stand out. We'll add single lines above and below Income and Expense totals and a double line beneath the Net Income amounts.

1 Select cells B6 to E6, and B27 to E27. Remember, you must hold down the Control (Windows) or Command (Mac OS) key to select multiple ranges.

	A	B	C	D	E
1	Item Name	Budget	Actual	Difference	% Diff
2	Income Items				
3	Sales	$8,200.00	$9,103.00	$903.00	11.0%
4	Interest Income	100.00	83.00	-17.00	-17.0%
5	Other Income	200.00	115.00	-85.00	-42.5%
6	Total Income	$8,500.00	$9,301.00	$801.00	9.4%
7	Expense Items				
8	Automobile	$150.00	$182.00	$32.00	21.3%
9	Bank Fees	25.00	25.00	0.00	0.0%
10	Contributions	30.00	50.00	20.00	66.7%
11	Depreciation	300.00	300.00	0.00	0.0%
12	Insurance	120.00	120.00	0.00	0.0%
13	Interest Expense	75.00	94.00	19.00	25.3%
14	Office Supplies	200.00	215.00	15.00	7.5%
15	Postage	360.00	427.00	67.00	18.6%
16	Professional Fees	180.00	180.00	0.00	0.0%
17	Rent	1,200.00	1,200.00	0.00	0.0%
18	Repairs	120.00	245.00	125.00	104.2%
19	Taxes	360.00	365.00	5.00	1.4%
20	Telephone	275.00	209.00	-66.00	-24.0%
21	Travel & Entertainment				
22	Entertainment	500.00	412.00	-88.00	-17.6%
23	Meals	250.00	342.00	92.00	36.8%
24	Travel	600.00	269.00	-331.00	-55.2%
25	Utilities	800.00	741.00	-59.00	-7.4%
26	Other Expenses	150.00	248.00	98.00	65.3%
27	Total Expenses	$5,695.00	$5,624.00	-$71.00	-1.2%
28	Net Income	$2,805.00	$3,677.00	$872.00	31.1%

In Windows:

2 Click the triangle on the Borders button on the Formatting toolbar to display a menu of options.

3 Choose the Top and Bottom Border button.

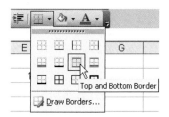

In Mac OS:

2 Click the triangle on the Type button in the Borders and Shading area of the Formatting Palette to display a menu of options.

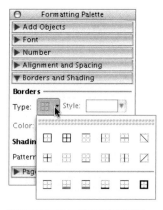

3 Choose the Top and Bottom Border button.

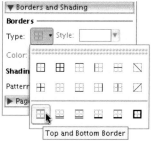

Borders are applied to the top and bottom of all selected cells.

	A	B	C	D	E
1	Item Name	Budget	Actual	Difference	% Diff
2	Income Items				
3	Sales	$8,200.00	$9,103.00	$903.00	11.0%
4	Interest Income	100.00	83.00	-17.00	-17.0%
5	Other Income	200.00	115.00	-85.00	-42.5%
6	Total Income	$8,500.00	$9,301.00	$801.00	9.4%
7	Expense Items				
8	Automobile	$150.00	$182.00	$32.00	21.3%
9	Bank Fees	25.00	25.00	0.00	0.0%
10	Contributions	30.00	50.00	20.00	66.7%
11	Depreciation	300.00	300.00	0.00	0.0%
12	Insurance	120.00	120.00	0.00	0.0%
13	Interest Expense	75.00	94.00	19.00	25.3%
14	Office Supplies	200.00	215.00	15.00	7.5%
15	Postage	360.00	427.00	67.00	18.6%
16	Professional Fees	180.00	180.00	0.00	0.0%
17	Rent	1,200.00	1,200.00	0.00	0.0%
18	Repairs	120.00	245.00	125.00	104.2%
19	Taxes	360.00	365.00	5.00	1.4%
20	Telephone	275.00	209.00	-66.00	-24.0%
21	Travel & Entertainment				
22	Entertainment	500.00	412.00	-88.00	-17.6%
23	Meals	250.00	342.00	92.00	36.8%
24	Travel	600.00	269.00	-331.00	-55.2%
25	Utilities	800.00	741.00	-59.00	-7.4%
26	Other Expenses	150.00	248.00	98.00	65.3%
27	Total Expenses	$5,695.00	$5,624.00	-$71.00	-1.2%
28	Net Income	$2,805.00	$3,677.00	$872.00	31.1%

4 Select cells B28 to E28.

25	Utilities	800.00	741.00	-59.00	-7.4%
26	Other Expenses	150.00	248.00	98.00	65.3%
27	Total Expenses	$5,695.00	$5,624.00	-$71.00	-1.2%
28	Net Income	$2,805.00	$3,677.00	$872.00	31.1%

In Windows:

5 Click the triangle on the Borders button on the Formatting toolbar to display a menu of options.

6 Choose the Top and Double Bottom Border button.

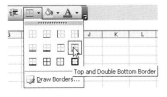

In Mac OS:

5 Click the triangle on the Type button in the Borders and Shading area of the Formatting Palette to display a menu of options.

6 Choose the Top and Double Bottom Border button.

A double border appears beneath the selected cells.

Here's what it should look like when you're done, with the selection area removed.

	A	B	C	D	E
1	Item Name	Budget	Actual	Difference	% Diff
2	Income Items				
3	Sales	$8,200.00	$9,103.00	$903.00	11.0%
4	Interest Income	100.00	83.00	-17.00	-17.0%
5	Other Income	200.00	115.00	-85.00	-42.5%
6	Total Income	$8,500.00	$9,301.00	$801.00	9.4%
7	Expense Items				
8	Automobile	$150.00	$182.00	$32.00	21.3%
9	Bank Fees	25.00	25.00	0.00	0.0%
10	Contributions	30.00	50.00	20.00	66.7%
11	Depreciation	300.00	300.00	0.00	0.0%
12	Insurance	120.00	120.00	0.00	0.0%
13	Interest Expense	75.00	94.00	19.00	25.3%
14	Office Supplies	200.00	215.00	15.00	7.5%
15	Postage	360.00	427.00	67.00	18.6%
16	Professional Fees	180.00	180.00	0.00	0.0%
17	Rent	1,200.00	1,200.00	0.00	0.0%
18	Repairs	120.00	245.00	125.00	104.2%
19	Taxes	360.00	365.00	5.00	1.4%
20	Telephone	275.00	209.00	-66.00	-24.0%
21	Travel & Entertainment				
22	Entertainment	500.00	412.00	-88.00	-17.6%
23	Meals	250.00	342.00	92.00	36.8%
24	Travel	600.00	269.00	-331.00	-55.2%
25	Utilities	800.00	741.00	-59.00	-7.4%
26	Other Expenses	150.00	248.00	98.00	65.3%
27	Total Expenses	$5,695.00	$5,624.00	-$71.00	-1.2%
28	Net Income	$2,805.00	$3,677.00	$872.00	31.1%

apply shading

Shading can also improve the appearance of a worksheet. We'll apply dark colored shading to worksheet cells containing headings so they really stand out, then apply a lighter color shading to the rest of the worksheet.

1 Select cells A1 to E1 and A2 to A28. Remember, you must hold down the Control (Windows) or Command (Mac OS) key to select multiple ranges.

	A	B	C	D	E
1	Item Name	Budget	Actual	Difference	% Diff
2	Income Items				
3	Sales	$ 8,200.00	$ 9,103.00	$ 903.00	11.0%
4	Interest Income	100.00	83.00	(17.00)	-17.0%
5	Other Income	200.00	115.00	(85.00)	-42.5%
6	Total Income	$ 8,500.00	$ 9,301.00	$ 801.00	9.4%
7	Expense Items				
8	Automobile	$ 150.00	$ 182.00	$ 32.00	21.3%
9	Bank Fees	25.00	25.00	-	0.0%
10	Contributions	30.00	50.00	20.00	66.7%
11	Depreciation	300.00	300.00	-	0.0%
12	Insurance	120.00	120.00	-	0.0%
13	Interest Expense	75.00	94.00	19.00	25.3%
14	Office Supplies	200.00	215.00	15.00	7.5%
15	Postage	360.00	427.00	67.00	18.6%
16	Professional Fees	180.00	180.00	-	0.0%
17	Rent	1,200.00	1,200.00	-	0.0%
18	Repairs	120.00	245.00	125.00	104.2%
19	Taxes	360.00	365.00	5.00	1.4%
20	Telephone	275.00	209.00	(66.00)	-24.0%
21	Travel & Entertainment				
22	Entertainment	500.00	412.00	(88.00)	-17.6%
23	Meals	250.00	342.00	92.00	36.8%
24	Travel	600.00	269.00	(331.00)	-55.2%
25	Utilities	800.00	741.00	(59.00)	-7.4%
26	Other Expenses	150.00	248.00	98.00	65.3%
27	Total Expenses	$ 5,695.00	$ 5,624.00	$ (71.00)	-1.2%
28	Net Income	$ 2,805.00	$ 3,677.00	$ 872.00	31.1%

2 In Windows, click the triangle on the Fill button on the Formatting toolbar to display a menu of colors and choose a dark color…

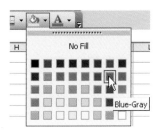

…or in Mac OS, click the triangle on the Color button in the bottom part of the Borders and Shading area of the Formatting Palette to display a menu of colors and choose a dark color.

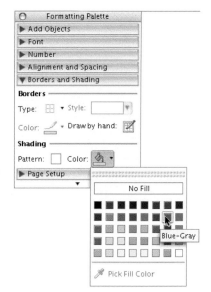

The color is applied to selected cells. Here's what it might look like with the selection area removed.

	A	B	C	D	E
1	Item Name	Budget	Actual	Difference	% Diff
2	Income Items				
3	Sales	$ 8,200.00	$ 9,103.00	$ 903.00	11.0%
4	Interest Income	100.00	83.00	(17.00)	-17.0%
5	Other Income	200.00	115.00	(85.00)	-42.5%
6	Total Income	$ 8,500.00	$ 9,301.00	$ 801.00	9.4%
7	Expense Items				
8	Automobile	$ 150.00	$ 182.00	$ 32.00	21.3%
9	Bank Fees	25.00	25.00	-	0.0%
10	Contributions	30.00	50.00	20.00	66.7%
11	Depreciation	300.00	300.00	-	0.0%
12	Insurance	120.00	120.00	-	0.0%
13	Interest Expense	75.00	94.00	19.00	25.3%
14	Office Supplies	200.00	215.00	15.00	7.5%
15	Postage	360.00	427.00	67.00	18.6%
16	Professional Fees	180.00	180.00	-	0.0%
17	Rent	1,200.00	1,200.00	-	0.0%
18	Repairs	120.00	245.00	125.00	104.2%
19	Taxes	360.00	365.00	5.00	1.4%
20	Telephone	275.00	209.00	(66.00)	-24.0%
21	Travel & Entertainment				
22	Entertainment	500.00	412.00	(88.00)	-17.6%
23	Meals	250.00	342.00	92.00	36.8%
24	Travel	600.00	269.00	(331.00)	-55.2%
25	Utilities	800.00	741.00	(59.00)	-7.4%
26	Other Expenses	150.00	248.00	98.00	65.3%
27	Total Expenses	$ 5,695.00	$ 5,624.00	$ (71.00)	-1.2%
28	Net Income	$ 2,805.00	$ 3,677.00	$ 872.00	31.1%

3 Select cells B2 to E28.

	A	B	C	D	E
1	Item Name	Budget	Actual	Difference	% Diff
2	Income Items				
3	Sales	$ 8,200.00	$ 9,103.00	$ 903.00	11.0%
4	Interest Income	100.00	83.00	(17.00)	-17.0%
5	Other Income	200.00	115.00	(85.00)	-42.5%
6	Total Income	$ 8,500.00	$ 9,301.00	$ 801.00	9.4%
7	Expense Items				
8	Automobile	$ 150.00	$ 182.00	$ 32.00	21.3%
9	Bank Fees	25.00	25.00	-	0.0%
10	Contributions	30.00	50.00	20.00	66.7%
11	Depreciation	300.00	300.00	-	0.0%
12	Insurance	120.00	120.00	-	0.0%
13	Interest Expense	75.00	94.00	19.00	25.3%
14	Office Supplies	200.00	215.00	15.00	7.5%
15	Postage	360.00	427.00	67.00	18.6%
16	Professional Fees	180.00	180.00	-	0.0%
17	Rent	1,200.00	1,200.00	-	0.0%
18	Repairs	120.00	245.00	125.00	104.2%
19	Taxes	360.00	365.00	5.00	1.4%
20	Telephone	275.00	209.00	(66.00)	-24.0%
21	Travel & Entertainment				
22	Entertainment	500.00	412.00	(88.00)	-17.6%
23	Meals	250.00	342.00	92.00	36.8%
24	Travel	600.00	269.00	(331.00)	-55.2%
25	Utilities	800.00	741.00	(59.00)	-7.4%
26	Other Expenses	150.00	248.00	98.00	65.3%
27	Total Expenses	$ 5,695.00	$ 5,624.00	$ (71.00)	-1.2%
28	Net Income	$ 2,805.00	$ 3,677.00	$ 872.00	31.1%

4 Follow step 2 to select a lighter color.

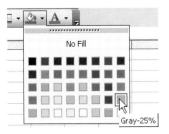

No Fill

Gray-25%

The color is applied to selected cells.

	A	B	C	D	E
1	Item Name	Budget	Actual	Difference	% Diff
2	Income Items				
3	Sales	$ 8,200.00	$ 9,103.00	$ 903.00	11.0%
4	Interest Income	100.00	83.00	(17.00)	-17.0%
5	Other Income	200.00	115.00	(85.00)	-42.5%
6	Total Income	$ 8,500.00	$ 9,301.00	$ 801.00	9.4%
7	Expense Items				
8	Automobile	$ 150.00	$ 182.00	$ 32.00	21.3%
9	Bank Fees	25.00	25.00	-	0.0%
10	Contributions	30.00	50.00	20.00	66.7%
11	Depreciation	300.00	300.00	-	0.0%
12	Insurance	120.00	120.00	-	0.0%
13	Interest Expense	75.00	94.00	19.00	25.3%
14	Office Supplies	200.00	215.00	15.00	7.5%
15	Postage	360.00	427.00	67.00	18.6%
16	Professional Fees	180.00	180.00	-	0.0%
17	Rent	1,200.00	1,200.00	-	0.0%
18	Repairs	120.00	245.00	125.00	104.2%
19	Taxes	360.00	365.00	5.00	1.4%
20	Telephone	275.00	209.00	(66.00)	-24.0%
21	Travel & Entertainment				
22	Entertainment	500.00	412.00	(88.00)	-17.6%
23	Meals	250.00	342.00	92.00	36.8%
24	Travel	600.00	269.00	(331.00)	-55.2%
25	Utilities	800.00	741.00	(59.00)	-7.4%
26	Other Expenses	150.00	248.00	98.00	65.3%
27	Total Expenses	$ 5,695.00	$ 5,624.00	$ (71.00)	-1.2%
28	Net Income	$ 2,805.00	$ 3,677.00	$ 872.00	31.1%

Save your work.

Click the Save button on the Standard toolbar.

Microsoft Exc

File   Edit

Save

format worksheets

change text color

When we applied a dark border to the worksheet's headings, we created a problem: The black text may not be legible with the dark cell shading. We can fix this problem by making the heading text a lighter color.

1 Select cells A1 to E1 and A2 to A28. Remember, you must hold down the Control (Windows) or Command (Mac OS) key to select multiple ranges.

2 In Windows, click the triangle on the Font Color button on the Formatting toolbar to display a menu of colors and choose a light color...

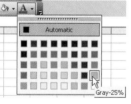

...or in Mac OS, click the triangle on the Color button in the Font area of the Formatting Palette to display a menu of colors and choose a light color.

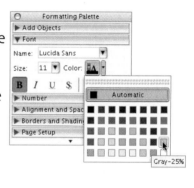

The color you selected is applied to the contents of selected cells. Here's what it might look like with the selection area removed.

format all worksheets

So far, all we've done is format one of the four worksheets in our workbook file: January. You can follow the steps on pages 70–84 to apply the same formatting to the other worksheets in the file: February, March, and Quarter 1.

Here are a few things to keep in mind:

- To activate a worksheet, click its sheet tab.

- Not all worksheets have the same number of columns and rows, so you won't be able to use the cell selections exactly as written in this chapter. Be sure to select the correct areas when applying formatting.

- In the February worksheet, Annual Party should be indented with the other Travel & Entertainment row headings.

- For the Quarter 1 worksheet, keep the consolidation's detail hidden. You can also hide column B by setting its column width to 0 (zero).

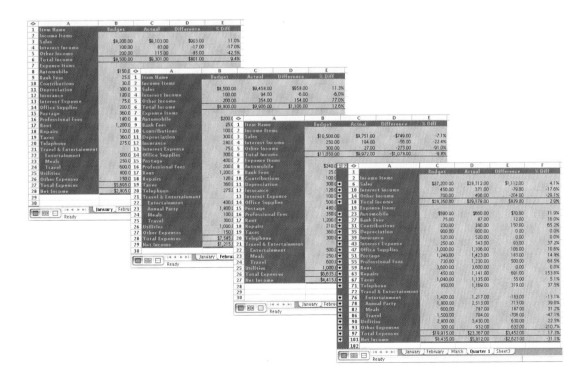

format worksheets

extra bits

set font formatting pp. 70–71

- A font is basically a typeface.

- A point is a unit of measurement roughly equal to 1/72 of an inch. Fonts are measured in points. The bigger the point size, the bigger the characters.

- Choose your font carefully! Some fonts are designed for display purposes only and can be difficult to read.

- Don't get carried away with font formatting. Too much formatting can distract the reader.

- Want more font formatting options? Choose Cells from the Format menu to display the Format Cells dialog, then click the Font tab. Use this dialog to set font formatting options and click OK to apply them to selected cells.

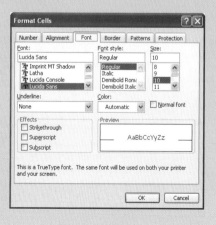

format values pp. 72–73

- Note that the number formatting applied with the Comma Style button in Windows is slightly different from the one applied with the Format Cells dialog in Mac OS as instructed on page 72.

- There are some subtle differences between number formatting as applied here in Windows and Mac OS. For example, in Windows, comma and currency formatting display dashes for zero values and put parentheses around negative values.

set column widths pp. 76–77

- In Windows, you enter column widths in characters; in Mac OS, you enter column width in inches. I don't know why they're different, but there it is.

- You can hide a column by setting its width to 0. To unhide a column, select the columns on either side of it and set the column width to anything but 0. The column reappears between the other two columns.

format worksheets

set alignment p. 78

- Depending on column width settings, you may find that column headings look better when right-aligned over the numbers beneath them rather than centered. Click the Align Right button to try it and decide for yourself.

add borders p. 80

- Don't confuse borders with underlines. Underlines are part of a cell's font formatting and, when applied, appear only beneath characters in a cell. Borders appear for the entire width of the cell.

- Don't confuse cell gridlines with borders, either. Gray cell gridlines appear onscreen to help you see cell boundaries. Normally, they don't print—although you can elect to print them in the Page Setup dialog. Cell borders always print.

7. add a chart

Excel includes a powerful and flexible charting feature that enables you to create charts based on worksheet information. Its Chart Wizard makes it easy to create charts to your specifications. Best of all, if any of the data in a source worksheet changes, the chart automatically changes accordingly.

In Excel, charts can be inserted into a workbook file in two ways:

- A chart sheet, as discussed in Chapter 2 and shown below, displays a chart on a separate workbook sheet.

- An embedded chart is a chart that is added as a graphic object to a worksheet.

In this chapter, we'll create a pie chart of actual expenses for the quarter as a separate sheet within our Budget workbook file.

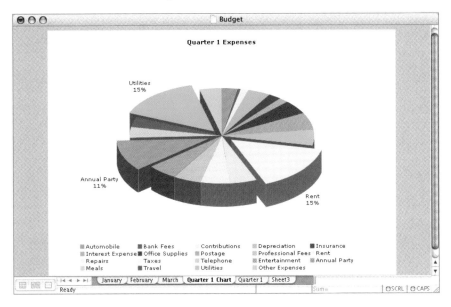

hide a row

Our chart will include all expense categories from the Quarter 1 file. Before we select the information to chart, however, we'll hide the row labeled Travel & Entertainment, which has no values, so it does not appear in the chart.

1 Click the Quarter 1 sheet tab to activate that sheet.

3 Choose Hide from the Row submenu under the Format menu.

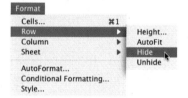

2 Click on the row heading number for row 72 to select it.

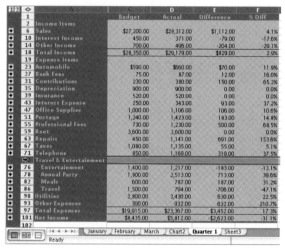

The row disappears.

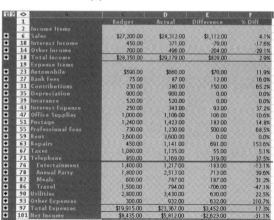

start the chart wizard

The first step in creating a chart is to select the information you want to include in the chart. This includes both values and corresponding labels. Then start the Chart Wizard.

1 Select cells A23 to A93 and cells D23 to D93. Remember, you must hold down the Control (Windows) or Command (Mac OS) key to select multiple ranges.

	A	C	D	E	F
1		Budget	Actual	Difference	% Diff
2	Income Items				
6	Sales	$ 27,200.00	$ 28,312.00	$ 1,112.00	4.1%
10	Interest Income	450.00	371.00	(79.00)	-17.6%
14	Other Income	700.00	496.00	(204.00)	-29.1%
18	Total Income	$ 28,350.00	$ 29,179.00	$ 829.00	2.9%
19	Expense Items				
23	Automobile	$ 590.00	$ 660.00	$ 70.00	11.9%
27	Bank Fees	75.00	87.00	12.00	16.0%
31	Contributions	230.00	380.00	150.00	65.2%
35	Depreciation	900.00	900.00	.	0.0%
39	Insurance	520.00	520.00	.	0.0%
43	Interest Expense	250.00	343.00	93.00	37.2%
47	Office Supplies	1,000.00	1,106.00	106.00	10.6%
51	Postage	1,240.00	1,423.00	183.00	14.8%
55	Professional Fees	730.00	1,230.00	500.00	68.5%
59	Rent	3,600.00	3,600.00	.	0.0%
63	Repairs	450.00	1,141.00	691.00	153.6%
67	Taxes	1,080.00	1,135.00	55.00	5.1%
71	Telephone	850.00	1,169.00	319.00	37.5%
76	Entertainment	1,400.00	1,217.00	(183.00)	-13.1%
78	Annual Party	1,800.00	2,513.00	713.00	39.6%
82	Meals	600.00	787.00	187.00	31.2%
86	Travel	1,500.00	794.00	(706.00)	-47.1%
90	Utilities	2,800.00	3,430.00	630.00	22.5%
93	Other Expenses	300.00	932.00	632.00	210.7%
97	Total Expenses	$ 19,915.00	$ 23,367.00	$ 3,452.00	17.3%
101	Net Income	$ 8,435.00	$ 5,812.00	$ (2,623.00)	-31.1%

2 Click the Chart Wizard button on the Standard toolbar.

Windows

Mac OS

The first step of the Chart Wizard dialog appears, as shown on the next page.

add a chart

select a chart type

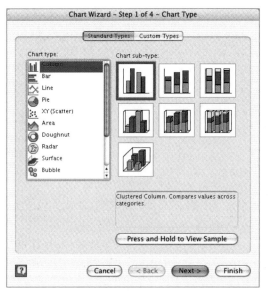

Step 1 of the Chart Wizard prompts you to select a type of chart. We'll be creating a 3-D pie chart.

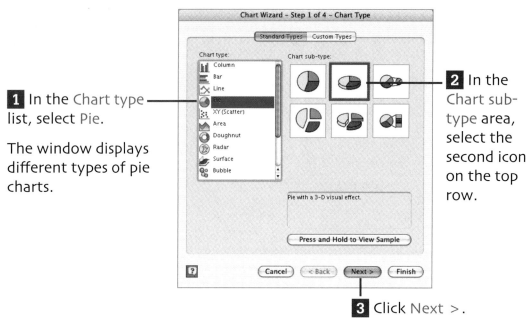

1 In the Chart type list, select Pie.

The window displays different types of pie charts.

2 In the Chart sub-type area, select the second icon on the top row.

3 Click Next >.

The second step of the Chart Wizard dialog appears, as shown on the next page.

add a chart

check the source data

Step 2 of the Chart Wizard enables you to enter the range of data to be charted. But if you correctly selected the right ranges of cells as instructed on page 91, the data range should already be entered.

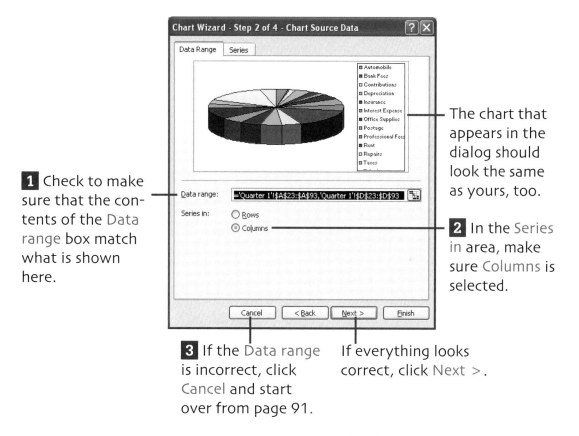

The chart that appears in the dialog should look the same as yours, too.

1 Check to make sure that the contents of the Data range box match what is shown here.

2 In the Series in area, make sure Columns is selected.

3 If the Data range is incorrect, click Cancel and start over from page 91.

If everything looks correct, click Next >.

The third step of the Chart Wizard dialog appears, as shown on the next page.

set chart options

Step 3 of the Chart Wizard has three parts for setting chart options. Click a tab (Windows) or button (Mac OS) at the top of the dialog to set each type of option.

1 Click the Titles tab or button.

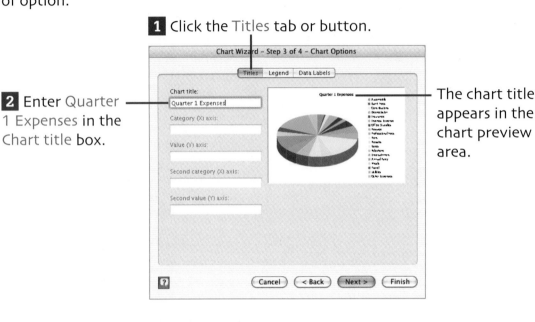

2 Enter Quarter 1 Expenses in the Chart title box.

The chart title appears in the chart preview area.

3 Click the Legend tab or button.

4 Make sure the Show legend check box is turned on.

5 Select the Bottom option.

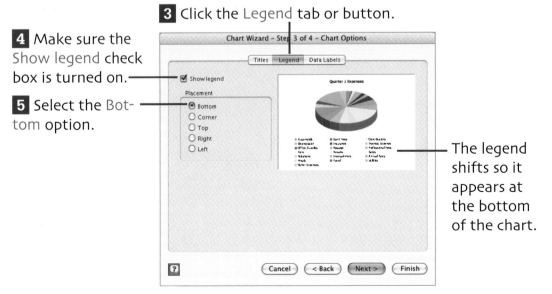

The legend shifts so it appears at the bottom of the chart.

add a chart

6 Click the Data Labels tab or button.

7 In Windows, make sure all Label Contains area check boxes are turned off...

...or in Mac OS, make sure None is selected.

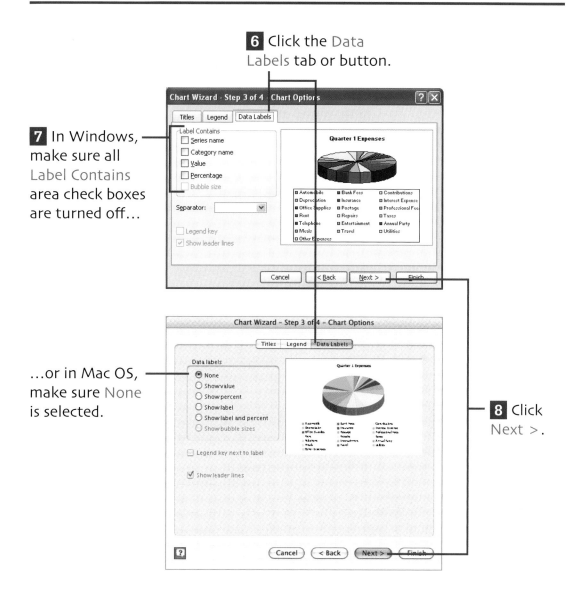

8 Click Next >.

The fourth step of the Chart Wizard dialog appears, as shown on the next page.

add a chart

set the chart location

Step 4 of the Chart Wizard lets you specify whether the chart will be on its own chart sheet or inserted as an object in a worksheet. Our chart will be on its own worksheet.

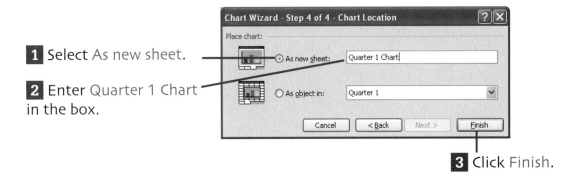

1 Select As new sheet.

2 Enter Quarter 1 Chart in the box.

3 Click Finish.

The chart appears in a chart sheet window.

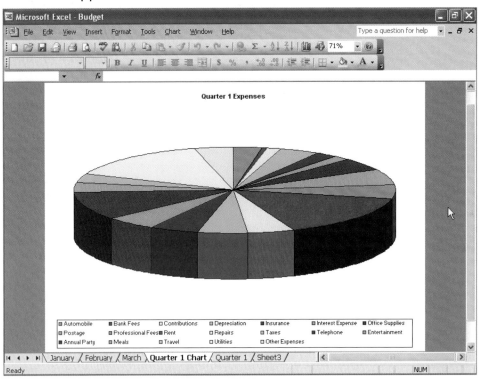

add a chart

explode a pie

You can make one or more pieces of a pie chart really stand out by "exploding" them away from the pie. In our example, we'll emphasize the pie pieces that represent the top three expense items: Rent, Utilities, and Annual Party.

1 Click the piece of pie representing Rent. (You'll know you have the right one when "Rent" appears in its tooltip.) The entire pie chart becomes selected.

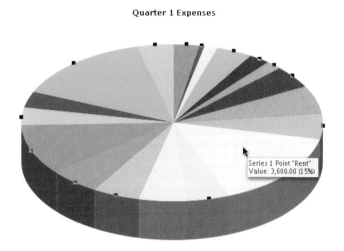

Quarter 1 Expenses

2 Click the pie piece so selection handles appear around it.

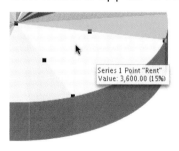

3 Drag the piece of pie away from the center of the pie. An outline of the pie moves as you drag.

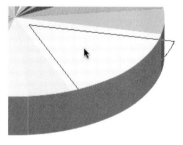

explode a pie (cont'd)

4 Release the mouse button. The pie is redrawn with the piece you dragged "exploded" away.

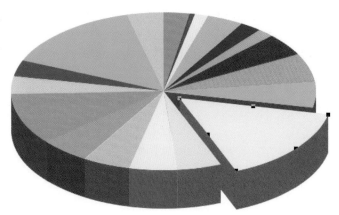

5 Repeat steps 2 through 4 for the pie pieces representing Utilities and Annual Party.

When you're finished, the pie chart should look like this.

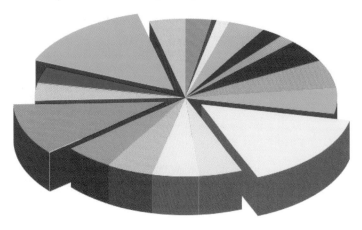

add a chart

add data labels

Data labels provide information about data in a chart. Although this chart includes a color-coded legend, we'll provide additional information about the three biggest expenses using data labels.

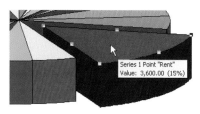

1 Click the pie piece for Rent. If the entire chart becomes selected, click it again so only the Rent piece is selected.

2 Double-click the selected pie piece.

The Format Data Point dialog appears.

Important Note: If the Format Data Series dialog appears instead, click Cancel and start over with step 1.

3 Click the Data Labels tab (Windows) or Labels button (Mac OS).

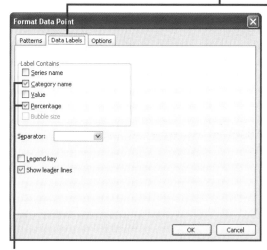

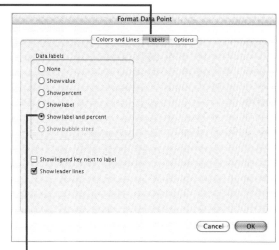

4 In Windows, turn on the check boxes for Category name and Percentage...

...or in Mac OS, select Show label and percent.

add data labels (cont'd)

5 Click OK.

The name of the category and its percentage appear beside the pie piece.

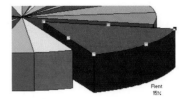

6 Repeat steps 1 through 5 for Utilities and Annual Party.

When you're finished, the pie chart should look like this.

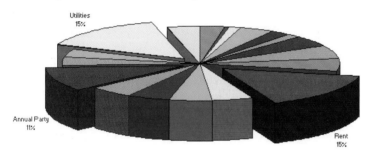

Save your work.

Click the Save button on the Standard toolbar.

add a chart

extra bits

select a chart type p. 92

- If you point to the Press and Hold to View Sample button and hold the mouse button down, you can view a sample of the chart type you selected with your data plotted.

set chart options pp. 94-95

- The number and type of options that appear in Step 3 of the Chart Wizard vary depending on the type of chart you selected in Step 1.
- The position of a chart's legend will impact the size of the chart. You can see this for yourself by trying different Placement settings for the legend.

add data labels pp. 99-100

- If you wanted data labels to appear for all pieces of the pie, you could set Data Label options in Step 3 of the Chart Wizard, as shown on page 95.

8. print your work

In many instances, when you're finished creating and formatting a worksheet or chart, you'll need to print it.

Although you can just use the Print command (or toolbar button) to send a sheet to your printer for hard copy, Excel offers a wide variety of page setup options you can use to customize your printout. For example, you can change page orientation and scaling, set margins, add headers and footers, and specify a print area. All of these settings affect the way your sheet will appear when printed. Fortunately, Excel's Print Preview feature (shown here) enables you to see what your sheets will look like before you print them, so you can fine-tune their appearance without wasting a lot of paper.

This chapter explores many of Excel's page setup options to prepare our worksheets for printing and to print them.

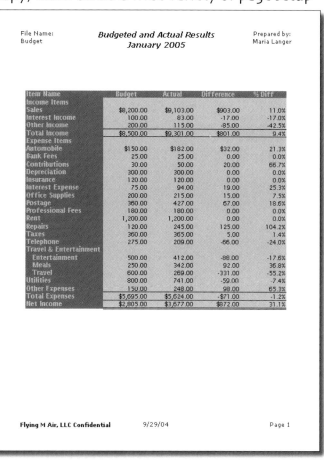

| File Name: Budget | Budgeted and Actual Results January 2005 | | Prepared by: Maria Langer |

Item Name	Budget	Actual	Difference	% Diff
Income Items				
Sales	$8,200.00	$9,103.00	$903.00	11.0%
Interest Income	100.00	83.00	-17.00	-17.0%
Other Income	200.00	115.00	-85.00	-42.5%
Total Income	$8,500.00	$9,301.00	$801.00	9.4%
Expense Items				
Automobile	$150.00	$182.00	$32.00	21.3%
Bank Fees	25.00	25.00	0.00	0.0%
Contributions	30.00	50.00	20.00	66.7%
Depreciation	300.00	300.00	0.00	0.0%
Insurance	120.00	120.00	0.00	0.0%
Interest Expense	75.00	94.00	19.00	25.3%
Office Supplies	200.00	215.00	15.00	7.5%
Postage	360.00	427.00	67.00	18.6%
Professional Fees	180.00	180.00	0.00	0.0%
Rent	1,200.00	1,200.00	0.00	0.0%
Repairs	120.00	245.00	125.00	104.2%
Taxes	360.00	365.00	5.00	1.4%
Telephone	275.00	209.00	-66.00	-24.0%
Travel & Entertainment				
Entertainment	500.00	412.00	-88.00	-17.6%
Meals	250.00	342.00	92.00	36.8%
Travel	600.00	269.00	-331.00	-55.2%
Utilities	800.00	741.00	-59.00	-7.4%
Other Expenses	150.00	248.00	98.00	65.3%
Total Expenses	$5,695.00	$5,624.00	-$71.00	-1.2%
Net Income	$2,805.00	$3,677.00	$872.00	31.1%

Flying M Air, LLC Confidential   9/29/04   Page 1

select the sheets

To print a sheet or set print options for it, you must activate it. Because our workbook includes several worksheets which will all have the same settings, we can select them all and set options for all of them at once.

1 Click the sheet tab for the January sheet.

2 Hold down the Control (Windows) or Command (Mac OS) key and click the sheet tabs for the Feburary, March, and Quarter 1 sheets.

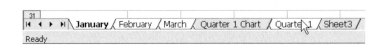

All of the sheet tabs you clicked become selected.

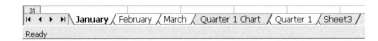

open page setup

The Page Setup dialog is a goldmine of options for setting up worksheets and charts for printing. Its options are organized into five categories:

- Page options control page orientation and scaling.

- Margins options control margin measurements and the centering of the sheet on the page.

- Header/Footer options enable you to choose from predefined headers or footers or create your own.

- Sheet options (which appear for worksheets only) enable you to specify what prints and how it prints.

- Chart options (which appear for chart sheets only) enable you to specify how a chart will print.

This chapter explores some of these options. But first, let's open that dialog.

Choose Page Setup from the File menu.

Windows

Mac OS

set page options (Windows)

Page options affect page orientation and scaling, as well as a few other settings. We'll set Page options for Portrait orientation, 100% scaling, and Letter size paper. These options should be set by default, but we'll check them, just in case they aren't.

1 In the Page Setup dialog, click the Page tab.

2 Select Portrait.

3 Select Adjust to and enter 100 in the box.

4 Choose Letter from the Paper size drop-down list.

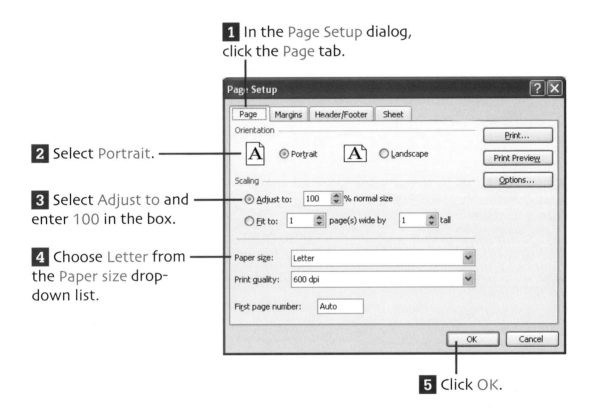

5 Click OK.

print your work

set page options (Mac OS)

Page options affect page orientation and scaling, as well as a few other settings. We'll set Page options for Portrait orientation, 100% scaling, and Letter size paper. These options should be set by default, but we'll check them, just in case they aren't.

1 In the Page Setup dialog, click the Page button.

2 Select Portrait.

3 Select Adjust to and enter 100 in the box.

4 Click Options.

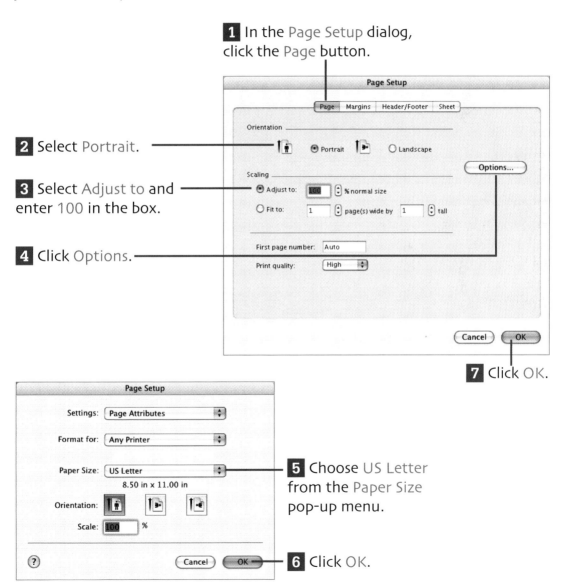

7 Click OK.

5 Choose US Letter from the Paper Size pop-up menu.

6 Click OK.

adjust margins

A margin is the amount of space between the printable area on a page and the edge of the paper. In Excel, Margins options enable you to control the space between the edge of the paper and the sheet contents, as well as the header or footer. Margins settings also enable you to center a sheet horizontally or vertically on a page.

1 In the Page Setup dialog, click the Margins tab (Windows) or button (Mac OS).

2 Enter 2 in the Top box.

3 Enter 1.5 in the Bottom box.

4 Turn on the Horizontally check box.

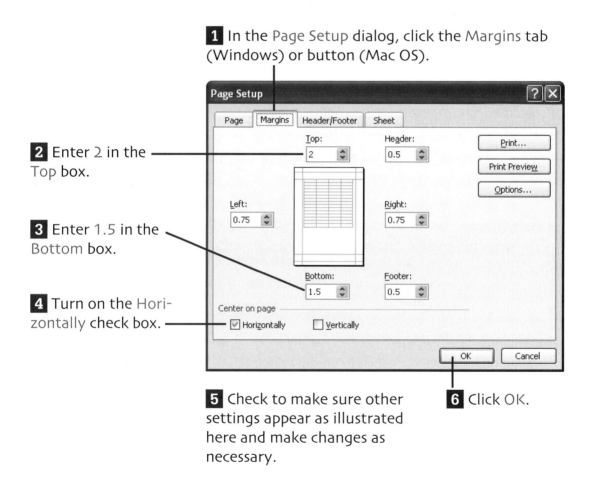

5 Check to make sure other settings appear as illustrated here and make changes as necessary.

6 Click OK.

add a standard footer

A footer is text that appears at the bottom of every page. In Excel, you add a footer with the Header/Footer options of the Page Setup dialog, which gives you a choice of predefined or custom headers and footers. For our example, we'll add a standard, predefined footer.

1 In the Page Setup dialog, click the Header/ Footer tab (Windows) or button (Mac OS).

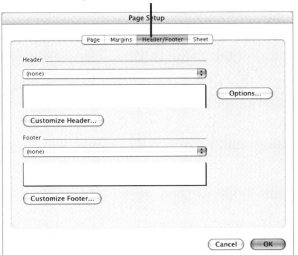

2 Choose the fifth option on the drop-down list (Windows) or pop-up menu (Mac OS) under Footer. It should display your company name followed by the word Confidential, the current date, and Page 1.

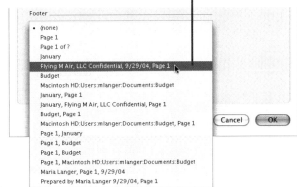

The footer appears in the Footer preview area.

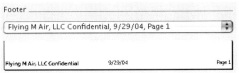

add a custom header

A header is text that appears at the top of every page. In Excel, you add a header with the Header/Footer options of the Page Setup dialog, which gives you a choice of predefined or custom headers and footers. For our example, we'll add a custom header.

1 In the Page Setup dialog, click the Header/Footer tab (Windows) or button (Mac OS).

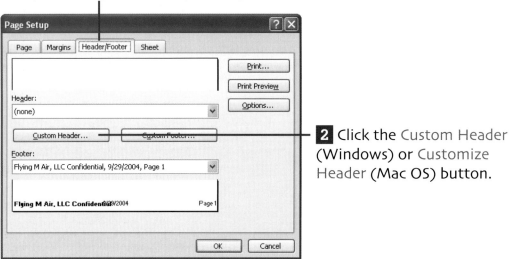

2 Click the Custom Header (Windows) or Customize Header (Mac OS) button.

The Header dialog appears.

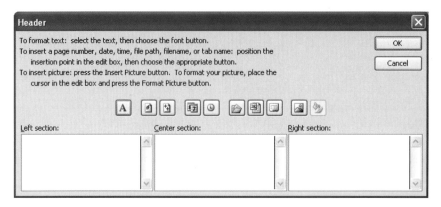

3 In the Left section box, type File Name: and press Enter (Windows) or Return (Mac OS).

4 Click the Insert File Name button. &[File] should appear on the next line.

5 In the Center section box, type Budgeted and Actual Results and press Enter or Return.

6 Click the Insert Sheet Name button. &[Tab] should appear on the next line.

7 Press the Spacebar and type 2005.

8 In the Right section box, type Prepared by:, press Enter or Return, and type your name.

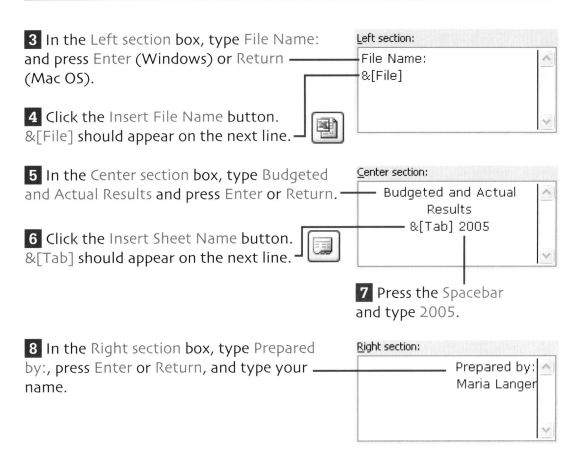

Left section:

File Name:
&[File]

Center section:

Budgeted and Actual
Results
&[Tab] 2005

Right section:

Prepared by:
Maria Langer

At this point, the Header dialog should look like this.

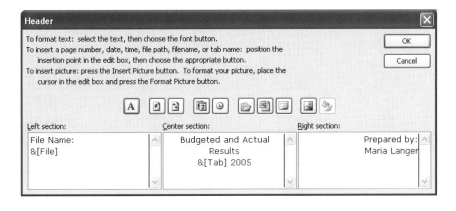

add custom header (cont'd)

9 Select the contents of the Center section box.

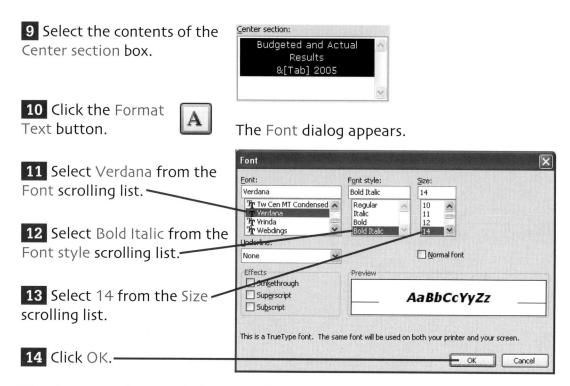

10 Click the Format Text button.

The Font dialog appears.

11 Select Verdana from the Font scrolling list.

12 Select Bold Italic from the Font style scrolling list.

13 Select 14 from the Size scrolling list.

14 Click OK.

The Center section text is formatted to your specifications.

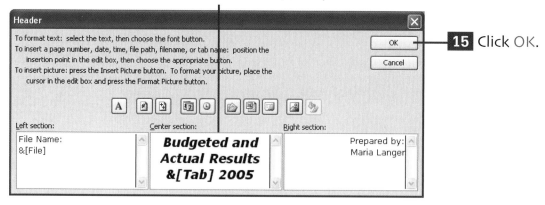

15 Click OK.

Your custom header appears in the Header preview area.

print your work

save settings

We've made a bunch of changes in the Page Setup dialog. It's time to save them.

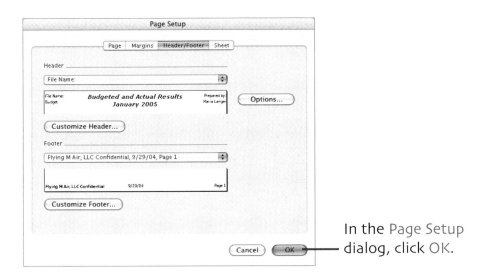

In the Page Setup dialog, click OK.

Save your work.

Click the Save button on the Standard toolbar.

preview the sheets (Win)

Excel's Print Preview feature saves time and paper by enabling you to see what a document will look like on paper without actually printing it. If it looks good, you can click a Print button to send it to your printer. If it doesn't look good, you can click a Setup button to go back to the Page Setup dialog and fix it.

Click the Print Preview button on the Standard toolbar.

A Print Preview window opens.

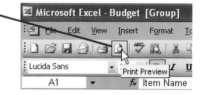

Click Print to open the Print dialog.

Click Setup to open the Page Setup dialog.

Click Close to close the window.

Click Next or Previous to scroll through pages.

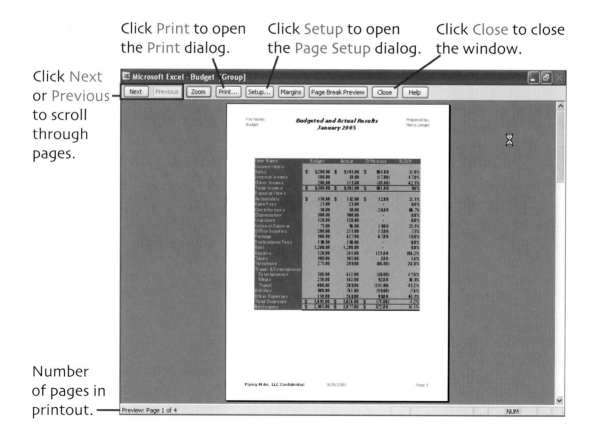

Number of pages in printout.

print your work

preview the sheets (Mac)

Excel's Print Preview feature saves time and paper by enabling you to see what a document will look like on paper without actually printing it. If it looks good, you can click a Print button to send it to your printer. If it doesn't look good, you can click a Setup button to go back to the Page Setup dialog and fix it.

Click the Print Preview button on the Standard toolbar.

A Print Preview window opens.

Click the Next or Previous button to scroll through pages.

Click Setup to open the Page Setup dialog.

Click the Print button to open the Print dialog.

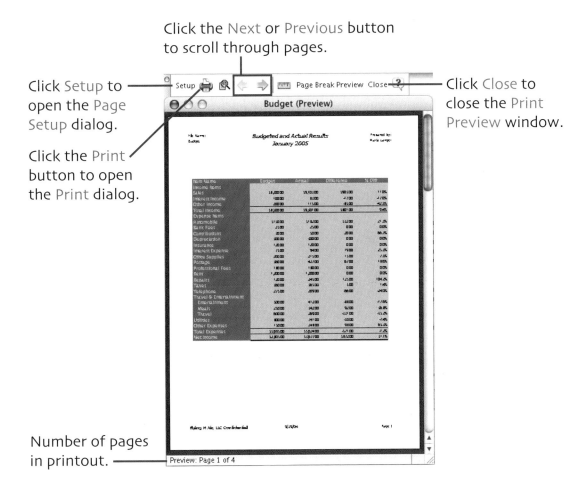

Click Close to close the Print Preview window.

Number of pages in printout.

print your work

print your work (Windows)

Once you're satisfied that the worksheets will look good on paper, you can print them.

1 Choose Print from the File menu.

The Print dialog appears.

2 Choose a printer from the Name drop-down list.

3 Select All in the Print range area.

4 Select Active sheet(s) in the Print what area.

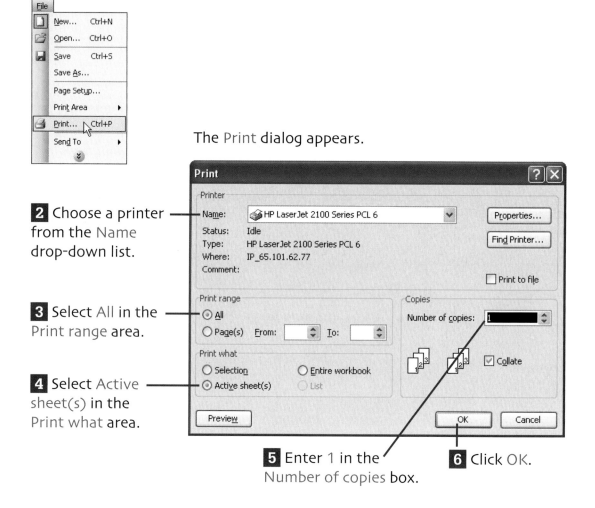

5 Enter 1 in the Number of copies box.

6 Click OK.

The worksheets are sent to the printer where they print.

print your work (Mac OS)

Once you're satisfied that the work-sheets will look good on paper, you can print them.

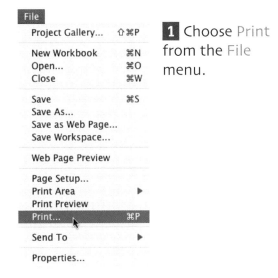

1 Choose Print from the File menu.

The Print dialog appears.

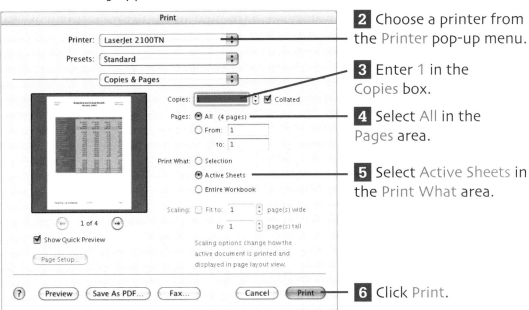

2 Choose a printer from the Printer pop-up menu.

3 Enter 1 in the Copies box.

4 Select All in the Pages area.

5 Select Active Sheets in the Print What area.

6 Click Print.

The worksheets are sent to the printer where they print.

extra bits

set page options pp. 106–107

- If you discover, when previewing your worksheet, that it doesn't quite fit on a single page, you can force it to fit on that page. Select Fit to in the Page options of the Page Setup dialog and make sure 1 is entered in both boxes beside it.

add a standard footer p. 109

- Excel gets your company name from information you entered when you installed it.

add a custom header pp. 110-112

- Excel left-aligns the Left section text, centers the Center section text, and right-aligns the Right section text.

- It isn't necessary to enter text in all three sections of a custom header or footer. Just use the sections you need.

save settings p. 113

- Page Setup options are automatically saved with a workbook file when you save the workbook. So once you've set options for a file, you don't have to reset them unless you want to change them.

print your work pp. 116–117

- Clicking the Print button on the Standard toolbar sends the selected sheets to the printer without displaying the Print dialog.

- In Windows, clicking the Properties button in the Print dialog displays additional options that are specific to your printer. Consult the manual that came with your printer for additional information about these options.

print your work

index

index

index

Mac interface, 6
    Windows interface, 5
Hide command (Format
    menu), 90
hiding rows, 90
Home folder (Mac), saving
    workbook file, 20

I

icons, 2
income calculations, 37
Increase Decimal button, 75
Increase Indent button, 79
Indent box, 79
indent text, formatting, 79
information, entering in
    worksheets, 26
Insert File Name button, 111
Insert menu commands
    Columns, 57
    Rows, 53, 57
Insert Sheet Name button, 111
inserting rows, 53
interface elements, 5–6

L

Label Contains area check
    boxes, 95
labels
    chart data, 99–100
    worksheet information, 26
Legend tab, 94
Lucinda Sans font, 71

M

Mac
    10 point Verdana font, 70
    changing views, 14
    column widths, 86
    creating blank workbook
        file, 16
        setting view
            preferences, 21
    dialogs, 11
    Finder, 2
    formatting borders, 80–81
    formatting text color, 84
    interface elements, 5
    mouse buttons, 3, 13
    naming sheets, 24
    opening program, 4
    percentage formatting,
      74–75
    previewing sheets, 115
    printing, 117
    quitting Excel, 12
    saving workbook files, 20
      sharing with Windows
        user, 21
    scroll bars, 8
      customizing, 14
    setting page options, 107
    views, 7
margins, 108
Margins option, Page Setup
    dialog, 105
Margins tab, 108
menu, 9

menu bar
    Mac interface, 6
    Windows interface, 5
Microsoft Office command
    (Start menu), 4
Microsoft Office Excel 2003
    command (Start menu), 4
mouse, 3, 13
My Documents button, 19
My Documents folder
    (Windows), 19

N

naming worksheets, 24, 44
net income calculations, 37
New button, creating
    workbook file, 16
Normal view, 7
Normal View button (Mac), 16
Normal View icon (Mac), 14
Number button, 72

O

opening program, 4, 13
option buttons (Windows),
    dialogs, 11
Options command (Tools
    menu), 17
Options dialog (Windows), 17
outline symbol, 65

index

index

Ready to Learn More?

If you enjoyed this project and are ready to learn more, pick up a *Visual QuickStart Guide*, the best-selling, most affordable, most trusted, quick-reference series for computing.

With more than 5.5 million copies in print, *Visual QuickStart Guides* are the industry's best-selling series of affordable, quick-reference guides. This series from Peachpit Press includes more than 200 titles covering the leading applications for digital photography and illustration, digital video and sound editing, Web design and development, business productivity, graphic design, operating systems, and more. Best of all, these books respect your time and intelligence. With tons of well-chosen illustrations and practical, labor-saving tips, they'll have you up to speed on new software fast.

> "When you need to quickly learn to use a new application or new version of an application, you can't do better than the *Visual QuickStart Guides* from Peachpit Press."
>
> Jay Nelson
> *Design Tools Monthly*

www.peachpit.com

Full-color projects from the folks who bring you Visual QuickStart Guides…

Visual QuickProject

Creating a Presentation
in PowerPoint

TOM NEGRINO

creating a presentation in powerpoint

Visual QuickProject Guide

by Tom Negrino

Peachpit
Press

Visual QuickProject Guide
Creating a Presentation in PowerPoint
Tom Negrino

Peachpit Press

1249 Eighth Street
Berkeley, CA 94710
510/524-2178
800/283-9444
510/524-2221 (fax)

Find us on the World Wide Web at: www.peachpit.com
To report errors, please send a note to errata@peachpit.com
Peachpit Press is a division of Pearson Education

Editor: Nancy Davis
Production Editor: Connie Jeung-Mills
Compositor: Owen Wolfson
Proofreader: Ted Waitt
Indexer: James Minkin
Cover design: The Visual Group with Aren Howell
Interior design: Elizabeth Castro
Cover photo credit: Getty One

ISBN 0-321-27844-5

Printed and bound in the United States of America

For Dori, Sean,
and Pixel the Cat

Special Thanks to...

The Board of Directors and Staff of
Access Healdsburg, community television
for Healdsburg and Northern Sonoma
County, CA. It's great working with you.
Visit AHTV's Web site at www.ahtv.org.

My superb editor, Nancy Davis.

The book's production editor, Connie
Jeung-Mills.

Thanks to Lockie Gillies, Brett Pollard,
and Vince Dougherty of Wine Country
Computers, www.winecomputers.com,
for the use of their computers.

contents

contents

contents

introduction

The Visual QuickProject Guide that you hold in your hands offers a unique way to learn about new technologies. Instead of drowning you in theoretical possibilities and lengthy explanations, this Visual QuickProject Guide uses big, color illustrations coupled with clear, concise step-by-step instructions to show you how to complete one specific project in a matter of hours.

Our project in this book is to create a compelling and colorful presentation using Microsoft PowerPoint. We'll use either PowerPoint 2003 for Windows or PowerPoint 2004 for Macintosh. These are the latest versions, but if you haven't upgraded yet, don't fret; things will look pretty familiar if you have PowerPoint 2000 or XP for Windows or PowerPoint X for Mac.

We will create a fundraising presentation for a real non-profit organization, Access Healdsburg, which is a community television station located in Sonoma County, California. But because the presentation showcases all the basic

techniques, you'll be able to use what you learn to create your own presentations, whether it be a talk for your annual sales meeting, a lecture for a class you're teaching, or a slide show for your department detailing your latest work.

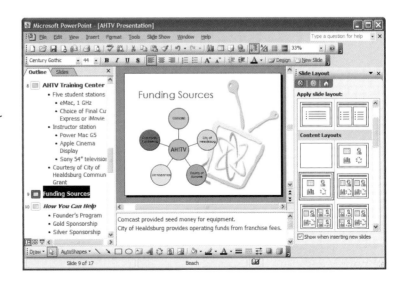

what you'll create

Write your presentation in PowerPoint's Outline View.

Apply slide layouts from the gallery.

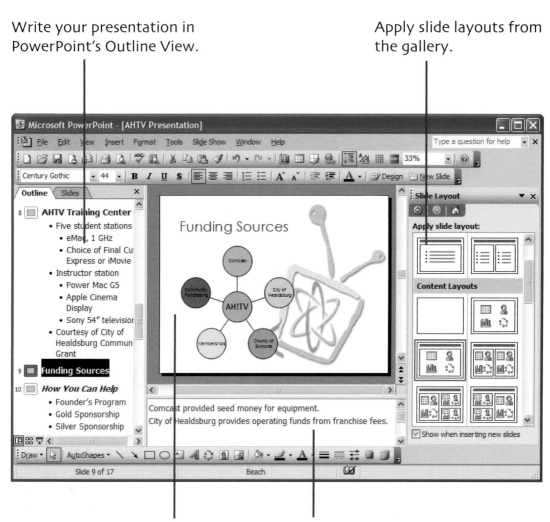

Create colorful, attractive diagrams with the Drawing toolbar to illustrate your message.

Add Speaker Notes to help keep your presentation on track when you give it.

Change the look and style of text on your slides.

Add photographs or other images.

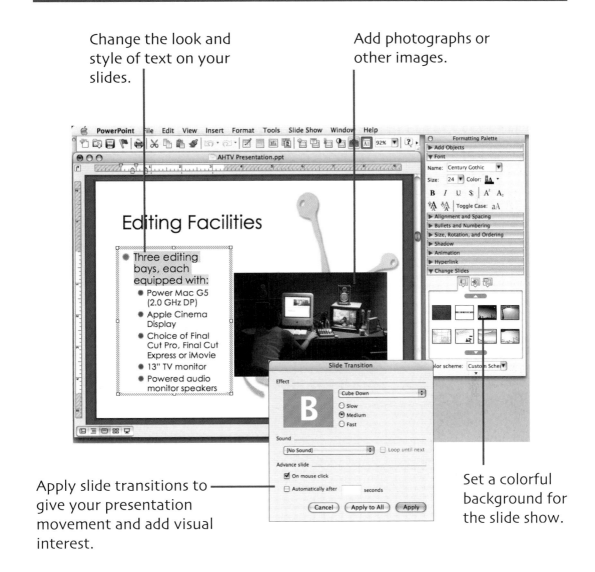

Apply slide transitions to give your presentation movement and add visual interest.

Set a colorful background for the slide show.

how this book works

The title of each section explains what is covered on that page.

Important terms and Web site addresses are shown in orange.

Numbered steps explain actions to perform in a specific order.

Captions explain what you're doing and why. They also point to items of interest.

set slide effects (Mac)

Like its Windows sibling, PowerPoint for Mac gives you two ways to control slide effects. Preset animations apply simple animations to the elements on the slide; custom animation gives you more control over each element (though not, alas, as much control as PowerPoint for Windows).

To use a preset animation, first choose View > Normal, then display the slide to which you want to apply the preset. Next, choose Slide Show > Preset Animations, then choose a preset from the cascading menu. The animation is applied to the slide.

Custom animations are a bit more complex to apply, but are much more flexible.

1 Begin by choosing View > Normal, then display the slide to which you want to apply the animation.

2 Choose Slide Show > Custom Animation. The Custom Animation dialog appears.

Preview pane

make it move

The extra bits section at the end of each chapter contains additional tips and tricks that you might like to know—but that aren't absolutely necessary for creating the presentation.

The heading for each group of tips matches the section title.

extra bits

rearrange slides p. 82

- If you want to move a group of slides at one time, in Slide Sorter View, click on the first slide, hold down the Shift key, and click the last slide. Those two slides and all slides in between will be selected, and you can drag and drop them as a group.

set slide transitions p. 84

- You can also select multiple slides in the Slide Sorter by clicking in a blank space between slides, then dragging over the slides you want.
- By default, PowerPoint is set so ~~ggered~~ ~~se dur-~~ ~~But you~~ ~~he~~ ~~the~~ ~~ne to~~ ~~ically~~ ~~after~~ ~~nds.~~ ~~little~~ ~~hen it~~ ~~ions.~~ ~~k Pane~~ ~~review~~ ~~humb-~~ ~~, but~~ ~~y button~~

to trigger the preview manually, and the Slide Show button puts PowerPoint into Slide Show mode, allowing you to see the slides and transitions full screen.

Mac users must apply a transition, then test it in the Slide Show or the small Animation Preview window.

To open the Animation Preview

window, choose Slide Show > Animation Preview. Click anywhere in the window to see the preview play.

- You can purchase add-ins (programs that extend PowerPoint) that give you additional slide transitions beyond the ones that come with PowerPoint. One well-known maker of these add-ins is Crystal Graphics (www.crystalgraphics.com), with their PowerPlugs series.

93

set slide transitions

Transitions between slides can enhance your presentation's message and add visual interest to your show. You can add transitions to one or more slides at one time in either the Normal or Slide Sorter View (though I find it's usually easier to use Slide Sorter View). PowerPoint includes dozens of special transition effects to choose from, ranging from subtle to the polar opposite of subtle. With slide transitions, as with any animation in PowerPoint, you should live by the principle "less is more" when choosing transitions, because the flashier they are, the more quickly your audience will become tired of them.

1 Switch to Slide Sorter View to begin setting the transition; choose View > Slide Sorter.

2 Select the slides to which you want to apply the transitions. To select multiple slides, click on the first slide, hold down the Shift key, and click the last slide. Those slides and all slides in between are selected.

3 Choose Slide Show > Slide Transition.

On Windows, the Slide Transition Task Pane opens.

Transition list

Transition speed

Sound pop-up menu

The page number next to the heading makes it easy to refer back to the main content.

make it move

useful tools

PowerPoint comes with most of what you need to create a terrific presentation, but you can improve the presentation with an image editor, which allows you to touch up and resize photos, modify images, and create custom backgrounds for your presentation.

Many digital cameras and scanners come bundled with some kind of image editor, such as Adobe Photoshop Elements. There are also low-cost or even free image editors, such as Windows Paint or GraphicConverter X for the Mac, as shown.

If you'll be adding links to your slides, you'll want to preview what happens when you click on those links in a Web browser. On Windows, you'll probably use Internet Explorer, and on the Mac, Safari (shown).

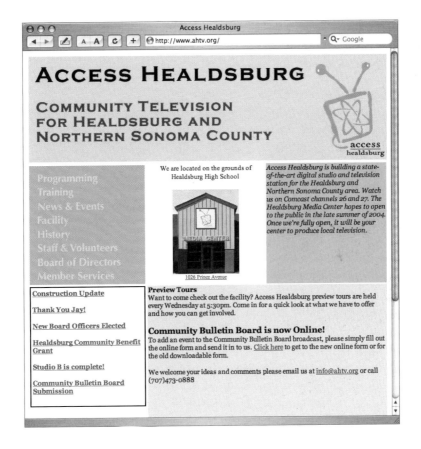

the next step

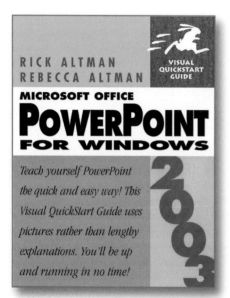

While this Visual QuickProject Guide will walk you through all of the steps required to create a presentation and deliver it to an audience, there's more to learn about PowerPoint. After you complete your QuickProject, consider picking up one of two books, also published by Peachpit Press, as an in-depth, handy reference.

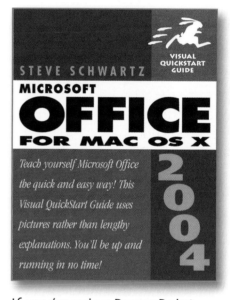

If you're using PowerPoint for Windows, check out Microsoft Office PowerPoint 2003 for Windows: Visual QuickStart Guide, by Rick and Rebecca Altman.

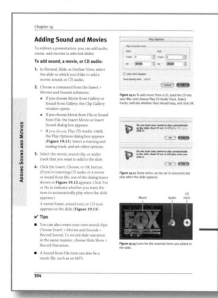

If you're using PowerPoint for Macintosh, take a look at Microsoft Office 2004 for Mac OS X: Visual QuickStart Guide, by Steve Schwartz.

Both books give you clear examples, concise, step-by-step instructions, and many helpful tips that will help you improve your presentations.

1. explore powerpoint

Before you get started on your presentation, you need to see the tools that PowerPoint gives you. In this chapter, you'll explore the user interface from two versions of PowerPoint: PowerPoint 2003 for Windows and PowerPoint 2004 for Macintosh. You'll see that they aren't terribly different.

Start up PowerPoint. On Windows, point at the Start menu, choose Programs, then choose Microsoft Office, then choose Microsoft Office PowerPoint 2003.

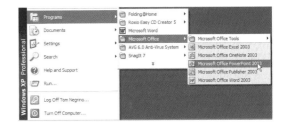

On the Mac, open the Applications folder, then open the Microsoft Office 2004 folder, and double-click on the Microsoft PowerPoint icon.

When PowerPoint starts, it creates a new presentation document. In this chapter, you'll create your presentation file, set it up for subsequent chapters, and save the file. You'll add text and graphics to this new document as you build the presentation throughout the rest of the book.

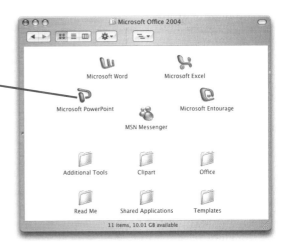

2003 for windows

PowerPoint 2003 for Windows has a main document window where you'll write your presentation and dress up your slides. In this picture, the Power-Point window is in the Normal view.

A The Menu Bar

B The Standard Toolbar has buttons and pop-up menus with the most-used commands, such as Save, Print, and Undo.

C The Formatting Toolbar allows you to style text on your slides, as well as change the slide design and create a new slide.

D The Normal View Pane has two tabs. The Slides tab that is shown here displays thumbnails of the presentation's slides, including the slide's graphics. The Outline tab shows you just the text on each slide; you'll learn more about how to use this tab in Chapter 2.

E The Slide Pane shows you what the current slide looks like. In this case, the slide is showing placeholders for text that you'll put on the slide later.

explore powerpoint

F This is the Task Pane, which changes its contents depending on what you are doing. You don't need to use it at this point in the project, so close it by clicking the X in its upper-right corner, or by pressing Control-F1.

G The Notes Pane is where you can type speaker notes for each slide. These notes will appear on printed handouts, but not in the onscreen presentation.

H The View Buttons let you switch between three different ways to look at your presentation.

I The Drawing Toolbar allows you to draw shapes on your slides, such as circles, lines, and arrows.

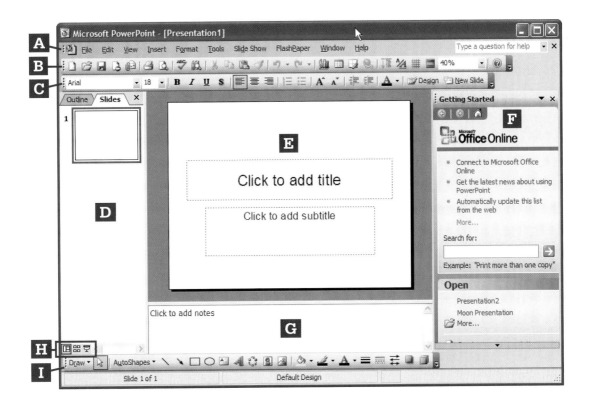

2004 for macintosh

Like its Windows counterpart, PowerPoint 2004 for Macintosh has a main document window, where you have the slide, the outline, and the space for speaker notes.

A The Standard Toolbar has buttons and pop-up menus with the most-used commands, such as Save, Print, and Undo.

In the Normal View shown here, the PowerPoint window is split into three panes.

B The Outline Pane is where you'll type the text of your presentation.

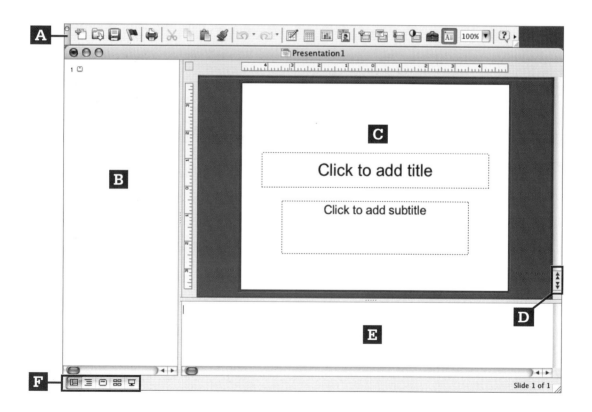

C The Slide Pane shows you what the current slide looks like. The slide is surrounded by the horizontal and vertical rulers, which can help you position graphics and text on the slide. You don't need to use the rulers at this point in the project, so choose View > Ruler to hide them.

D The Previous Slide and Next Slide buttons let you step through the slides in the presentation.

E The Notes Pane is where you can type speaker notes for each slide. These notes will appear on printed handouts, but not in the onscreen presentation.

F The View Buttons let you switch between five different ways to look at your presentation.

The Formatting Palette contains most of the commands and buttons you need to modify the look of your slides and the text and graphics on the slides. It changes to match what you're doing, and has different sections that appear and disappear as needed. See Chapter 5 for more about using the Formatting Palette.

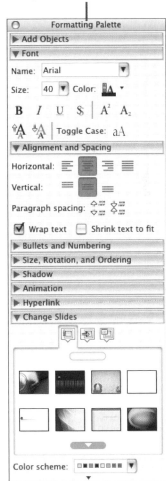

explore toolbars

In PowerPoint you'll use many toolbars to change the look of your slides and the things that you put on the slides. For now, we'll look at the buttons in the Standard Toolbar that you will use the most in your project.

Use the New button to create a new presentation.

The Open button lets you open existing presentation files.

Click the Save button at any time to save your work.

Use the Cut, Copy, and Paste buttons to move text or graphics from one place to another in your presentation, or even to other presentations (or other programs).

The Undo and Redo buttons help you recover from mistakes.

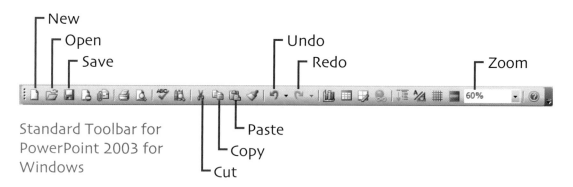

Standard Toolbar for PowerPoint 2003 for Windows

New
Open
Save
Undo
Redo
Zoom
Paste
Copy
Cut

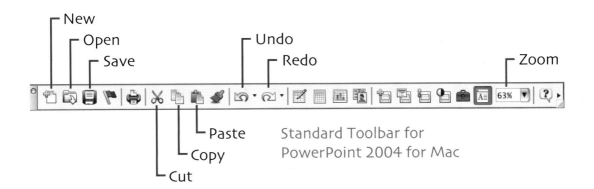

New
Open
Save
Undo
Redo
Zoom

Paste
Copy
Cut

Standard Toolbar for
PowerPoint 2004 for Mac

Use the Zoom menu to make the slide in the Slide Pane larger or smaller.

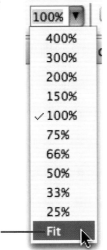

100%

400%
300%
200%
150%
✓ 100%
75%
66%
50%
33%
25%
Fit

Use the Fit choice in this menu to make the slide fill the pane.

explore powerpoint

powerpoint views

PowerPoint 2003 for Windows has three view buttons.

You saw the Normal View earlier in this chapter.

The Slide Sorter View allows you to rearrange slides by dragging and dropping them into a different order. Each slide is shown as a thumbnail, along with the slide's number. You'll learn more about this view in Chapter 7.

The Slide Show View starts the slide show, allowing you to preview your presentation full-screen. This is also the view you use to actually give the presentation.

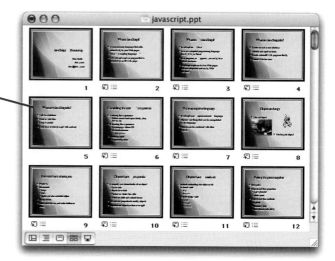

PowerPoint 2004 for Mac uses five view buttons.

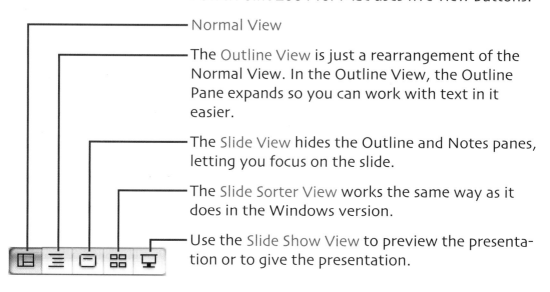

Normal View

The Outline View is just a rearrangement of the Normal View. In the Outline View, the Outline Pane expands so you can work with text in it easier.

The Slide View hides the Outline and Notes panes, letting you focus on the slide.

The Slide Sorter View works the same way as it does in the Windows version.

Use the Slide Show View to preview the presentation or to give the presentation.

anatomy of a slide

To make it easier to create your slides, PowerPoint provides placeholders on its slides into which you can put text, graphics, or charts. These placeholders are arranged into preset slide layouts, and every slide in your presentation is based on one of these layouts. Besides the slide layout, each presentation also has a single design template, which provides the visual look of the slide, including things like the background image for the slides and the style and color of the text you put on the slides.

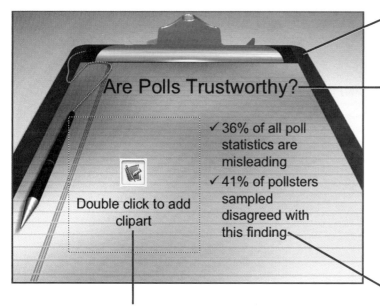

The Background is an image that is part of the design template.

A Title is included on each slide layout (except for the Blank layout). The title corresponds to the main heading for each slide in the presentation's outline. You'll learn more about outlines in Chapter 2.

Slide layouts with slots for graphics, charts, or movies come with Placeholders that tell you where to add the object.

A slide's Body Text is contained in one or more text boxes. The body text can be bulleted or numbered lists, a caption for an image, or plain text.

save the presentation

Save your presentation file before you continue to the next chapter. Choose File > Save.

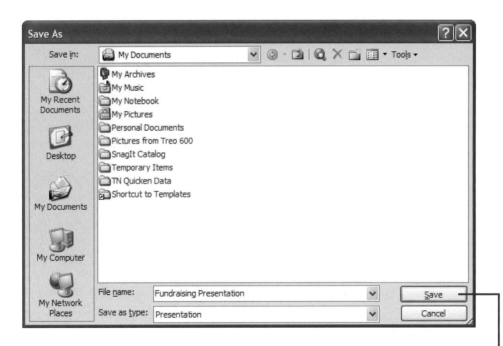

The first time you save, the Save As box appears. This is where you name the presentation. Type the name you want in the File name box (on the Mac, in the Save As box), then click the Save button.

extra bits

2004 for macintosh p. 4

- Don't be thrown by the Drawing Toolbar that's in the figure for PowerPoint for Windows. The Mac version has a Drawing Toolbar, too; it's just not shown at the moment.

anatomy of a slide p. 9

- Not shown on page 4 are a slide's header or footer. You can have one or both of these on each slide. Headers (at the top of each slide) and footers (at the bottom) can contain slide numbers, the date and time, a copyright notice, or any other information you want to include.

save the presentation p. 10

- Save all of the files used in the project in a single folder you create inside your My Documents folder (Windows) or Documents folder (Mac). That way, everything you need for the presentation is in one place.

2. write your presentation

Now that you've created your presentation file, you need to write the presentation. And the best place to write the presentation is not on the slides, but in PowerPoint's Outline View. Now, it's possible that, like many of us, you were scared off of outlines by your sixth grade teacher. You should reconsider, because Outline View is PowerPoint's secret weapon for making better presentations. When you write in the outline, you can focus on the content of your presentation, rather than getting distracted by the look of the presentation. Text that you write in the Outline pane will also appear on your slides, and vice versa.

We've all seen PowerPoint presentations where the presenter spent more time on the appearance than the message. But your message is the most important part of your presentation. PowerPoint's biggest trap is seducing you with flashy pictures, distracting you from your message. By writing the presentation in the outline before you even consider the look, you'll avoid that pitfall—and you'll be way ahead of most other presenters.

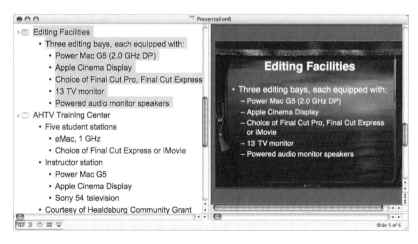

You don't need to do anything extra to get an outline; every presentation has an outline underneath, so it makes sense to start in the outline, rather than on the slide.

write the outline

Switch to Outline View by clicking the Outline tab in the Normal View pane (Windows) or by clicking the Outline View button at the bottom of the PowerPoint window (Mac).

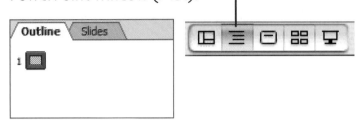

When Outline View becomes active, the Outline pane becomes bigger, to make room for you to work, but you can still see a preview of the slide in the Slide pane. If you need even more room in the outline, point at the border between the Outline pane and the Slide pane; when the cursor becomes a double-headed arrow, drag the border so the pane is as wide as you want.

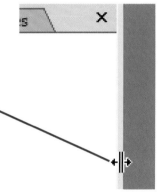

The first slide is a Title slide, which contains the title and subtitle for the presentation. The first line, or heading, in your outline is the title of your presentation. Type it, then press Enter (Return).

Hey, what's this? PowerPoint created a new slide, rather than letting you type the subtitle on the first slide.

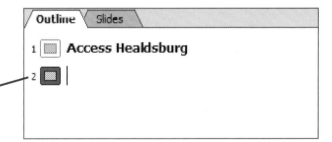

No problem; press the Tab key. That tells PowerPoint that you want to create a subheading, which is a heading indented below an existing heading.

You can see from the slide preview that your slide is looking the way that you want.

You're done for now with the Title slide (we'll dress it up with graphics in later chapters), so choose Insert > New Slide. PowerPoint creates the new slide, and automatically assigns it the Title and Text layout (which is called Bulleted List on Mac).

Type the title of the second slide, press Enter (Return), then press Tab and type the bullet points for your second slide, pressing Return between each bullet point. As you type, the slide preview updates. When you're done with the slide, press Enter (Return), then press Shift-Tab to get a new slide. Continue for the rest of your presentation.

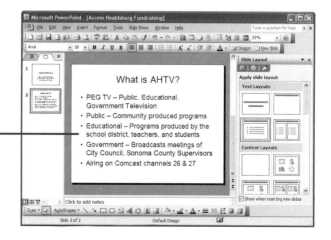

work with outline text

The flexibility of PowerPoint's Outline View is that it makes it easy to rearrange your ideas as you work on your presentation. Let's look at the outline for the last slide we wrote:

2 **What is AHTV?**
- PEG TV – Public, Educational, Government Television
- Public – Community produced programs
- Educational – Programs produced by the school district, teachers, and students
- Government – Broadcasts meetings of City Council, Sonoma County Supervisors
- Airing on Comcast channels 26 & 27

It's okay, but it needs better organization. Some headings can move up and others would be better as subheadings. To move headings around, use the Outlining toolbar. Display it by choosing View > Toolbars > Outlining.

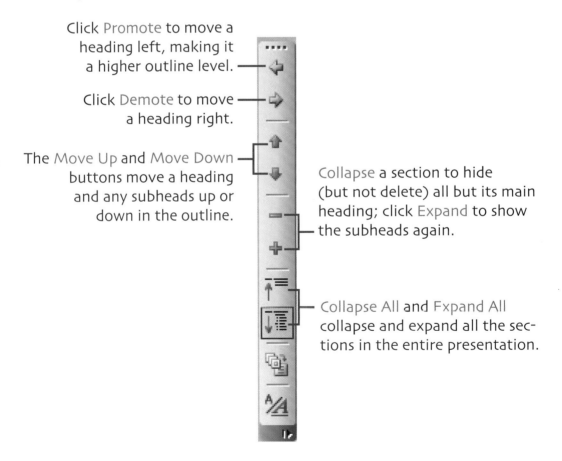

Click Promote to move a heading left, making it a higher outline level.

Click Demote to move a heading right.

The Move Up and Move Down buttons move a heading and any subheads up or down in the outline.

Collapse a section to hide (but not delete) all but its main heading; click Expand to show the subheads again.

Collapse All and Fxpand All collapse and expand all the sections in the entire presentation.

write your presentation

Click anywhere in a heading, then use a button in the Outlining toolbar to move it. After a few strategic moves, the outline is better organized.

Outline

This heading moved up. ─────

These headings ───── became subheads.

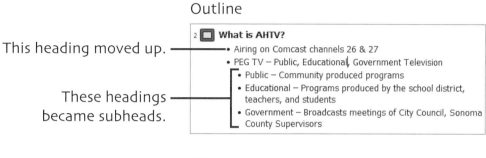

Slide

write outline in Word

If you prefer to do your writing in Word, that's no problem; you can create an outline in Word, save it, then import the outline into PowerPoint.

In Word, Choose View > Outline. Word's Outlining toolbar (which resembles the one in PowerPoint) appears automatically.

You can write the outline and move headings around in much the same way that you can in PowerPoint.

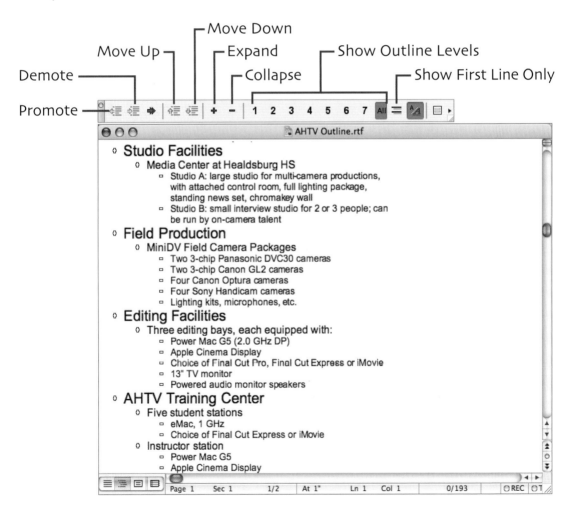

write your presentation

When you're done in Word, you must save the document in a format that PowerPoint can read, called Rich Text Format (RTF). Choose File > Save As, then from the Save as type pop-up menu (the Format pop-up menu on Mac), choose Rich Text Format, then click Save.

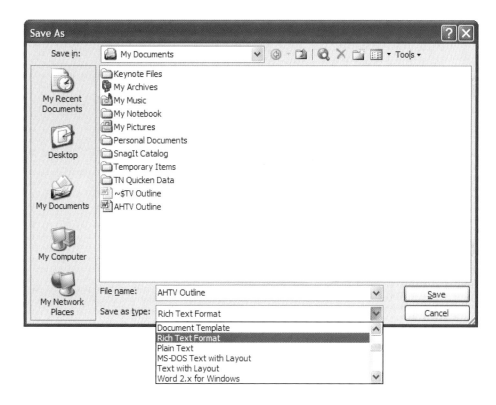

Back in PowerPoint, choose File > Open, select the RTF file, and click Open. PowerPoint converts the file into a presentation.

use the research pane

When you're writing a presentation, you often need to look up a bit of information here, check a fact there, or use a thesaurus to find a better word. The Research pane, found in PowerPoint 2003 for Windows, gives you instant access to reference materials, both online and on your machine.PowerPoint for Macintosh does not include this feature.

Open the Research pane by choosing View > Task Pane (Ctrl-F1), and then choose Research from the pop-up menu at the top of the Task Pane.

If you want to look up a word, the easiest way to do it is to hold down the Alt key and click the word. It will appear in the Search for field of the Research pane, with the Encarta Dictionary definition.

You can also type a word or phrase in the Search for field and press Enter to start a search.

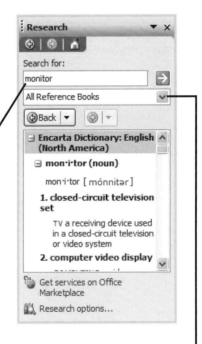

If you want to use a different reference source (say, you would rather do a thesaurus lookup, or search the online Encarta Encyclopedia), choose the source from the Source pop-up menu (the one directly under the search field).

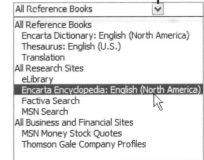

extra bits

write your presentation p. 13

- Having problems getting started writing the presentation? PowerPoint's AutoContent Wizard provides you with the basic outline for many types of presentations, such as Selling a Product or Service, Marketing Plan, Company Meeting, Recommending a Strategy, and many more. These outlines are a good starting point when you're in a hurry, or when you're just not feeling inspired. To use the AutoContent Wizard in PowerPoint for Windows, choose File > New (or press Ctrl-N), then in the Task Pane, click From AutoContent Wizard. The Wizard will start up. In PowerPoint for Macintosh, choose File > Project Gallery, or press Cmd-Shift-P. In the Blank Documents group, double-click AutoContent Wizard.

write the outline p. 14

- If the text in the outline is too small to work with comfortably, choose a larger value from the Zoom menu in the Standard toolbar. Don't change the font size in the Formatting Toolbar (Windows) or Formatting palette (Mac); that changes the size of text on the slides, but doesn't affect the outline text.

work with outline text p. 16

- If you prefer, you can move headings around with the mouse. When you place the pointer over the icon of a slide or a bullet in the outline, the pointer changes to a four-headed arrow. Click and drag the heading to a new location. You can move headings this way in either PowerPoint or Word.

extra bits

write outline in Word p. 18

- If you're dealing with a large presentation, you have a large outline. And Word, being a full-fledged word processor, has better tools for working with larger outlines. For example, you have more control over the number of heading levels that you show or hide at any given time, which lets you concentrate on the points that are important without being distracted by supporting information.

use the research pane p. 20

- To look up words another way, right-click a word in your presentation, then choose Look Up from the shortcut menu. The word will be transferred to the Research pane and will be looked up in the reference source you last used.

- The Research pane has a Translation reference source. You can use it to translate a word or short phrase to and from a very wide variety of languages.

3. gather image and sound files

Now that you've written your presentation outline, I'll let you in on a secret: The hardest part of creating your presentation is behind you. From this point, you're adding more elements to the presentation to add impact to the story you're telling and making the slides look good. But before we plunge into the nitty-gritty of changing the look of your slides, there's still one more important bit of planning to do. You need to decide what parts of your presentation will be enhanced with the addition of pictures and media files such as sounds and video. We've all seen PowerPoint presentations where the speaker threw in pictures and sounds seemingly at random, and that tends to turn audiences off. A quick review of your slides helps you avoid this pitfall.

In this chapter, we'll figure out where images, sounds, and even video clips could enhance your presentation, find images, and talk a bit about using sound in PowerPoint slideshows.

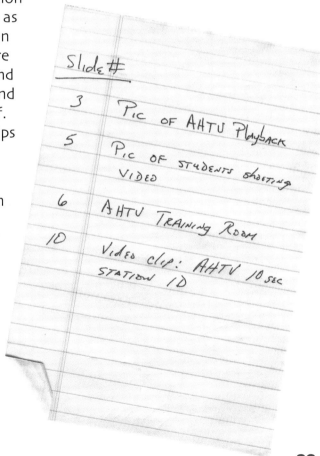

review your slides

For the first time, we're going to look at material on the slides, rather than in the outline, with an eye to deciding where we want to add images or sounds. You'll need a notepad or scratch paper to take notes as you browse the slides.

On Windows, click the Slides tab, and if needed, drag the border between the Normal View pane and the Slide pane to make the slide thumbnails easier to read.

Click the Normal View button at the bottom of the PowerPoint window, or choose View > Normal.

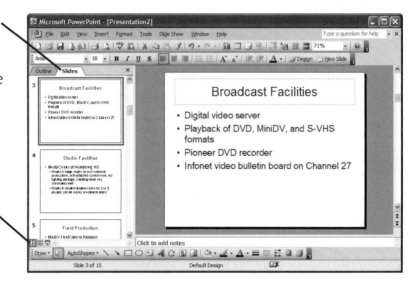

On Mac, you'll use the Normal View as is, working with the Outline and Slide panes.

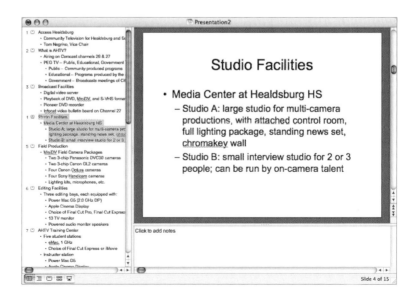

If you want more room for
the slide, point at the border
between the Slides and Notes
panes and drag it down
to hide the Notes pane.

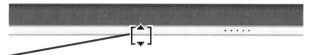

Using the Previous Slide and Next Slide buttons, browse through your slides, and as you re-read the contents of each slide, think about what pictures you could add to the slide that would help your audience better grasp your message. Some slides won't need any help from images; others will benefit from an added image. For example, on the slide in my presentation about the Training Facility, a picture of the facility would be helpful, because it's a good-looking facility.

As you browse, jot down notes with the slide number and what sorts of images, sound files, or even video clips you could add that would enhance the slide.

view slide layouts

Now that you know what sorts of images you might want to use, it's time to start thinking about how those images will appear on your slides. You'll do this by looking at the slide layouts PowerPoint provides for slides that contain images, or images and text.

On Windows, display the Task Pane by choosing View > Task Pane, or press Ctrl-F1. From the pop-up menu at the top of the Task Pane, choose Slide Layout. The Slide Layouts appear.

Scroll down to Content Layouts, which have placeholders for one or more pictures, or a title and pictures.

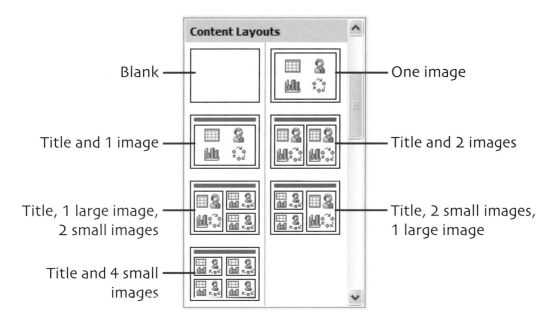

Blank ——

One image ——

Title and 1 image ——

Title and 2 images ——

Title, 1 large image, 2 small images ——

Title, 2 small images, 1 large image ——

Title and 4 small images ——

For your slides, you might find the Text and Content Layouts more useful; these include placeholders for a title, bulleted text, and one or more pictures.

Title, text, and 1 image

Title, text, and 2 small images

Title and text over 1 image

Title and 2 small images over text

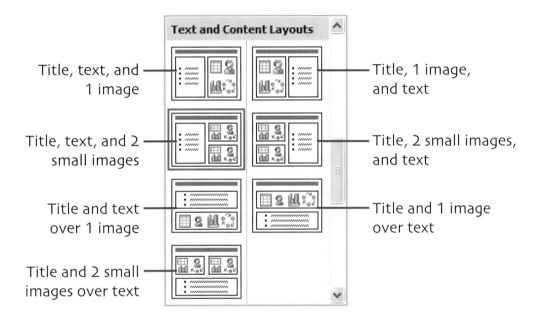

Title, 1 image, and text

Title, 2 small images, and text

Title and 1 image over text

Mac PowerPoint users will find slide layouts in the Change Slides section of the Formatting Palette. If the Formatting Palette isn't visible, choose View > Formatting Palette.

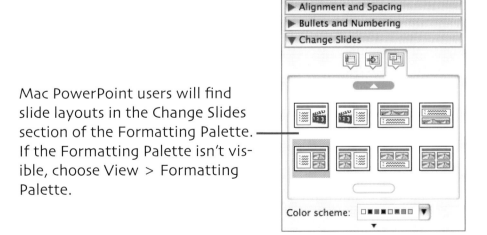

view slide layouts (cont.)

As you browse through the slide layouts, you can see how a slide will look with that layout applied by displaying the slide, then clicking on the thumbnail of a layout. The slide will change to the new layout, reformatting the slide's text if necessary.

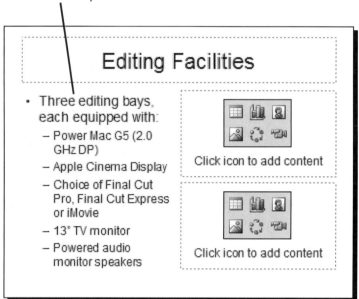

gather image and sound files

find images

Images you use in your presentations can come from many possible sources: digital pictures you take yourself; scanned photographs or drawings; stock photography that you purchase online; or clip art. Some clip art comes with Microsoft Office. You can find it by choosing Insert > Picture > Clip Art. The Clip Art pane of the Task Pane opens (Windows). On the Mac, it opens the Clip Gallery.

On Windows, search the clip art by entering a word in the Search for field, then click Go. On the Mac, enter a word in the Search field, then click Search.

find images (cont.)

You'll add images to your slides in Chapter 6. For now, look through the available images in the clip art collections to find images that you may want to use.

If you're not happy with the selection of clip art that comes with the program, there's a lot more available for free at Microsoft Office Online, at http://office.Microsoft.com/clipart/.

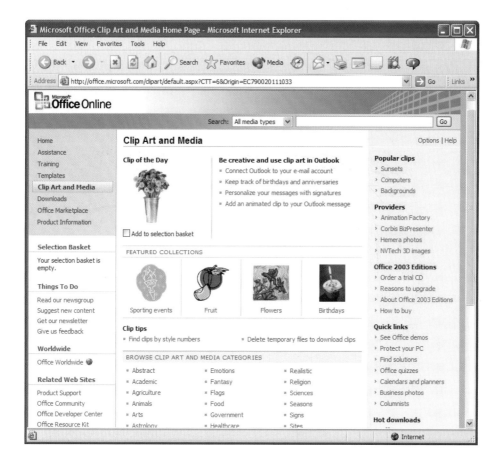

If you find any images that you like among the vast collection on Microsoft Office Online, download them to your local machine for later use.

choose sounds

Finding sounds is a bit trickier than finding images. The Windows version of PowerPoint includes sound files in its clip art collection, but the Mac version does not.

To find sounds on Windows, restrict your search to just sounds in the Results should be pop-up menu in the Clip Art pane.

Uncheck the Clip Art, Photographs, and Movies choices.

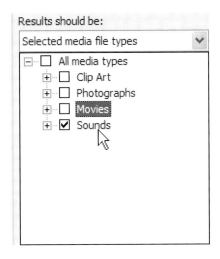

Search the collection by entering a word in the Search for field, then click Go. The sounds will appear in the results field as icons.

choose sounds (cont.)

Once you find sounds, you'll want to hear them. Right-click on a sound, and from the shortcut menu, choose Preview/Properties. The Preview/Properties dialog appears and plays your sound.

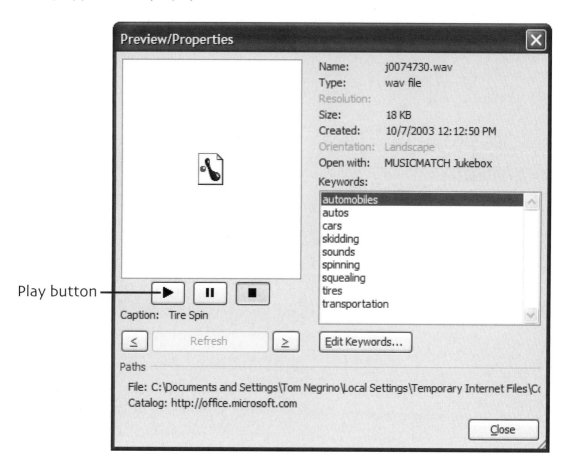

Play button

If you need to play the sound again, click the Play button.

You'll add sounds to slides in Chapter 6. For now, make note of the sounds that would work with your presentation.

extra bits

view slide layouts p. 26

- Windows users have 27 preset slide layouts; Mac users have 24.

find images p. 29

- Images you use in your presentations should be royalty free, meaning they can be used without additional payments to the image's producer.

- Clip art and other media found at the Microsoft Office Online site are subject to certain restrictions, which are listed at the site. At the bottom of the clip art page, you'll find a link called "Legal." Click it, and be prepared to be stunned into submission by legal-eze.

- There are many places online to find images for your presentations. Rather than singling out just a few companies, do a Google search on all of the following search terms: "images" "royalty-free" "clip art". You'll get a wealth of choices, some free, some not.

- Besides online resources, you can find many excellent clip art packages on the market. These come on CD or DVD, and are usually royalty free. Some good ones are from Hemera (www. hemera.com), in their Photo-Object collections, and Nova Development's Art Explosion (www.novadevelopment.com). Digital Juice (www.digitaljuice. com) has the Presenters Toolkit package, which contains thousands of images, video clips, animations, and backgrounds.

choose sounds p. 31

- You can find many Web sites that sell royalty-free sound collections, such as SoundRangers (www.soundrangers.com). These sites sell individual sounds for as little as $1.50. You'll find more sites with a Google search on "sounds" "royalty-free". Most of these sites work equally well for both Windows and Mac users.

- Just because Mac Office's Clip Gallery doesn't come with sounds, it doesn't mean that you can't either add sounds to the Clip Gallery, or use sounds from any sound file in your presentations.

4. pick a design

With your presentation's content set, it's time to start dressing up your slides. You'll do that in this chapter by selecting a design template for your presentation. That template provides the visual look of the slides—the slide design—throughout the whole presentation, including elements like a background image for the slides and the style and color of the text you put on the slides.

You'll also apply a slide layout to each slide in your presentation, matching the layout to the content of the slide. For example, you'll apply the Title layout to the first slide, and add one of the layouts that contains image placeholders for slides where you will add pictures.

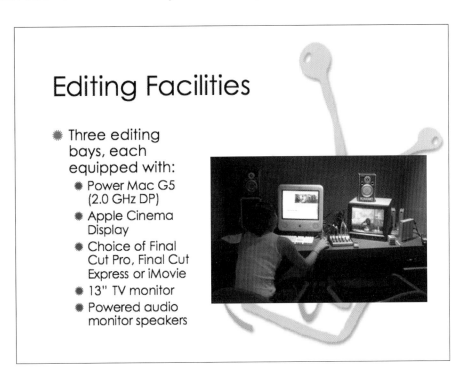

pick a slide design

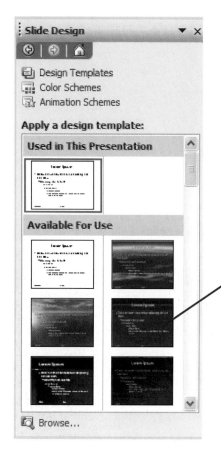

When you pick a slide design, PowerPoint applies it to all of the slides in the presentation, so that they will have a consistent look. Begin adding a slide design by displaying one of the presentation's slides in Normal View. Any slide will do, but I usually use one of the slides that contains a title and bulleted text, because those are the most common in presentations.

On Windows, display the Task Pane by choosing View > Task Pane, or press Ctrl-F1. From the pop-up menu at the top of the Task Pane, choose Slide Design. The slide designs appear as small thumbnail images.

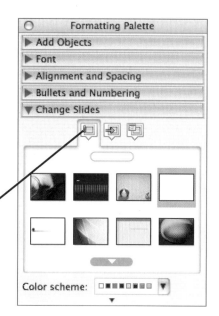

On the Mac, you'll find the slide templates in the Change Slides section of the Formatting Palette.

Click the Slide Design tab.

Scroll through the slide designs until you find one that you like. Click the thumbnail of the slide design, and PowerPoint applies it to your slide.

Broadcast Facilities

- Digital video server
- Playback of DVD, MiniDV, and S-VHS formats
- Pioneer DVD recorder
- Infonet video bulletin board on Channel 27

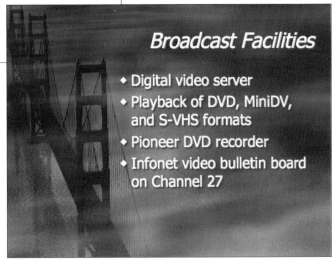

You can see how applying the slide design has changed the font and styles of the text on the slide; the positioning of the text on the slide; the slide's background image; and the style of the bullets used on the slide (from dots to diamonds).

apply slide layouts

Now it's time to go through all of your slides and apply the proper slide layout to each one.

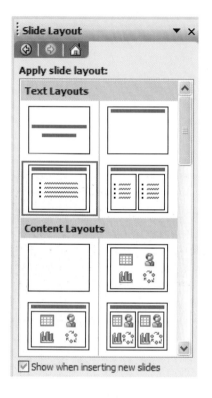

On Windows, from the pop-up menu at the top of the Task Pane, choose Slide Layout.

Scroll to the first slide in your presentation, which is the title slide. The slide should be using the Title Slide or Title Only layout. If it is not (it usually isn't if you imported the slide outline from Word, for example), click the layout you want.

On the Mac, click the Slide Layout tab in the Change Slides section of the Formatting Palette.

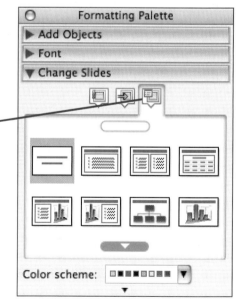

pick a design

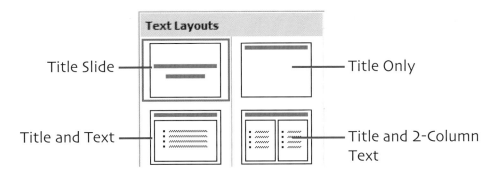

Title Slide ———— ————— Title Only

Title and Text ———— ———— Title and 2-Column Text

The slide changes to the new layout.

Slide with Title and Text layout

Slide with Title Slide layout

Use the Next Slide button (at the right edge of the PowerPoint window) to move through your slides, applying the appropriate layout to each one. This is where the notes you took in Chapter 3 will come in handy; because you've already figured out where images will go in your presentation, you can apply picture layouts where it is appropriate. If you're doing a presentation that includes charts, apply one of the layouts that has chart placeholders.

customize background

Let's say you like the font and bullet styles of a slide design, but not the background image—you can choose the slide design, then change just the background to one more appropriate for your presentation. Of course if you're happy with the background, you can skip this step.

For my presentation for Access Healdsburg, I found a slide design that was pretty good, but it had a wildly inappropriate background image for a community television station.

So I replaced that image with an image of the organization's logo that I prepared in Adobe Photoshop.

To use your own background image, choose Format > Background (Format > Slide Background), which brings up the Background dialog.

From the pop-up menu at the bottom of the dialog, choose Fill Effects. In the resulting Fill Effects dialog, click the Picture tab, then click the Select Picture button.

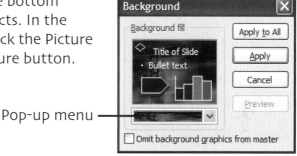

Pop-up menu

The Select Picture dialog will appear. Find the image file you want to use as the background and click Insert. You'll return to the Fill Effects dialog, which displays a preview of the picture you just chose.

Click OK to return to the Background dialog. You want the new background to appear on all your slides, so click Apply to All.

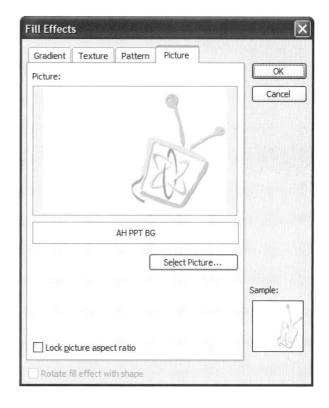

adjust text location

After applying the slide design and possibly customizing the background, you may find that some of the text on your slides isn't quite where you want it. For example, the title slide of my presentation had the two placeholders containing the title and subtitle covering the organization's logo.

The text on the slide is in placeholders, and you can move the placeholders as you like.

Text placeholders —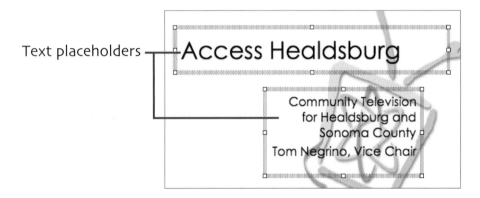

Move the pointer towards the text on a slide. As you get near the text, the pointer will change to a four-headed arrow (on the Mac it will change to a grabber hand).

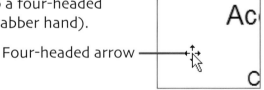

Four-headed arrow

Selection handles —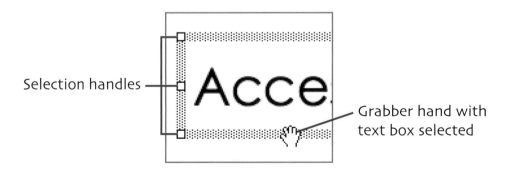

Grabber hand with text box selected

pick a design

When the pointer changes, click the mouse button. The text placeholder will be selected, showing a thick dotted border. You can drag the placeholder from any spot on the border. Clicking and dragging any of the placeholder's selection handles resizes the placeholder.

After the placeholders are moved around, the logo is mostly uncovered, and the slide looks much better.

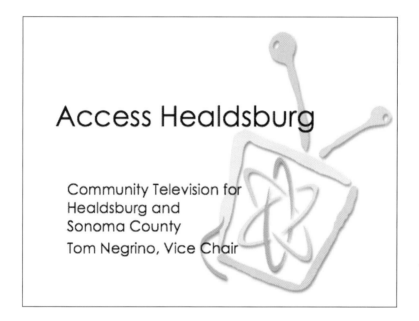

extra bits

pick a slide design p. 36

- The little thumbnails of the design templates in the Task Pane (Windows) or Formatting Palette (Mac) might not be large enough for you to get a good feel for the template. To get a bigger view, click the Browse link at the bottom of the Task Pane, or on the Mac, choose Format > Slide Design. You'll get a dialog box that shows you a larger preview of the template.

- The Windows and Mac versions of PowerPoint don't come with the same set of design templates. Windows PowerPoint comes with 63 different templates, and the Mac version checks in with 110 templates. All templates are compatible across platforms, and are part of the presentation file, so if you start working on a presentation on a Mac, then copy it to Windows, the slide template will come right along.

pick a design

apply slide layouts p. 38

- To apply a slide template that is different from the main template that you're using to more than one slide, switch to Slide Sorter View, and select the slides you want to change. You can Shift-click slide thumbnails to select multiple consecutive slides, or Ctrl-click (Cmd-click) multiple nonconsecutive slides.

- Not happy with the slide templates that come with Power-Point? There are many places to find more templates on the Web. The first place to look is Microsoft Office Online, at http://office.microsoft.com/templates/. Click the Power-Point link to display additional design templates, background slides, and useful templates for things like calendars, charts and diagrams, and awards and certificates. All of these templates are free, and work on both Windows or Mac.

- There are many online sites that sell additional templates. Search for "PowerPoint templates" using Google or another search engine.

customize background p. 40

- PowerPoint can use just about any graphic file (in a standard format such as JPEG, TIFF, or PNG) as a slide background. To make a new background, you'll need a graphic editing program, such as Adobe Photo-shop or Macromedia Fireworks. Those programs are terrific, but they're not cheap, and you can get by with less expensive alternatives. Windows Paint, which comes with Windows, can do the job of creating a background, and on the Mac, the shareware GraphicConverter (www.lemkesoft.com) is a good choice.

- Just as there are sites that sell slide templates, others sell slide backgrounds. One of my favorites is PowerPoint Art (www.powerpointart.com), which sells a subscription that allows you to use any of their thousands of backgrounds. Again, a Google search will turn up many others.

pick a design   **45**

extra bits

adjust text location p. 42

- You can often make your slides look even better by changing the font size or text alignment. You'll see how to do that in Chapter 5.

5. work with text

Even though you did most of the writing of your presentation in the outline, now that you see the text on the slides with your preferred slide design, you probably want to make some changes on the slides themselves.

In this chapter, you'll learn how to edit and format text on the slides, add hyperlinks, and even add extra text to a slide for special purposes like adding captions to images. Finally, you'll learn how to avoid a major presentation embarrassment: misspellings on your slides.

Challenges

* Equipment funding
  1. Studio A build out
  2. Additional channel capacity
  3. Remote vehicle
* Staff funding
  1. Administrative assistant
  2. Additional instructor
  3. Broadcast scheduler

edit slide text

If you want to add text to a slide, move the mouse pointer over the text. The cursor will change into an I-beam, indicating that clicking will set the insertion point where you can start typing.

Click the mouse button, and add or delete text.

You can also use the I-beam cursor to select text inside a text placeholder. Click and drag over the text you want to select. Once it is selected, you can type to replace the selected text.

The most common reason to want to edit text on a slide is to make the text work better with your slide design, which usually means getting a line of text to break in a different spot. A line break is the point on a line at which the text wraps down to the next line.

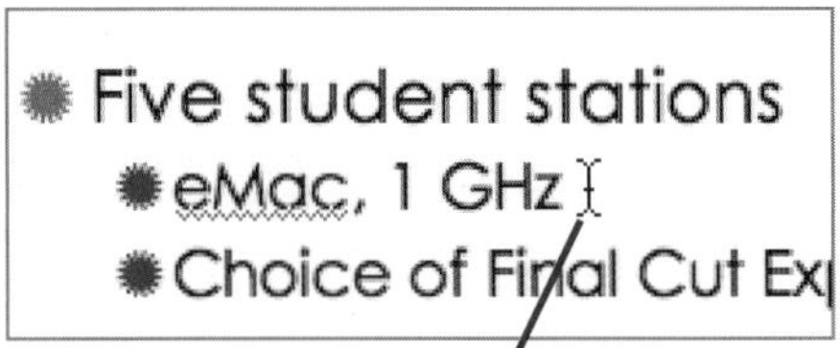

* Five student stations
  * eMac, 1 GHz I
  * Choice of Final Cut Ex|

I-beam cursor

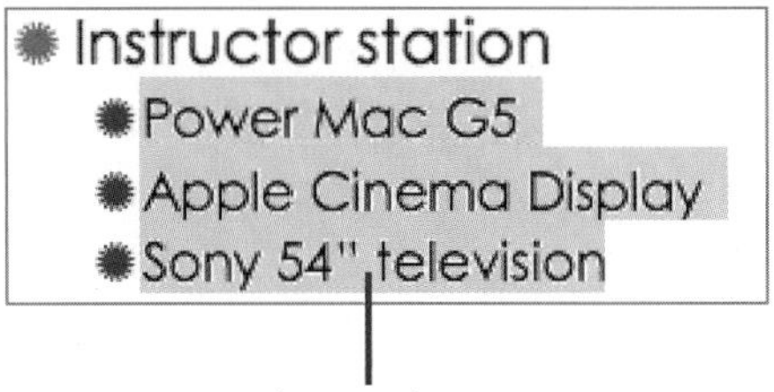

* Instructor station
  * Power Mac G5
  * Apple Cinema Display
  * Sony 54" television

Selected text

For example, let's look again at the title slide of my presentation. For this first slide, it would look better if none of the text in the subhead or my name covered up any of the organization's logo.

To change the text so that it wraps more attractively, we'll add manual line breaks to the text. Click to set the insertion point before the word where you want the break to happen.

You can't just press Enter (Return), because PowerPoint will think that you want to create a new paragraph, which on slides with bulleted text would result in a new bullet point. Instead, press Shift-Enter (Shift-Return), which adds a line break without adding a paragraph break. On the next line, I deleted the comma after my name and added a manual line break. The result is considerably more pleasing to the eye.

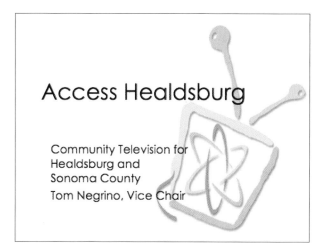

Insertion point

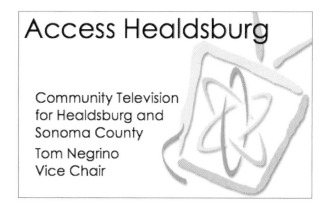

format slide text

Another way to change the text on your slides is to change its formatting, including the size and look of the text, the alignment, and the spacing between the lines.

Most text changes are done in much the same way that you would do them in a word processor: Select the text, then make a choice from the Formatting Toolbar (Windows) or Formatting Palette (Mac).

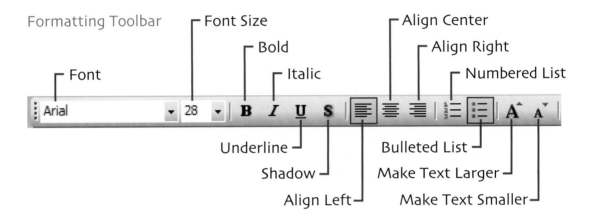

work with text

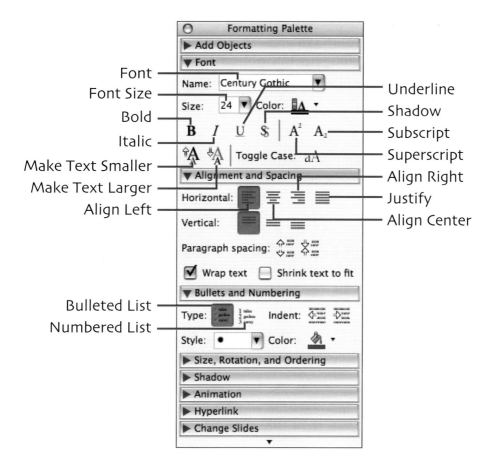

Font — Name: Century Gothic

Font Size — Size: 24

Bold — **B**

Italic — *I*

Make Text Smaller

Make Text Larger

Align Left

Underline

Shadow

Subscript

Superscript

Align Right

Justify

Align Center

Bulleted List

Numbered List

For example, let's say that you want to emphasize some text on one of your slides. First, click and drag to select the text.

Then click the Italic button on the Formatting Toolbar (Formatting Palette).

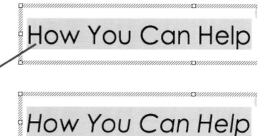

work with text

align slide text

When you're working with graphics, you may want to change text alignment in text boxes so that they work better with the image. Or you may decide that left-aligned or right-aligned text looks better on your title slide, instead of the center alignment that is the setting on most design templates.

For example, this left-aligned text overlaps the graphic, so the solution is to right-align it.

Select the text, then click one of the text alignment buttons.

change line spacing

You can spread the line spacing on a slide if it is too tight for the content, or reduce the line spacing if you need to get a little more text on the slide.

On this slide, the indented text would be easier to read if the lines were a bit further apart.

What is AHTV?

* Airing on Comcast channels 26 & 27
* PEG TV – Public, Educational, Government Television
  * Public – Community produced programs
  * Educational – Programs produced by the school district, teachers, and students
  * Government – Broadcasts meetings of City Council, Sonoma County Supervisors

Select all of the lines of indented text, then choose Format > Line Spacing. The Line Spacing dialog appears.

Use this to change the line spacing. ⎯

Use this to change the amount of space before each paragraph.

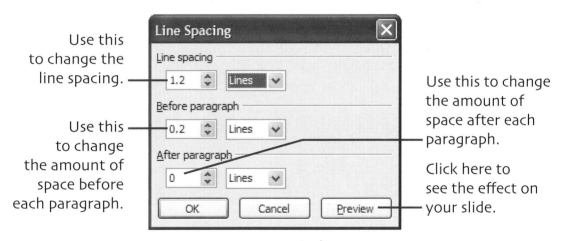

Use this to change the amount of space after each paragraph.

Click here to see the effect on your slide.

Use the spacing controls, then click the Preview button. If you like the new look, click OK. The slide text changes to reflect your new line spacing.

* PEG TV – Public, Educational, Government Television
  * Public – Community produced programs
  * Educational – Programs produced by the school district, teachers, and students
  * Government – Broadcasts meetings of City Council, Sonoma County Supervisors

use numbered lists

Bulleted lists are standard in presentations, but sometimes you want to show a process with a clear beginning and end. For that, a numbered list is better. You can easily change the bulleted list that PowerPoint gives you into a numbered list, and customize the numbering as you wish.

First, select the bulleted text. ——

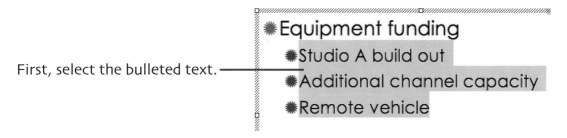

Click the Numbering button in the Formatting Toolbar (Windows) or in the Bullets and Numbering section of the Formatting Palette (Mac).

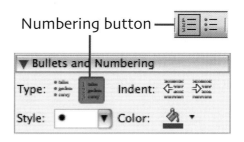

The text changes to a numbered list.

If you want a different numbering system (maybe you would prefer letters rather than numbers, i.e., A, B, C...), with the text still selected, choose Format > Bullets and Numbering. From the resulting dialog, choose a numbering system, then click OK.

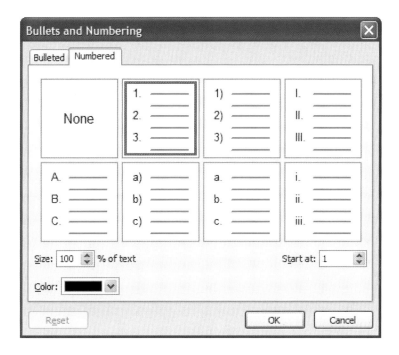

add hyperlinks

You're already familiar with hyperlinks; they're the underlined text that you click on in a Web browser to take you to another Web page. You can use two kinds of hyperlinks in your PowerPoint presentations. The first kind, when clicked during your presentation, leaves PowerPoint, opens the Web browser on your machine, and brings you to the hyperlink's destination. The other kind of hyperlink makes PowerPoint jump to a different slide in your presentation. Either kind of hyperlink only works while you are actually presenting; you don't have to worry about accidentally opening your Web browser while you are working on your presentation.

If you type a Web address into the outline or a PowerPoint slide—such as www.peachpit.com—PowerPoint is smart enough to automatically turn it into a hyperlink. In many instances, that's all you'll need,

✳Join at our Website
www.ahtv.org

because the link shows your audience the Web address you want them to use and also allows you to click it to display the site.

If you want text on your slide to be the link instead, follow these steps:

1 Select the text that you want to make into a hyperlink.

* Join at our Website

2 Choose Insert > Hyperlink, or press Ctrl-K (Cmd-K).
The Insert Hyperlink dialog appears.

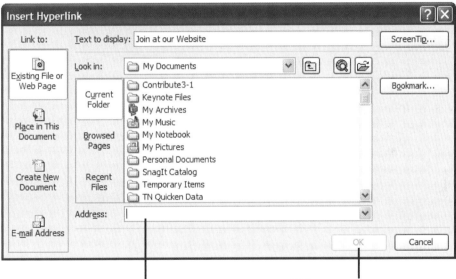

3 In the Address field, type the full Web address for the hyperlink. If the address starts with www., PowerPoint will automatically add the http:// before the address. If it does not, as in office.microsoft.com, you must add the http:// manually.

4 Click OK. The text is colored and underlined, indicating that it has become a hyperlink.

work with text

add hyperlinks (cont.)

To make the other kind of hyperlink—the kind that jumps to a different slide in your presentation—follow these steps (this works only in PowerPoint for Windows):

1 Select the text you want to use as the hyperlink and choose Insert > Hyperlink.

2 In the Link section of the Insert Hyperlink dialog, in the Link to section, click Place in This Document. The dialog changes to reflect your choice.

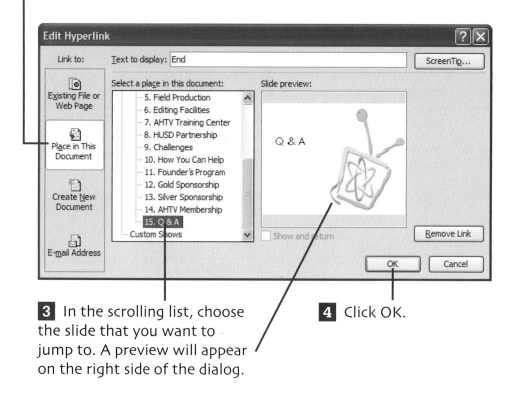

3 In the scrolling list, choose the slide that you want to jump to. A preview will appear on the right side of the dialog.

4 Click OK.

work with text

add text boxes

There are many reasons why you might want text on your slides that isn't part of the outline, but the most common reason to add text is that it will be a label or caption for a picture. To add this text, you'll first need to add a text box to the slide.

 Choose Insert > Text Box.
The cursor changes into the
Insert Text Box cursor.

Click and drag where you want the new text box in order to define its shape of the new text box. When you release the mouse button, the text box appears with a blinking insertion point. Type the text you want in the new text box.

Visit the Media Center at Healdsburg High School!

After you create the text box, you can apply any formatting you like to the text it contains, or adjust the position of the text box on the slide.

check your spelling

Aside from those dreams that you had when you were a kid that you were naked in front of your geometry class (uh, maybe that was just me), there's nothing much more embarrassing than doing a presentation with a misspelled word. Your mistake is there for everyone to see, and it's projected 10 feet wide, to boot! Avoid this nightmare by using PowerPoint's spelling tools.

The nice thing is that PowerPoint is always watching you like a hawk as you write, looking for spelling mistakes. If it finds one, it puts a wavy red underline under the suspected mistake. To fix it, right-click (Control-click) the word. You'll get a shortcut menu with one or more suggested corrections.

Choose the correction you want from the menu, and PowerPoint replaces the misspelling.

You can also check spelling throughout your whole presentation. Choose Tools > Spelling. The Spelling dialog appears, and finds the first questionable word.

In the Suggestions list, click the correct spelling, then click the Change button. If the word is correct (just not in PowerPoint's dictionary), click Ignore. If you know the word is used more than once in your presentation, you can click the

Change All or Ignore All button, which fixes or ignores all occurrences of the word. When the spelling check is complete, the Spelling dialog closes automatically, and PowerPoint displays an alert box, telling you that it is done.

work with text

extra bits

format slide text p. 50

- When you want to emphasize text, use italic rather than underline. People tend to interpret underlined text as a Web link.

- If you have applied multiple formatting changes to text and you want to make the same changes to other text, you don't have to do all those formatting steps again. Instead, use the Format Painter on the Standard Toolbar, which copies text formatting. First, select the text that has the formatting you want to copy. Then click the Format Painter button.

Click the text you want the formatting copied to, and that text changes to match the first text formatting. If you want to use the Format Painter to apply formatting to more than one text selection, double-click the Format Painter button. This locks the tool on, and whatever text you select will take on the copied formatting. When you're finished applying formatting, click the Format Painter button once to turn it off.

- If you want to change the fonts throughout your presentation, choose Format > Replace Fonts.

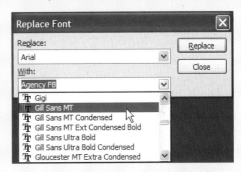

In the resulting dialog, pick the font you want to replace from the Replace pop-up menu, and the new font that you want to use from the With pop-up menu. This is a much faster way to change fonts throughout your presentation, rather than formatting text in individual text boxes.

extra bits

align slide text p. 52

- Sometime it's better to move a text placeholder on the slide, rather than mess with text alignment. See "adjust text location" in Chapter 4 for more information.

use numbered lists p. 54

- In the Bullets and Numbering dialog, you can change the starting number of the list, which is handy when you're continuing a list from a previous slide. You can also change the size of the number relative to the text, and change the number's color.

- When you choose a numbering system, pick one that matches the flavor of your presentation. For example, in a formal presentation, you might want to consider using Roman numerals as the numbering system. But that would probably be inappropriate (not to mention pompous) in a presentation about softball teams. Whatever you choose, be consistent from slide to slide; you don't want to use numbers (1, 2, 3…) on one slide and letters (A, B, C…) on the next.

add hyperlinks p. 56

- To remove a hyperlink, select the link, open the Insert Hyperlink dialog, and click the Remove Link button. The text of the link will remain, but it will no longer be a hyperlink.

work with text

6. illustrate your presentation

Images add an important spice to any presentation. Some information is better presented in a graphic form, and often you'll find that your audience will better grasp your message with graphical help. Your presentation can include many different kinds of information that isn't text, such as pictures, charts, diagrams, tables, clip art, sound effects, or video clips. Very few, if any, presentations include all of these elements, but you'll probably want to add at least some to every presentation.

This chapter is where you'll use the images and other media files that you gathered in Chapter 3. If you made a list of files and where they go, find and refer to it as you work through the chapter.

In this chapter, you'll learn how to add images and media clips to your presentation; use PowerPoint's drawing tools to add interest to your slides; and add tables, diagrams, and charts to your presentation.

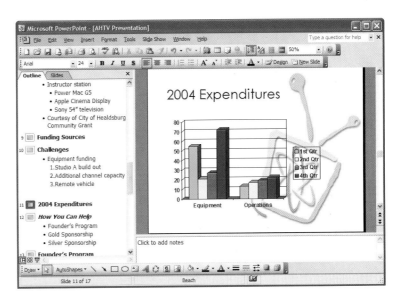

add images from disk

You can add pictures to your PowerPoint presentation by using files on your hard disk or on a CD and inserting them in the presentation.

Display the slide that you want the image on. It should already have a slide layout with a placeholder ready to accept the image. If it doesn't, apply such a layout using the instructions in Chapter 4.

If you used one of the Content layouts in PowerPoint for Windows, click the Insert Picture icon in the Content box.

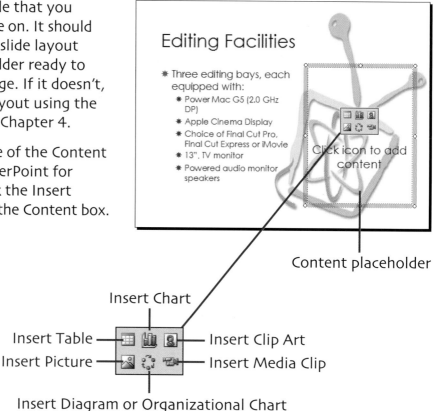

Content placeholder

Insert Chart

Insert Table — Insert Clip Art

Insert Picture — Insert Media Clip

Insert Diagram or Organizational Chart

illustrate your presentation

The Mac version of PowerPoint doesn't use the Content box, so double-click the Picture placeholder.

The Insert Picture (Choose a Picture) dialog appears. Navigate to the picture you want, then click Insert. PowerPoint automatically scales the image to fit inside the placeholder, and the image appears on your slide.

Double click to add picture

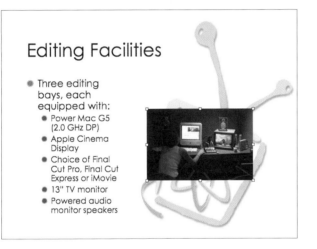

If you don't like the position and size of the image, click on the image and drag it to where you want it to be. Then click one of the selection handles on the image and drag to resize it. As you drag, you'll see a dashed line indicating how large the picture will be when you release the mouse button.

add clip art

Another way to add images to your presentation is by using an image that's in the Clip Organizer (called the Clip Gallery on the Mac).

Display the slide that you want the image on. If it doesn't already have a slide layout with a placeholder ready to accept the image, apply such a layout using the instructions in Chapter 4.

On Windows, click the Insert Clip Art icon in the Content box. The Select Picture dialog will appear. Type a search term into the Search text field and click the Go button.

On the Mac, double-click the Clip Art placeholder. The Clip Gallery will appear. Type a search term into the Search box and click the Search button.

When you find the clip art that you like, click the OK button (Insert button on the Mac). The clip art appears on your slide.

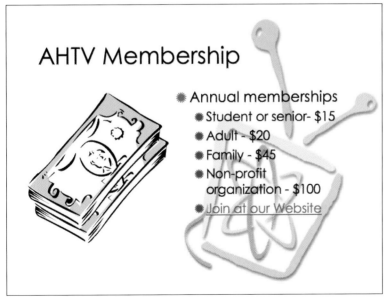

illustrate your presentation

use the drawing tools

If you're the kind of person that can't draw a straight line, much less a circle or an octagon, then PowerPoint's drawing tools are for you. PowerPoint offers tools in the Drawing toolbar (and on the Mac, also in the Add Objects section of the Formatting Palette) with many ready-made shapes that can be easily drawn onto your slides. These AutoShapes include lines, arrows, stars, flowchart symbols, callout boxes, and more.

On Windows, click the AutoShapes pop-up menu on the Drawing toolbar, then choose the shape you want from one of the categories of AutoShapes.

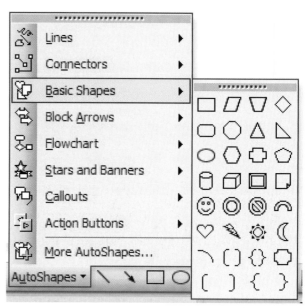

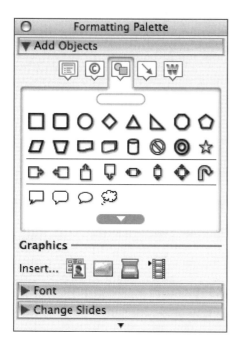

On the Mac, in the Add Objects section of the Formatting Palette, click the AutoShapes tab, then select the shape that you want.

The cursor becomes a cross.

illustrate your presentation

Click and drag on the slide to draw the AutoShape object as large as you wish. Here, I'm using a Cloud callout shape, which serves as a thought bubble for a photo.

Position the drawn AutoShape where you want it, and resize it as needed.

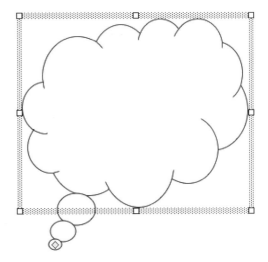

add sound files

Usually, there's no quicker way to annoy your audience than by adding sounds to your slides. It's a big tip-off of novice PowerPoint jockeys. But there are certainly valid reasons for using sounds in presentations. For example, a presentation about music might use brief clips, or anthropologists could include snippets of a language they are studying.

To use a sound, you'll need the sound files to be on your hard disk in a format that your computer can play.

Choose Insert > Movies and Sounds > Sound from File. The Insert Sound dialog appears.

Navigate to the sound file you want, select it, and click OK (Insert).

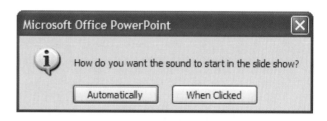

PowerPoint asks if you want the sound to start automatically when you switch to the slide, or only when you click a button on the slide. Make your choice.

Sound icon

The sound icon appears on the slide. Move it to where you want it. To preview the sound, double-click the sound icon. During the presentation, you will need to click the icon to play the sound, unless you previously told PowerPoint to start the sound automatically.

• **Bengal tiger - recorded 9/03**

use video clips

Video clips can be very effective in a presentation. You could include a video quote from your product manager, or show a brief tutorial. In the presentation for Access Healdsburg, I used a video clip to take audiences on a tour of the television station's studios.

Video clips must be on your hard disk in a format that your computer can play.

Choose Insert > Movies and Sounds > Movie from File. The Insert Movie dialog appears.

Navigate to the movie file you want, select it, and click OK (Insert).

PowerPoint asks if you want the movie to start automatically when you switch to the slide, or only when you click the movie. Decide which you want.

The movie appears on your slide. You might have to reposition and resize it, especially on a Mac.

Filmstrip icon

If you want to play the movie to preview it, right-click the movie and choose Play Movie from the shortcut menu (Windows) or click the filmstrip icon to display the familiar QuickTime movie controller (Mac). When you give the presentation, click the movie to play it, unless you told PowerPoint to automatically play it when you switched to the slide.

Play button   Movie controller

illustrate your presentation   **71**

add diagrams (Win)

PowerPoint for Windows lets you easily insert a variety of predesigned diagrams, such as organization charts and Venn diagrams. You can then customize the diagram for your needs. Here, I've used a radial diagram to show the funding sources for Access Healdsburg. PowerPoint for Mac does not have this feature.

Start by clicking the Insert Diagram or Organization Chart button on the Drawing toolbar.

From the resulting Diagram Gallery dialog, choose the chart that you want.

The diagram appears on the slide, and the Diagram toolbar also appears. This toolbar changes, depending on what sort of diagram you've inserted.

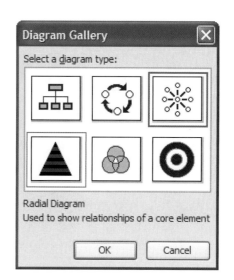

Using the Diagram toolbar, adjust the look of the diagram, changing the number of elements as necessary. For example, I needed more circles in the radial diagram, so I added them.

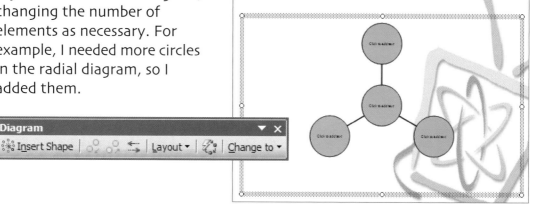

The diagram contains placeholders for text. Click in each one and enter your own text.

Double-click on an element in the diagram to bring up the Format AutoShape dialog to change its coloring. The resulting diagram gets the message across.

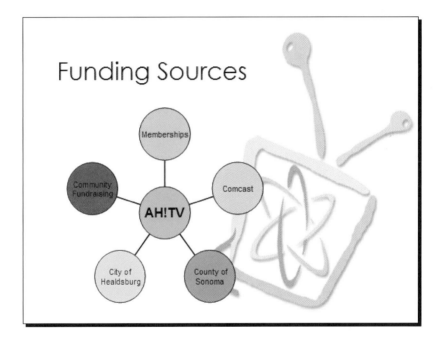

add charts

Many slide presentations include a set of numbers of some kind—for example, projected fundraising for next year, or a look back at last year's budget versus actual numbers. It's difficult for an audience to understand long columns of numbers, especially in the short time they would be on the screen during your presentation. A chart offers a much better way to let people quickly grasp the relationship between numbers and helps them spot trends.

Insert Chart

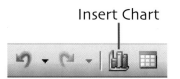

To add a chart to one of your slides, start by clicking the Insert Chart button on the Standard toolbar.

On the Mac, a new program, Microsoft Graph, starts up, displaying a new menu bar, a new set of toolbars, a datasheet where you enter data to be charted, and a preview of the chart. The datasheet is already populated with some sample data for you.

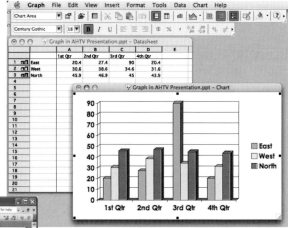

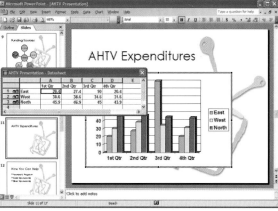

On Windows, Graph takes over the PowerPoint window.

Change the sample data in the datasheet one cell at a time, entering your own data. As you change the datasheet, the chart preview automatically updates.

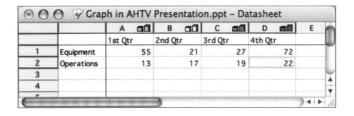

Use the Graph toolbars to make any other changes you need in the chart, such as changing the chart type, chart colors, and so on.

On Windows, click the slide background to close Graph and return to PowerPoint. On the Mac, choose Graph > Quit and Return to [presentation name]. The new chart appears on your slide.

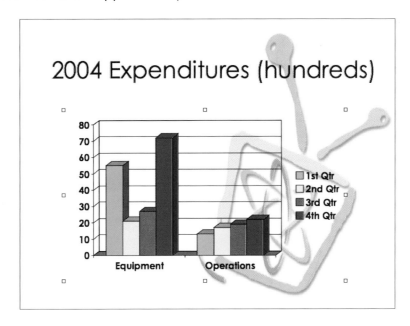

add tables

Tables are a great way to show relationships between groups of data, and to get a lot of information into your presentation in an easy-to-understand fashion. Tables can contain words, numbers, or both.

On the Standard toolbar, click Insert Table. The table grid appears. Drag to select the number of rows and columns that you need in your table.

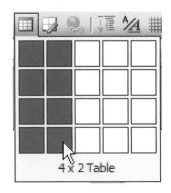

When you click, a blank table is inserted into the current slide.

If you want, point at the horizontal or verti-cal lines inside the table until the cursor turns into a double-headed arrow. Then click and drag to resize the rows or columns.

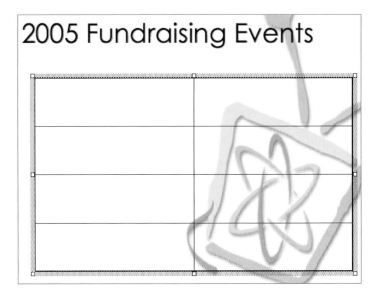

Click inside the first cell of the table to get an insertion point, then enter your data into the cells. You can press the Tab key to move between cells without using the mouse. When you're finished adding data to the table, click on the slide background to deselect the table.

2005 Fundraising Events

Q1	Winter Telethon
Q2	Spring Carnival
Q3	Harvest Time Telethon
Q4	Halloween Dinner & Ball

extra bits

add images from disk p. 64

- You can also add an image to a slide by dragging and dropping it from the desktop onto your slide. Sometimes this is faster than navigating through the Open dialog, but the disadvantage to dragging and dropping (as opposed to using a placeholder to insert the image) is that you'll have to resize the image yourself.

- Got a picture that's not as clear as you wish it could be? You can change the brightness and contrast of images that you import by double-clicking them to bring up the Format Picture dialog. Click the Picture tab, then use the Brightness and Contrast sliders to adjust the picture. Click the Preview button to see the effect on the image. When you're happy with the result, click OK.

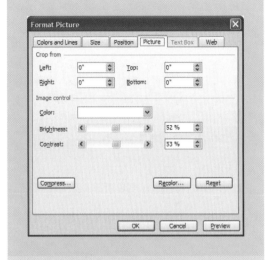

add clip art p. 66

- You can also store photographs and media clips, not just line art, in the Clip Organizer (Clip Gallery).

illustrate your presentation

use the drawing tools p. 68

- You can layer text and graphics, so if you want to, for example, put text inside a callout Auto-Shape, you would insert a Text Box over the callout shape.

- You can add colors to an AutoShape by double-clicking it, and then using the Fill and Line controls in the resulting Format AutoShapes dialog.

- The Mac has a Drawing toolbar, too; choose View > Toolbars > Drawing to display it. In fact, you'll find more drawing options in the Drawing toolbar than in the Formatting Palette.

- If you need to precisely line up objects, you'll find alignment and distribution commands in the Draw pop-up menu on the Drawing toolbar.

add sound files p. 70

- On Windows, PowerPoint can use the following kinds of sound files: AIFF, AU, MIDI, MP3, Windows Audio file (WAV), and Windows Media Audio file (WMA). On the Mac, Power-Point supports any audio type that QuickTime supports, including AAC, AIFF, AU, MIDI, MOV, MP3, SFIL, and WAV.

- Depending on your presentation setting, it can be effective to attach a music file to the first and last slides of your presentation, which helps introduce and end the show.

- You'll find additional sound effects in the Clip Organizer on Windows.

use video clips p. 71

- On Windows, PowerPoint can use the following kinds of video files: Windows Media file (ASF), Windows Video file (AVI), MPEG, and Windows Media Video files (WMV). On the Mac, PowerPoint supports any video type that QuickTime supports, including AVI, DV, Flash (SWF), MPEG, and MOV.

extra bits

add diagrams (Win) p. 72

- You can add an organizational chart on a Mac, though you don't get the other nice pre-designed diagrams. Choose Insert > Object, then from the resulting Object dialog, choose Microsoft Organization Chart and click OK. A separate program, also called Microsoft Organization Chart, opens and lets you create and adjust the org chart. When you're done, close the program, and the new org chart is automatically pasted into your PowerPoint slide.

add charts p. 74

- Besides entering chart data directly in PowerPoint's datasheet, you can also copy and paste spreadsheet data from Microsoft Excel into the datasheet.

- If you're more comfortable working with charts in Excel, you can create a chart in Excel, copy it, then paste it into a PowerPoint slide.

add tables p. 76

- When you're editing a table, the Tables and Borders toolbar appears. You can use this toolbar to draw new lines in your table; erase existing lines; add a fill color to table cells; and change the thickness of the lines in the table. It also contains two handy buttons to help you resize rows and columns: Distribute Rows Evenly and Distribute Columns Evenly.

7. make it move

Your presentation is nearly complete. You've written the content, chosen a design, set the layout of each slide, and added images and media files. The last major task before you give the presentation is to give it some movement, by adding slide transitions and slide effects.

Slide transitions are the animated effects the audience sees when you switch from one slide to the next in the presentation. PowerPoint provides many different transition effects, and you've probably seen them all (even the really tasteless ones). Slide effects are animations that occur within a slide. For example, you can have each bullet point fade onto the screen as you get to it, and then dim to gray text as you move to the next point. Or you can have an image, graph, or diagram glide onto the screen.

In this chapter, you'll rearrange the order of your slides in the Slide Sorter View and then set slide transitions and effects.

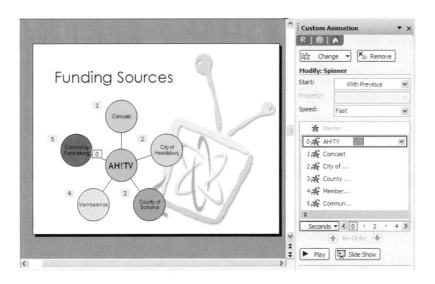

rearrange slides

As you've been developing your presentation, you've seen how the topic of one slide flows into the next, and perhaps that flow is perfect for your show. But maybe the presentation would be a bit better, a touch tighter, if you moved that slide there, and moved that other slide over here. PowerPoint's Slide Sorter View shows you many slides at once, and allows you to drag one or more slides to other places in the presentation. Slide Sorter View also offers a convenient way to apply slide transitions and slide effects to multiple slides in one operation (you'll see how to do that in the next section).

To enter Slide Sorter View, choose View > Slide Sorter, or click the Slide Sorter View button at the bottom of the PowerPoint window.

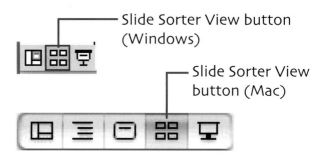

Slide Sorter View button (Windows)

Slide Sorter View button (Mac)

In Slide Sorter View, you see thumbnail views of the slides; the currently selected slide shows a darker border around it.

Selected slide

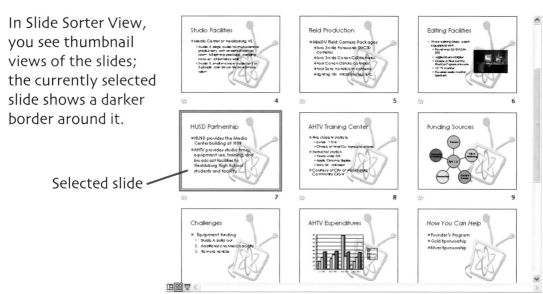

make it move

To move a slide, click on the slide you want to move, then drag it to the new location. As you drag, an indicator line will show you where the slide will go when you release the mouse button.

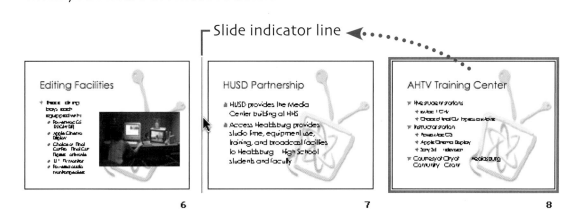

Slide indicator line

set slide transitions

Transitions between slides can enhance your presentation's message and add visual interest to your show. You can add transitions to one or more slides at one time in either the Normal or Slide Sorter View (though I find it's usually easier to use Slide Sorter View). PowerPoint includes dozens of special transition effects to choose from, ranging from subtle to the polar opposite of subtle. With slide transitions, as with any animation in PowerPoint, you should live by the principle "less is more" when choosing transitions, because the flashier they are, the more quickly your audience will become tired of them.

1 Switch to Slide Sorter View to begin setting the transition; choose View > Slide Sorter.

2 Select the slides to which you want to apply the transitions. To select multiple slides, click on the first slide, hold down the Shift key, and click the last slide. Those slides and all slides in between are selected.

3 Choose Slide Show > Slide Transition.

On Windows, the Slide Transition Task Pane opens.

Transition list ——

Transition speed ——

Sound pop-up menu ——

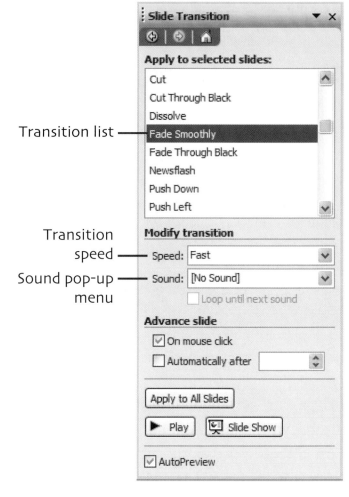

make it move

On the Mac, the Slide Transition dialog appears.

Transition pop-up menu ——

Preview area ——

Transition speed ——

Sound pop-up menu ——

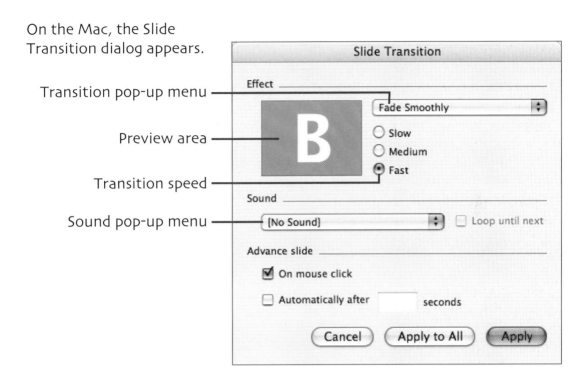

4 On Windows, choose a transition effect from the transition list which applies the effect. If the AutoPreview setting at the bottom of the Task Pane is checked, you'll see a preview of the effect on the slide thumbnails in the Slide Sorter.

On the Mac, choose the transition effect from the transition pop-up menu. You'll see the effect in the preview area of the dialog.

5 Choose the speed of the transition by selecting it from the Speed pop-up menu (Windows) or clicking one of the Speed radio buttons (Mac).

6 If you want, choose a sound from the Sound pop-up menu. This sound will play between each of the selected slides. Use this sparingly; many audiences hate sound effects in presentations.

7 Click Apply to add the transition to the selected slides, or click Apply to All Slides (Apply to All) to add the transition to the entire presentation.

set slide effects (Win)

You've seen slide effects in most presentations; these are the effects that are responsible for titles, bulleted text, charts, or diagrams that fade, wipe, or animate onto the screen when the presenter clicks the mouse button. PowerPoint for Windows has two ways to apply animation to objects on your slides. The first way is to use animation schemes, which are preset animations that are easy to apply. The other way is to create a custom animation, where you're in complete control of each of the elements on the slide.

To apply an animation scheme, first choose View > Normal, then display the slide to which you want to apply the animation scheme. Next, choose Slide Show > Animation Schemes. The Animation Schemes Task Pane opens.

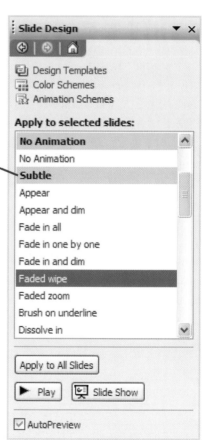

The scheme list is divided into categories: Subtle, Moderate, and Exciting, in rough order of how extreme the scheme is. At the subtle end, a scheme such as Wipe makes the title fade onto the screen, then each bullet point wipes onto the screen from left to right. At the extreme end, the motion sickness-inducing Neutron scheme makes each letter in the title spiral in an orbit to its final destination, then each bullet point slides up from the bottom of the screen. Ick. Unless you have a very specific reason, I suggest you stick with the schemes in the Subtle category.

Click on a scheme in the scheme list. The slide pane shows you a preview of the animation. To play it again, click the Play button at the bottom of the Task Pane. If you're happy with the effect, click Apply to All Slides, and the entire presentation will take on the animation scheme.

make it move

add custom animation

Sometimes animation schemes don't really do the trick; you need more control over moving items on or off the screen, or you want to apply an animated effect to a particular part of the slide. For example, in the Access Healdsburg presentation, the Funding Sources slide contains a diagram that can be enhanced with a little animation. PowerPoint for Windows has a terrific custom animation capability.

Because I'm going to talk about each of the funding sources, I'll build up the diagram a bubble at a time, starting with the green center bubble (which will appear on the screen first), then adding each of the source bubbles, beginning at the top and moving clockwise. Each bubble will appear after I click the mouse.

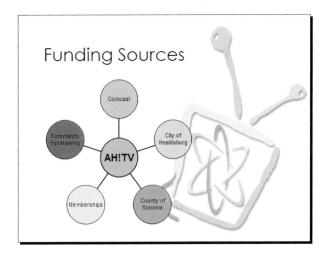

Begin by choosing Slide Show > Custom Animation, which opens the Custom Animation Task Pane.

Animation list ————

Select the first element you want to animate; I chose the center bubble in the diagram.

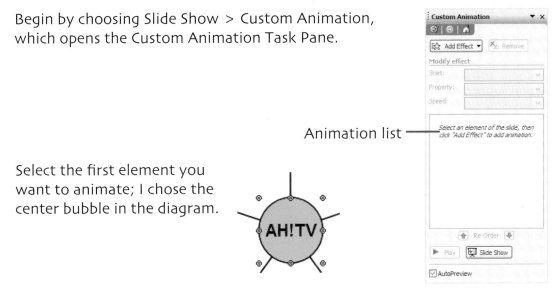

add custom animation

The Add Effect button in the Task Pane is really a pop-up menu; choose an effect from the Entrance category (because you're animating how the element will be entering the slide; if you want the element to fly off the screen later, you can add an effect from the Exit category). I chose Spinner, which fades up the element while spinning it.

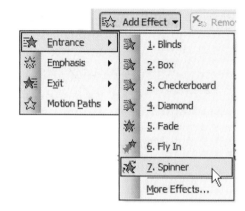

The effect preview shows that the entire diagram spins onto the screen, which isn't what we want; we want each bubble in the diagram to appear separately. A look at the animation list shows that the whole diagram is set to animate.

To split the elements of the diagram so that we can animate each one separately, right-click the item in the animation list, and choose Effect Options.

make it move

In the resulting Spinner dialog, click the Diagram Animation tab, then make a choice from the drop-down menu. I want the center bubble to appear first, followed by each bubble moving clockwise, so I chose Clockwise – Outward. Click OK.

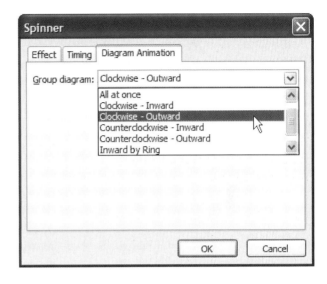

Each element of the diagram is now numbered separately, and the animation list contains an entry for each element. If you want, you can now add a separate animation effect for each element. Just right-click each element in the animation list and make changes.

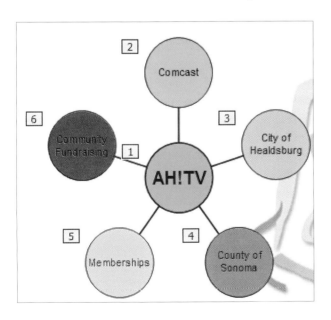

make it move

set slide effects (Mac)

Like its Windows sibling, PowerPoint for Mac gives you two ways to control slide effects. Preset animations apply simple animations to the elements on the slide; custom animation gives you more control over each element (though not, alas, as much control as PowerPoint for Windows).

To use a preset animation, first choose View > Normal, then display the slide to which you want to apply the preset. Next, choose Slide Show > Preset Animations, then choose a preset from the cascading menu. The animation is applied to the slide.

Custom animations are a bit more complex to apply, but are much more flexible.

1 Begin by choosing View > Normal, then display the slide to which you want to apply the animation.

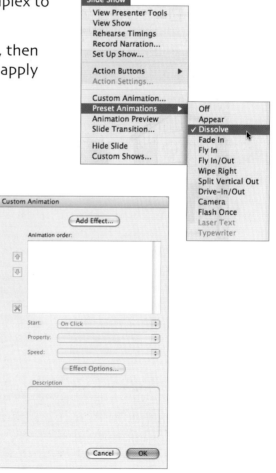

2 Choose Slide Show > Custom Animation. The Custom Animation dialog appears.

Preview pane

make it move

3 In the Select to animate list, which contains the elements of the slide that can be animated, select the element you want to animate.

4 Click Add Effect. The Animation Effects dialog appears. It is divided into four categories: Basic, Subtle, Moderate, and Exciting. It's a good idea to stick to items in the Basic or Subtle category; it's better for the audience. I chose a wipe effect for the bulleted text on my slides.

As you click an effect, you can see its result in the Preview pane of the Custom Animation dialog.

The elements appear in the Animation order list, and the animation controls become active.

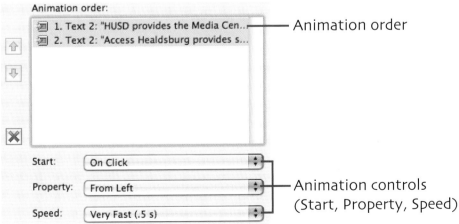

Animation order

Animation controls
(Start, Property, Speed)

set slide effects (Mac)

In this case, I want to change the wipe direction from From Bottom to From Left, so the text appears in the same way that people read. I choose this in the Property pop-up menu (this menu changes depending on the kind of effect you've set, so it may not look exactly like the one shown).

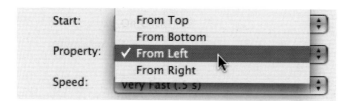

You can also change when the animation starts and its speed, from Very Slow (5 seconds) to Very Fast (.5 second), or you can set a custom time.

5 Click OK to apply the custom animation.

make it move

extra bits

rearrange slides p. 82

- If you want to move a group of slides at one time, in Slide Sorter View, click on the first slide, hold down the Shift key, and click the last slide. Those two slides and all slides in between will be selected, and you can drag and drop them as a group.

set slide transitions p. 84

- You can also select multiple slides in the Slide Sorter by clicking in a blank space between slides, then dragging over the slides you want.

- By default, PowerPoint is set so that the transition is triggered when you click the mouse during your presentation. But you can use the settings in the Advance slide section of the Slide Transition Task Pane to set the slide to automatically change to the next slide after a given number of seconds.

- Windows users have it a little better than Mac users when it comes to setting transitions. The Slide Transition Task Pane not only allows you to preview transition effects with thumbnails of the actual slides, but you can also use the Play button to trigger the preview manually, and the Slide Show button puts PowerPoint into Slide Show mode, allowing you to see the slides and transitions full screen.

Mac users must apply a transition, then test it in the Slide Show or the small Animation Preview window.

To open the Animation Preview

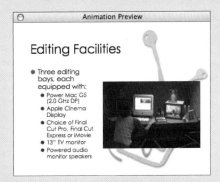

window, choose Slide Show > Animation Preview. Click anywhere in the window to see the preview play.

- You can purchase add-ins (programs that extend PowerPoint) that give you additional slide transitions beyond the ones that come with PowerPoint. One well-known maker of these add-ins is Crystal Graphics (www.crystalgraphics.com), with their PowerPlugs series.

extra bits

set slide effects (Win) p. 86

- If you're having problems controlling when images on your slides appear, it's probably because the image is using an image placeholder. The placeholder is part of the slide's master, and it can't be changed with the animation controls. The solution is to select the image, then choose Edit > Cut. The picture will disappear, and the placeholder will appear. Select the placeholder, then press Backspace (Delete) to get rid of it. Finally, choose Edit > Paste to bring back the picture. Now the picture is in the same layer as the rest of the slide elements, and it will respond to the animation controls.

add custom animation p. 87

- The choices in the Effect Options dialog will be different, depending on what you have selected. For example, if you're animating bulleted text, there will be a Text Animation tab in the dialog.

- You can change the timing for each element in the animation list separately. The orange bar in the list is the length of the animation for that element.

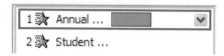

To change the length of the element's animation, point at the orange bar. The cursor will change to a double-headed arrow. Click and drag the bar to the desired length.

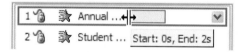

- PowerPoint for Windows can create and play animations that the Mac version can't match, including animation of elements along paths, and it has many more effects from which to choose. Motion path animation effects created in PowerPoint for Windows will play in PowerPoint 2004 for Mac, but not in earlier versions. Custom animations of diagrams created on Windows will not play in PowerPoint for Mac; the diagram will appear, but without its animation.

make it move

set slide effects
(Mac) p. 90

- To apply preset animations to all the slides in your presentation in one operation, switch to Slide Sorter View, and choose Edit > Select All or press Cmd-A. Then choose the preset animation from the Slide Show menu.

- Click the Effect Options button in the Custom Animation dialog to get more precise control over effects, timing, and specific animation controls for the selected kind of slide element.

8. prepare to present

Now that you've finished putting together your presentation, there are some things you can do to make it better before you step on stage. The easiest way to improve your talk is familiar to anyone who has done any kind of performance: Rehearse it before you get in front of your audience. You can also send your presentation to co-workers for their comments; it's amazing how often other people will suggest a great point that you missed.

To help you give the presentation, you can create and print speaker notes, and to help the audience, you can print handouts containing your slides. In this chapter, you'll see how a little final preparation can help make your presentation a smashing success.

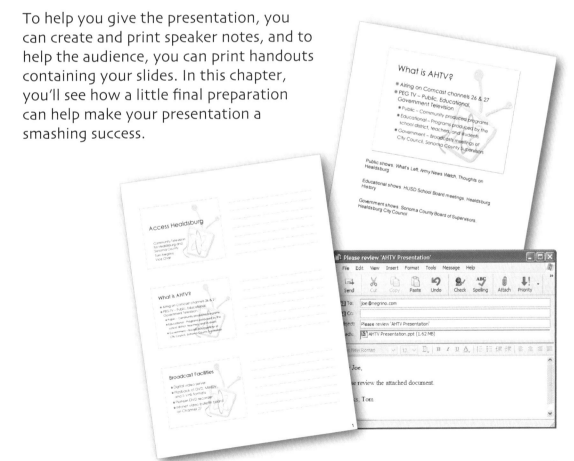

get colleague review

One easy way to improve your presentation is to show it to other people for their comments. You'll often gain valuable insights into your presentation by getting this feedback. I've had some co-workers suggest areas that I should have mentioned, and others give me some great images that I incorporated into my show. If possible, allow people to watch you rehearse, then solicit their constructive criticism. Believe me, your final presentation will be better for it.

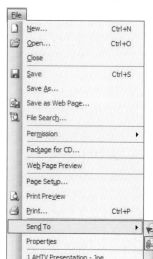

PowerPoint allows you to send your presentation file to colleagues as an email attachment. To do this, open the presentation. Then choose File > Send To > Mail Recipient (as Attachment).

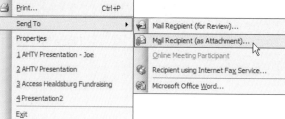

Your email program will open and create a new message with a subject filled in and the file attached. Address the email, enter a note for your recipient, and click Send.

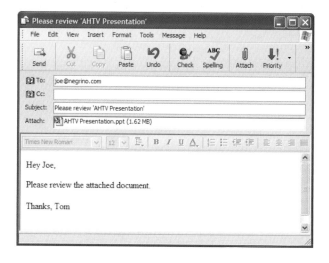

prepare to present

rehearse your show

Rehearsals are key to any production, whether it is a Broadway play, a concert, or your slide show. When you rehearse your presentation, you get a better feel for what you want to say to accompany the slides, and it helps you make sure that you stay within your allotted time. Being able to do the whole presentation at your own pace is infinitely preferable to trying to stretch if you run short, or worse, getting the hook if you run too long. Unless you have a lot of experience presenting, rehearsal is the best way to find out how long your presentation really is.

PowerPoint has a built-in rehearsal feature that can tell you how long you spend on each slide, and when you're done, it will tell you the total time for the presentation.

Choose Slide Show > Rehearse Timings. The slide show appears full-screen, covering up everything else on your monitor.

On Windows, the Rehearsal toolbar appears.

Next ——— Pause ——— Slide time ——— Total time

On the Mac, you get a small timer that changes for each slide. Clicking the timer advances the presentation to the next slide or next slide effect, the same as clicking the mouse.

0:01:10

rehearse your show

Give the presentation for each slide. To trigger the next slide effect or to advance to the next slide, click the mouse button or press the right arrow key on the keyboard. When you are done with the presentation, PowerPoint displays a dialog asking if you are happy with the slide timings, and if you want it to store them for future use. If you want, PowerPoint can use these timings to advance your presentation automatically when you give it, rather than you advancing it manually.

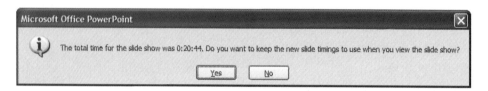

If you click yes, PowerPoint for Windows drops you into Slide Sorter mode, where you can review the timing for each slide. On the Mac, PowerPoint asks if you want to go to the Slide Sorter. You can see a variety of information about each slide in the Slide Sorter.

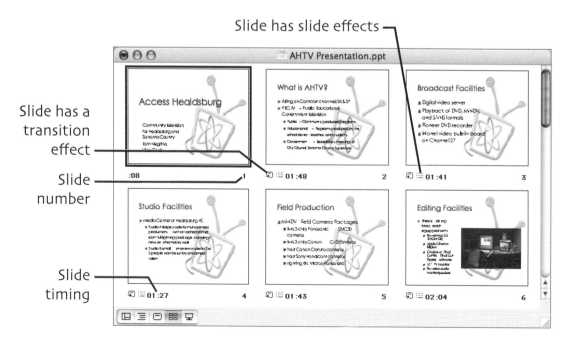

prepare to present

create speaker notes

Speaker Notes are printed notes that you'll use to help keep you on track while you're giving the presentation. As you saw way back in Chapter 1, PowerPoint has an area in Normal view where you can type in your notes for each slide.

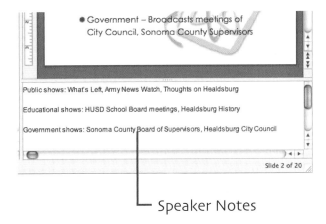

— Speaker Notes

These notes don't appear on the presentation screen, but if you're using a laptop to present with an external projector or monitor, the notes will appear on the laptop screen, so you can see them, but your audience can't.

If you prefer, you can also print Speaker Notes (let's say that you won't be operating the computer yourself) so that you can refer to notes without being tethered to your computer. When PowerPoint prints Speaker Notes, they appear one slide to a page, with your notes underneath.

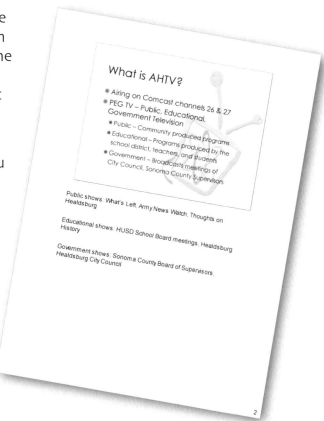

print speaker notes

To print the Speaker Notes, choose File > Print. From the Print what pop-up menu, choose Notes Pages (on the Mac, Notes), then click OK (on the Mac, click Print).

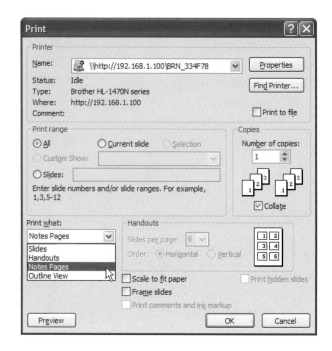

prepare to present

print slides & handouts

You can print slides and handouts for your use (or the audience's) in color (with a color printer, of course), grayscale, or black and white. When you print slides, just the slide appears on the page, filling the page, in landscape format (meaning the slide is rotated so that the wide side of the slide is aligned with the length of the printed page).

For handouts, PowerPoint gives you a choice of 1, 2, 3, 4, 6, or 9 slides per printed page, shrinking the slides to fit. If you want your audience to be able to take notes easily, I suggest that you use the 3-slides-per-page option; it's the only one that provides lines next to the slides for audience notes, and the slides are a good size for easy readibility.

To print slides, choose File > Print. In the Print dialog, choose Slides from the Print what pop-up menu. From the Color/grayscale (on the Mac it's called Output) pop-up menu, decide how you want the page to print. If you choose Grayscale or Pure Black and White, the background of the slide will not print. Click OK (Print) to print the slides.

print slides & handouts

To print handouts in Windows, choose File > Print. In the Print dialog, choose Handouts from the Print what pop-up menu. The handouts section of the Print dialog will become active. Choose the number of slides per handout page you want (a preview icon gives you an idea what the layout will look like). Make a choice from the Color/grayscale pop-up menu, then click OK to print the handouts.

Preview icon

To print handouts on the Mac, choose File > Print. In the Print dialog, choose Handouts from the Print What pop-up menu. A preview of the page appears in the Quick Preview area on the left side of the dialog. Make a color choice from the Output pop-up menu, then click Print to print the handouts.

Quick Preview

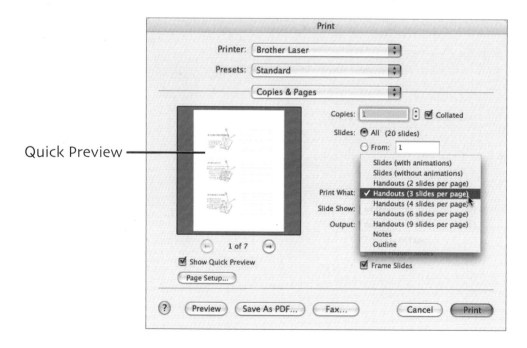

extra bits

get colleague review p. 98

- If your co-worker doesn't have PowerPoint installed on his or her machine, you have a few options. You could, for example, print the presentation, then send your colleague the paper. But if you want to send a file via email, you need to get the file into a format that can be easily read, such as PDF (Portable Document Format), which can be read by the free Adobe Reader on most operating systems, and also by Preview on the Mac.

  Mac users have it easy; they can print any file, including a PowerPoint file, to PDF simply by clicking the Save As PDF button at the bottom of the Print dialog. Windows users don't have this built-in PDF facility. If you want to print to PDF, I suggest that you look into Macromedia FlashPaper 2 ($79), which allows you to print any file in either PDF format or as a Macromedia Flash file. FlashPaper 2 even has plug-ins for Microsoft Office that allow you to easily convert any Office file to PDF or Flash.

- PowerPoint for Windows has a better (but more complex) way to get and incorporate reviewer's comments than the Mac version. You can save a presentation in a special format called "Presentation for Review," after which you send the presentation to others. They can then make changes to the file and email it back to you. When you open it, you can merge their changes with your original presentation file. Detailing this review process is beyond the scope of this book; to learn how to do it, choose Help > Microsoft Office PowerPoint Help, then search for "review." Click the topic "About sending a presentation for review."

rehearse your show p. 99

- When you're rehearsing timings, it's a good idea to speak your narration just as you would during the presentation. Stand up or sit up straight, breathe normally, and speak clearly without rushing.

extra bits

print slides & handouts p. 103

- The choice of 1 slide per handout is only available on PowerPoint for Windows.

- On the Mac, you have the option of printing slides with or without animations. If you print with animations, you will get as many slides printed as you have slide effects. For example, let's say you have a slide with a title and three bullet points. The bullet points wipe onto the screen one by one. Printing the slide with animations means that you'll get four pages, one for the slide with just the title, and then one more page for each bullet point. Most of the time, you'll want to print slides without animations.

9. deliver your presentation

Finally, you're ready to give your presentation. You've arrived at the room where you'll give the talk, and perhaps the audience is beginning to arrive. You need to connect your notebook computer to the projector, set up your computer so that it recognizes the two displays (the notebook screen and the projector), and run the show.

If you don't have a notebook, and you know that the presentation venue will have a computer and projector waiting for you, you can burn your presentation to a CD and just bring that. See Chapter 10 for how to burn a CD of your presentation.

During the presentation, you can use PowerPoint's Presenter Tools, which allow you to control your show and to display your Speaker Notes as you present, using an interface that only you see. You can also annotate your slides and make additional notes during the presentation.

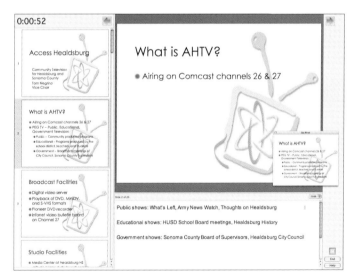

set up projector (Win)

You'll typically want to deliver a presentation with a notebook computer connected to a projector or large monitor. Your computer must support multiple monitors. To use multiple monitors on Windows, you must be running Windows XP (or Windows 2000 SP3 or later). Your notebook must also have a VGA video output (most do). You'll view the presentation on your notebook screen, and your audience will view the projected screen.

First, turn off the projector and computer.

Hook the projector (if you don't have a projector, you can use another external display, such as a monitor) up to the notebook. Most PC notebooks have a VGA port, but some require an adapter; check the documentation for your notebook.

Turn on the projector and the computer. The notebook should recognize the existence of a second display. To configure your computer for multiple monitors, right-click the desktop, then choose Properties from the shortcut menu. The Display Properties dialog will open. Click the Settings tab.

The two monitors will appear as icons in the dialog. The notebook screen is always the primary monitor (labeled with a 1), by default.

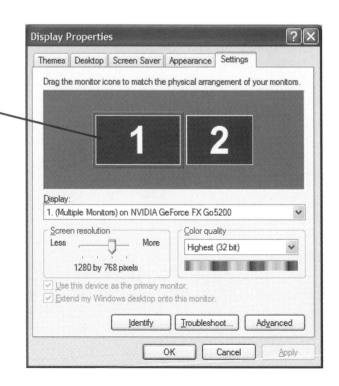

Click the icon for the second monitor, click "Extend my Windows desktop onto this monitor," and then click Apply. The second monitor should now show your desktop wallpaper. Click OK to save your settings.

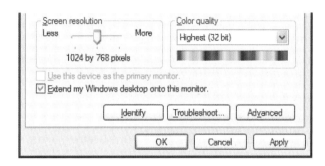

Now that you are set up for multiple monitors, you need to tell PowerPoint that you'll be using a projector. Open your presentation in PowerPoint, then choose Slide Show > Set Up Show. In the Multiple monitors section, choose the projector from the "Display slide show on" pop-up menu.

If you want to use the Presenter View, click the Show Presenter View checkbox, then click OK. To learn more about Presenter View, see use presenter view, later in this chapter.

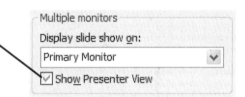

set up projector (Mac)

Setting up dual-display mode and hooking up a projector to a Mac is straight-forward; just follow these steps.

First, turn off the projector and computer.

Hook the projector up to the Mac. Apple notebooks usually need an adapter to connect their VGA output to the projector's VGA input. Older iBooks, iBook G4, and 12" PowerBook G4 machines use the Apple mini-DVI-to-VGA adapter; the 15" and 17" PowerBook G4 machines use the Apple DVI-to-VGA adapter. All of these machines come with their respective adapters. The older Titanium PowerBook G4 notebooks have a VGA port, so they don't need an adapter.

Turn on the projector and the computer. The Mac will recognize the existence of a second display and will go into mirrored mode, which puts the same image on the external display as is on the notebook's screen. Open System Preferences and choose Displays. In the Displays dialog, click the Display tab. Two windows will appear, one for each display.

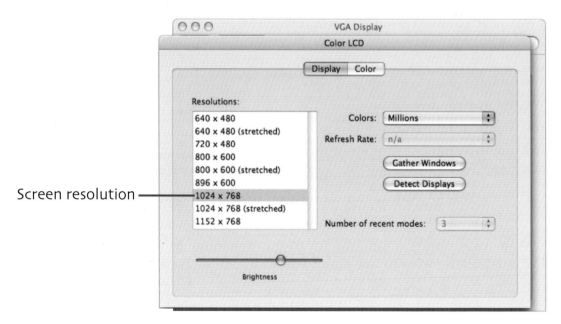

Click the screen resolution that matches the resolution of the projector. It will typically be either 800 X 600 or 1024 X 768. The two mirrored screens will change to the selected resolution.

If you don't want to use PowerPoint's Presenter Tools, your setup is done. To use Presenter Tools, you'll need to take the displays out of mirrored mode and into extended desktop mode, where the projector and notebook screen become one continuous desktop. If your Mac doesn't support extended desktop mode (iBooks, for example, only do mirroring), you can't use Presenter Tools.

Open System Preferences and choose Displays. In the Displays dialog, click the Arrangement tab, then clear the Mirror Displays checkbox.

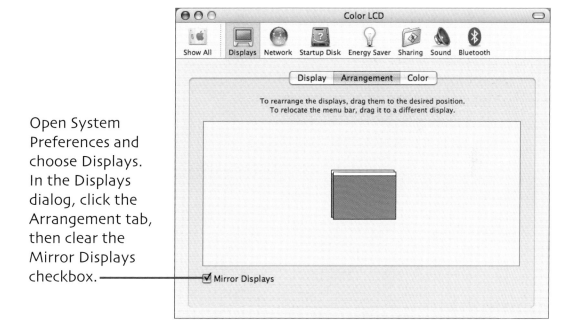

You can now set the resolution for each display separately. Click on the Display tab for each of the two display windows, and click the desired resolution.

prepare yourself

So now you have created a terrific presentation, your notebook and the projector are set up, and your audience is beginning to drift into the room, eager for the show. But what about you? What about your needs? If you're like most people, you're feeling a little stage fright at this point. Dealing with your butterflies is what this section is about. Here are some tips that can help you keep your presentation running smoothly.

- If you can, get to the presentation venue early. Sit or stand where you will be speaking, and make sure that your seating (or the podium) is adjusted the way that you want it. Take a moment to adjust the microphone (if any) and work with the venue's audio technician to get the levels right before the audience arrives. Make sure you have a spot to place a cup of water. Getting comfortable with the physical space and facilities helps a lot.

- If you have the opportunity to greet some of the audience members as they enter the room, you should do so. It's easier to speak to people you know, even if all you've done is said hello.

- Before you begin, visualize yourself giving a successful presentation. Imagine that you've spoken very well, and hear your audience's applause. Picture audience members coming up to congratulate you after the show. It sounds a bit silly, but visualizing success works.

- Concentrate on your message, not on the audience. If you focus on what you're saying, you will distract yourself from being nervous.

- If you are nervous, never apologize for it. Except in extreme cases, most audiences don't notice that speakers are nervous, and it doesn't help your case to point it out.

deliver your presentation

- Always keep in mind that your audience wants you to succeed. People don't go to a presentation thinking, "I sure hope this guy does a lousy talk and wastes my time." They want to get something out of your presentation as much as you do.

- Unless you are a professional comedian, keep the jokes to a minimum, or skip them altogether. A joke that falls flat isn't a good way to start a show.

- Never read straight from a script. Very few people can read from a script without putting their audience to sleep; we call those few people actors.

- Don't read your slides aloud word for word. Your slides should be signposts and reminders of what you want to say. Using your slides as a teleprompter is another way to lose audience interest. If you need prompting for your topics, use your Speaker Notes.

- After the presentation is over, thank your audience and make yourself available for questions. Make sure to get feedback from them so that you can improve your next show.

run the presentation

To run the presentation, choose View > Slide Show, or click the Slide Show button at the lower-left corner of the PowerPoint window. On Windows, you can also press F5 on your keyboard.

Slide Show button (Windows)   Slide Show button (Mac)

The presentation appears on the screen. If you are using a projector or external monitor, the presentation appears on whichever screen you selected during setup.

During the presentation, if you're not using the Presenter View (Presenter Tools), PowerPoint provides some onscreen tools that you can use to control your show. They include ways to move to the previous and next slides, a menu that allows you to jump to any slide or custom show in your presentation, and a way to pause your presentation or turn the screen black for a moment.

These controls appear at the bottom-left corner of the screen when you move the pointer over them. On Windows, they are unobtrusive icons.

Previous slide ——— ——— Next slide

Control menu

On the Mac, there is a pop-up menu with the controls; click the menu's icon to bring up the pop-up menu.

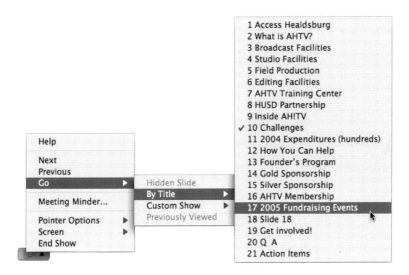

To advance to the next slide or slide effect, click the mouse button, or press the Right Arrow key on the keyboard. To return to a previous slide, press the Left Arrow key.

At the end of the show, PowerPoint for Windows will go to a black screen; click the mouse button to leave Slide Show mode and go back to the Power-Point window. On the Mac, you drop out of Slide Show mode and go back to the PowerPoint window automatically when you advance past the last slide. To end the slide show manually, press the Esc key on your keyboard.

use presenter view

Presenter View (called Presenter Tools on the Mac) is a new feature that gives you more control over the presentation as you are giving it. It gives you a control panel that you see on your notebook's screen, while the audience sees the regular slide show on the projector.

This mode is only available when you are using multiple monitors on Windows; on the Mac, choosing View > Presenter Tools allows you to use the Presenter Tools to rehearse your presentation without a second display.

In Presenter View, you get a scrolling list of your slide thumbnails, a large view of the current slide, buttons for Previous Slide and Next Slide, your Speaker Notes, and best of all, an onscreen timer that tells you the elapsed time of your presentation. This timer is a great tool to help you stay on track; by knowing how long you have been talking, you can speed up or slow down to keep within your allotted speaking time.

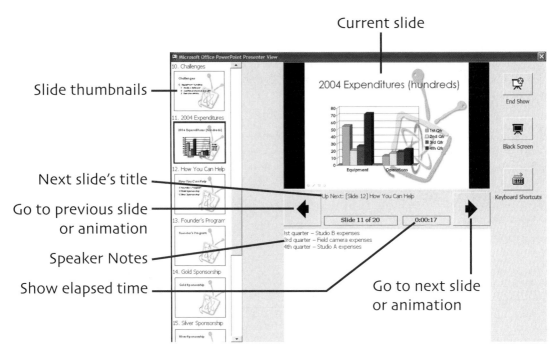

Presenter View for Windows

deliver your presentation

On the Mac, Presenter Tools works in much the same way, except that you get a small floating Up Next window that shows you the upcoming slide or slide animation effect.

Presenter Tools for Mac

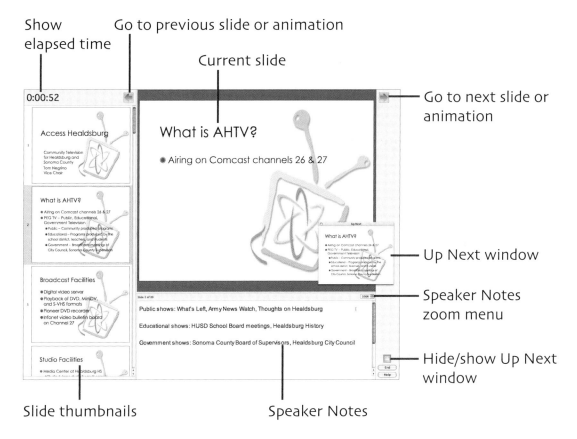

To jump ahead to any slide in your presentation, scroll the list of slide thumbnails, then click the slide you want. If there is a slide transition associated with the slide you clicked, it will trigger and the slide will appear on the projector.

create custom shows

Have you ever needed to show part of a presentation, but not all of it, for a particular audience? For example, let's say that you have a presentation about a new product that includes slides with commission rates for the sales department. When you give the presentation to the marketing department, you can omit the commission slides by creating a custom show. This is a subset of the presentation that includes just the slides you want. To create a custom show, open your presentation, then choose Slide Show > Custom Shows. The Custom Shows dialog appears.

Click the New button, and in the Define Custom Show dialog, name the custom show, then select slides from the list on the left, and click the Add button to add them to the list on the right.

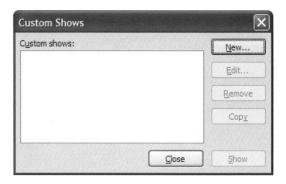

Click OK, and then, back in the Custom Shows dialog, click Close.

To run the custom show, choose Slide Show > Set Up Show. In the Show slides section of the resulting dialog, click Custom show, and then choose the show you want from the pop-up menu. Click OK. When you run the presentation, the custom show will run.

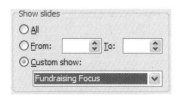

extra bits

set up projector (Win) p. 108

- If you're not sure which monitor is which, click the Identify button in the Settings tab of the Display Properties dialog. Large numbers will appear on each monitor.

set up projector (Mac) p. 110

- Unlike PowerPoint for Windows, you don't need to make any special settings in PowerPoint for the Mac so that it uses a second monitor. The Presenter Tools will appear on the monitor with the menu bar (usually the notebook screen), and the presentation will appear on the projector.

- Most of the time, you don't actually have to turn the computer and projector off before you hook them together. You can connect them, then open the Displays pane of System Preferences. If two display windows don't appear, click the Detect Displays button, which will scan for displays, after which the second display window will appear.

prepare yourself p. 112

- If you want to become a better presenter, there are some terrific online resources. I'm a fan of the Beyond Bullets weblog (www.beyondbullets.com), written by Cliff Atkinson. It's full of practical tips and information that will help you think about using PowerPoint in a different way.

- The best PowerPoint presentation I've ever seen didn't use a single bullet point. It was performed by Scott McCloud, who wrote Understanding Comics (1993, Perennial Currents), a brilliant, essential book that will help you understand all forms of visual communications, including PowerPoint. And it's mostly done as comics! Trust me on this one.

deliver your presentation

119

extra bits

run the presentation p. 114

- Besides clicking the mouse or pressing the Right Arrow key, you can also use the following keys to advance slides or perform the next animation: N, Page Down, Enter (Return), Down Arrow, or the spacebar. I usually use the spacebar when I present, because it's the biggest and easiest to find by touch while I'm talking.

- Besides pressing the Left Arrow key, you can also use the following keys to return to the previous slide or return to the previous animation: P, Page Up, Up Arrow, or Delete.

- To jump to a particular slide number, type number and Enter (Return).

- Press B or Period to turn the screen all black; press W or Comma to turn it all white. This is useful if you want to pause for a moment; press the key again to return to the presentation.

- PowerPoint for Mac has the ability to take notes and create action items while you're giving your presentation, using a feature called Meeting Minder. To use it, while your presentation is onscreen, choose Meeting Minder from the Actions pop-up menu at the lower-left corner of the screen.

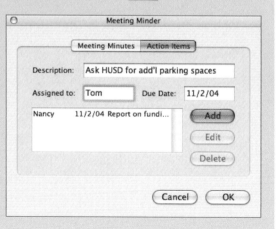

  The Meeting Minder window will appear. You can use it to take minutes or to record action items. If you create action items, they will appear on a new slide at the end of your presentation.

  PowerPoint for Windows eliminated the Meeting Minder feature beginning with PowerPoint 2003.

- There are a few great hardware accessories that can help almost any presentation. The first is an inexpensive laser pointer. These are essential for drawing your audience's attention to a part of your slide. I have a fancy (and pricey) laser pointer with a green beam, but that's because I'm a presentation geek. You can find the standard models with red beams for as little as $10. You can also benefit from a remote control for your computer, because they allow you to wirelessly roam anywhere on the stage, rather than being tied to your notebook. These units usually consist of a handheld control and a receiver that connects to your notebook via the USB port. Some of them, such as units from Keyspan (www.keyspan.com) and Targus (www.targus.com), have a built-in laser pointer. If you'll be presenting from a Mac, make sure that the remote is Mac-compatible (most are).

use presenter view p. 116

- On the Mac, you can use the Speaker Notes zoom menu to make the notes larger or smaller, so they are more comfortable to read.

- You can type new notes or change your Speaker Notes during the show on the Mac, but not on Windows. If you have the time while you're presenting, this allows you to incorporate audience feedback during the show.

- Those Previous Slide and Next Slide buttons in Presenter View are nice, but I find that it's easier to click on the much bigger current slide to move forward, or to keep a finger on the spacebar or Right Arrow key on the keyboard.

10. present everywhere

Given the smashing success of your presentation, chances are good that you'll be asked to provide it to others, or take it on the road. As usual, PowerPoint is up to the task. On Windows, you can turn your presentation into a CD that you can send anywhere; on the Mac, you can convert the presentation into a QuickTime movie; and you can even save the show as Web pages that can be viewed by anyone with a Web browser.

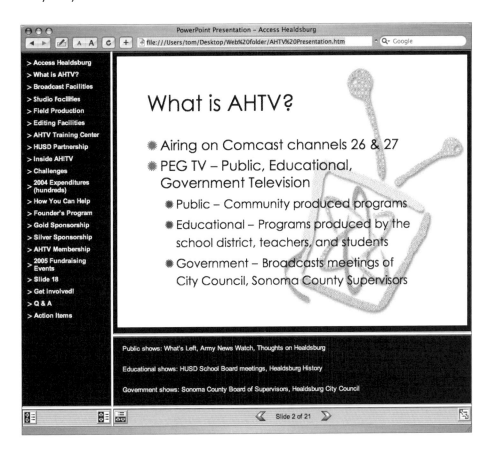

save to CD (Win)

PowerPoint for Windows allows you to turn your presentation into a package, which is a folder or a CD that contains all of the files associated with your presentation, including graphics, the PowerPoint file, fonts, external movies that are linked to the presentation, and sounds. The package will also contain a copy of the PowerPoint Viewer program, so the recipients of the CD don't even have to have PowerPoint installed to admire your work.

The reason why you want to create a package, rather than just copy the presentation file to a CD, is that you need to make sure that all of the elements of your presentation come along with the file. To be efficient and to make sure the PowerPoint presentation file doesn't get too big, PowerPoint will invisibly link large external files (especially video files) into the presentation, but will not copy those files into the presentation file. Similarly, fonts that you have on your system may not be available on another computer, and creating a PowerPoint package will copy the fonts used in the presentation for use by the PowerPoint Viewer.

With your presentation open, choose File > Package for CD. In the resulting dialog, if you don't like the default name of PresentationCD, you can change it.

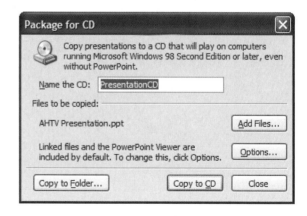

You're not limited to copying only one presentation file to the package; if you want to add additional presentations, click the Add Files button, then use the resulting Add Files dialog to choose the presentation files.

By default, the PowerPoint Viewer and linked external files will be included in the package, and all of the presentations in the package will play automatically when the CD is inserted. To change this, click Options.

present everywhere

If you don't want to include the PowerPoint Viewer, clear that checkbox in the Options dialog. If you want to change how the presentations play in the viewer, select one of the choices in the pop-up menu.

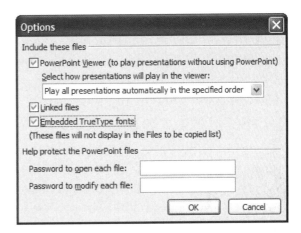

If you don't want to include linked files or embed fonts in the package, clear those checkboxes. Finally, you can optionally enter passwords that will be required to either open or modify the presentation files included in the package. When you're done setting options, click OK. You will return to the Package for CD dialog.

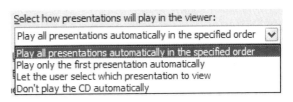

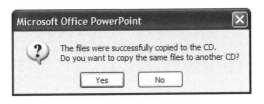

To burn the package to a CD, click Copy to CD. If there isn't a CD already in the drive, PowerPoint will ask you to insert a blank CD. Do so, then click the Retry button. The CD will be burned. PowerPoint will ask if you want to make additional CDs. Make your selection.

To save the package as a folder on your hard drive (which you can copy to a networked server, or even burn to a CD later), click Copy to Folder in the Package for CD dialog. In the resulting dialog, give the folder a

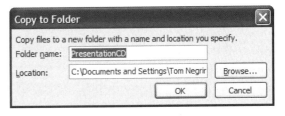

name and browse to the location on your hard drive where you want to save it.

save as movie (Mac)

On the Mac, you can save the presentation as a QuickTime movie, which can be played on any computer that has the QuickTime Player installed (all Macs have this, and QuickTime is often installed on Windows machines). This is PowerPoint for Mac's alternative answer to the PowerPoint Viewer program, but truth be told, it's a poor substitute.

PowerPoint presentations converted to QuickTime movies don't look as good as they do in PowerPoint; text is blocky and line art is noticeably lower in resolution. Worst of all, the resulting movies aren't interactive, which means that slide transitions and effects don't advance when you click the movie or press the Right Arrow key. Because of these fidelity problems, you should think carefully, run tests, and perhaps think about redesigning aspects of your presentation before you distribute it as a QuickTime movie.

To convert a presentation to a QuickTime movie, choose File > Make Movie. The Save dialog will appear. Navigate to where you want to save the movie.

You can change the name of the saved movie in the Save As box. You should adjust the movie settings. To do so, click Movie Options.

present everywhere

I recommend you use these movie settings:
Under Optimization, choose Quality;
choose movie dimensions of 640 x 480
(if you are going to edit this movie into
other video, click Custom and use 720 x
540); and leave the rest as shown. This
will give you a good-quality movie.

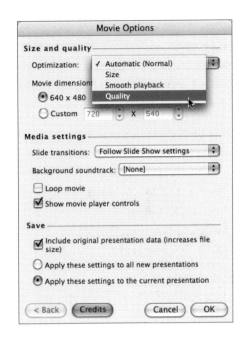

save as a web site

You can make your presentation available to the widest audience by converting it into a Web site and placing it on a Web server, either on the Internet or on your company's intranet. The presentation will be readable by anyone with a Web browser on any major computing platform (Windows, Mac, Linux, and others).

Presentations turned into Web sites resemble Normal View, with the outline on the left, a large area for the slide, and a space for Speaker Notes.

Web presentation from PowerPoint for Windows

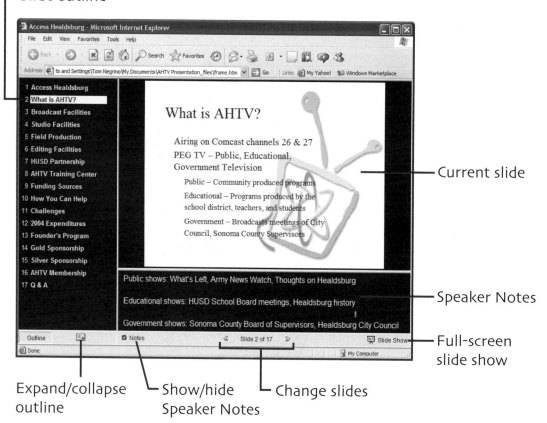

Slide outline

Current slide

Speaker Notes

Full-screen slide show

Expand/collapse outline

Show/hide Speaker Notes

Change slides

Presentations turned into Web sites from PowerPoint for Macintosh look similar to, but are not exactly the same as, presentations converted from PowerPoint for Windows.

Web presentation from PowerPoint for Mac

Slide outline

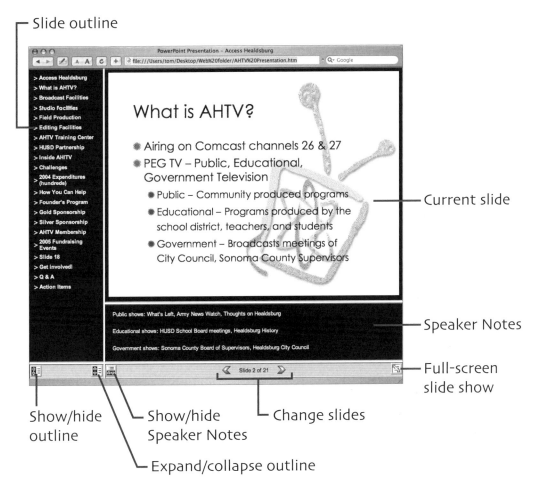

Current slide

Speaker Notes

Full-screen slide show

Show/hide outline

Show/hide Speaker Notes

Change slides

Expand/collapse outline

Besides the differences in the onscreen controls, you can see font differences on the slides, and the presentation converted from the Mac preserved the bullets on the slide, whereas the Windows version did not.

save as a web site (cont.)

To convert your presentation into a Web page, choose File > Save As Web Page. In the Save As dialog (Windows), Power-Point automatically fills in the file name and the Web page's title with the name of the presentation. You can edit the file name by changing it in the Save As dialog, and the page title by clicking the Change Title button.

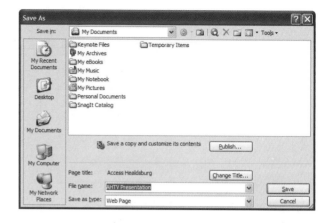

If you want to make adjustments to PowerPoint's default settings for Web pages, click Publish. The Publish as Web Page dialog appears, where you can choose whether or not to display your Speaker Notes on the Web. More advanced settings are available by clicking Web Options.

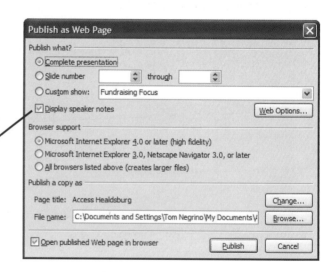

present everywhere

The Mac Save As dialog looks similar.

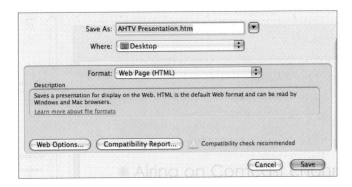

To change the page title or make other adjustments, click Web Options. In the resulting dialog, you can make a variety of useful changes to the look of the exported Web page.

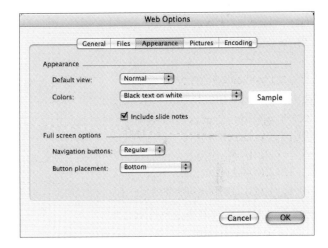

When you're done setting the options, click OK to leave the Web Options dialog, then click Save to save your Web page. The saved Web page will consist of two parts. One is the HTML file, and the other is a companion folder with the files that make up the presentation (text, graphics, etc.).

AHTV Presentation.htm

AHTV Presentation_files

You need to copy the Web page and the companion folder to a Web server for it to be viewable by others. If you don't know how to do that, ask your Web site's administrator.

extra bits

save to CD (Win) _{p. 124}

- If PowerPoint tells you that it isn't able to burn the CD, it may be because your computer has CD-burning software that is incompatible with direct burning from PowerPoint. That doesn't mean that you can't burn a CD with your presentation. The workaround is to save the package as a folder on your hard disk, then use your CD-burning program to copy the folder to a CD.

- Before you save the presentation to a CD, make sure that the presentation's settings are as you want them, especially if you have created Custom Shows. The show selected in Slide Show > Set Up Show will be the one that plays in the PowerPoint Viewer.

- Always preview the contents of the CD before you send it off!

- PowerPoint for Mac can save the presentation and associated files as a PowerPoint package, but the package works a little differently than a PowerPoint package on Windows, in that the PowerPoint Viewer program is not included. That's because Microsoft discontinued the PowerPoint Viewer program for Macintosh a few years back. The PowerPoint package on Macintosh is useful when you want to copy your presentation from one disk to another, and you want to make sure that any associated files that might be external to the presentation file (such as large movies or sounds) will be included. To create a PowerPoint package from your presentation on the Mac, choose File > Save As, and then choose PowerPoint Package from the Format pop-up menu in the Save As dialog.

present everywhere

- If you will be creating your presentations using PowerPoint 2004 for Mac and sharing them with Windows users (Power-Point files are largely compatible across platforms), it's a good idea to use the new Compatibility Report feature. This lets you know if your show will have any problems displaying on other (or older) versions of PowerPoint. Choose Tools > Compatibility Report, which opens the associated pane in the Toolbox. If the report shows any problems, you should consider making changes in the presentation.

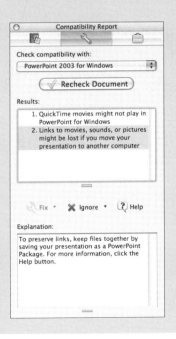

save as movie (Mac) p. 126

- If there are slide timings in your presentation, the QuickTime movie will use them for the duration of each slide. Most of the time, you'll want the movie to be run manually, meaning that viewers will advance through the presentation on their own. For manual operation, you'll need to clear the slide timings. To do that, switch to Slide Sorter View, and select all the slides in the presentation. Choose Slide Show > Slide Transition, then in the Advance Slide section of the Slide Transition dialog, clear the "Automatically after X seconds" checkbox, and then click Apply to All.

- If you need to install QuickTime for Windows (so you can play a presentation converted to a movie on a Windows machine), you can download the free player from http://www.apple.com/quicktime/download/.

extra bits

- Interestingly, Apple's competing presentation program, Keynote, does a better job of converting presentations to QuickTime movies than PowerPoint does. The movie looks better, plays more smoothly, and is fully interactive, working more like the file would in Keynote or PowerPoint. Keynote also does a very good job of importing PowerPoint files. So if you have Keynote and you need QuickTime movie output, consider first converting your Power-Point file to Keynote, then exporting the Keynote file to a QuickTime movie.

save as a web site p. 128

- If you have upgraded to Windows XP Service Pack 2, you will discover that Internet Explorer objects to viewing your exported PowerPoint presentation. That's because the presentation uses scripting and Active X controls to enhance the viewing experience. Internet Explorer will show the Information Bar, letting you know that the content you are trying to load may be unsafe.

> 🛡 To help protect your security, Internet Explorer has restricted this file from showing active content ✖
> that could access your computer. Click here for options...

Of course, your presentation content is OK, so click the word options and choose Allow Blocked Content from the pop-up menu. Your presentation will appear in the Internet Explorer window.

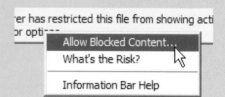

index

index

formatting text, 50–51, 61
Formatting Toolbar (Windows), 2
   Numbering button, 54
   text formatting with, 50–51

G

graphic files, 45
   See also images
GraphicConverter program, 45

H

handouts, printing, 103–104, 106
headers, 11
headings, 14
Hemera PhotoObject collections, 33
hyperlinks, 56–58, 62
   to slides, 58
   to Web sites, 56–57

I

I-beam cursor, 48
Identify button, 119
illustrating presentations, 63–80
   charts for, 74–75, 80
   clip art for, 66–67, 78
   diagrams for, 72–73, 80
   disk-based images for, 64–65, 78
   drawing tools for, 68–69, 79
   tables for, 76–77, 80
   video clips for, 71, 79
images
   clip art, 29–30, 33
   disk-based, 64–65, 78
   finding, 29–30, 33

resizing, 65
   royalty-free, 33
importing Word outlines, 19
Insert Chart button, 74
Insert Clip Art icon, 66
Insert Diagram or Organization Chart
   button, 72
Insert Hyperlink dialog, 57, 58
Insert Movie dialog, 71
Insert Picture icon, 64
Insert Sound dialog, 70
Insert Table button, 76
Internet Explorer, 134
italic text, 61

K

keyboard controls, 120
Keynote program, 134
Keyspan remote control, 121

L

laser pointers, 121
layouts. See slide layouts
Left Arrow key, 115, 120
line breaks, 48–49
line spacing, 53
links. See hyperlinks
lists
   bulleted, 54
   numbered, 54–55, 62

index

index

index

Ready to Learn More?